Understanding Social Anxiety

Understanding Social Anxiety

A Recovery Guide for Sufferers, Family, and Friends

Vera Sonja Maass

 PRAEGER™

An Imprint of ABC-CLIO, LLC

Santa Barbara, California • Denver, Colorado

Library of Congress Cataloging-in-Publication Data

Names: Maass, Vera Sonja, author.
Title: Understanding social anxiety : a recovery guide for sufferers, family, and
   friends / Vera Sonja Maass.
Description: Santa Barbara, California : Praeger, an Imprint of ABC-CLIO, LLC,
   [2017] | Includes bibliographical references and index.
Identifiers: LCCN 2016040338 (print) | LCCN 2016042933 (ebook) |
   ISBN 9781440841958 (hardcopy : alk. paper) | ISBN 9781440841965 (ebook)
Subjects: LCSH: Social phobia—Handbooks, manuals, etc. | Anxiety—Handbooks,
   manuals, etc.
Classification: LCC RC552.S62 M33 2017 (print) | LCC RC552.S62 (ebook) |
   DDC 616.85/22—dc23
LC record available at https://lccn.loc.gov/2016040338

ISBN: 978-1-4408-4195-8
EISBN: 978-1-4408-4196-5

21 20 19 18 17   1 2 3 4 5

This book is also available as an eBook.

Praeger
An Imprint of ABC-CLIO, LLC

ABC-CLIO, LLC
130 Cremona Drive, P.O. Box 1911
Santa Barbara, California 93116-1911
www.abc-clio.com

This book is printed on acid-free paper ∞

Manufactured in the United States of America

This book discusses treatments (including types of medication and mental health thera-pies), diagnostic tests for various symptoms and mental health disorders, and organ-izations. The author has made every effort to present accurate and up-to-date information. However, the information in this book is not intended to recommend or endorse particular treatments or organizations, or substitute for the care or medical advice of a qualified health professional, or be used to alter any medical therapy without a medical doctor's advice. Specific situations may require specific therapeutic approaches not included in this book. For those reasons, we recommend that readers follow the advice of qualified health care professionals directly involved in their care. Readers who suspect they may have specific medical problems should consult a physician about any suggestions made in this book.

Contents

Preface

Although social anxiety disorder is currently receiving increased public attention, it is by no means a new problem, as is outlined in this book. Sadly, the rekindled attention is due to an increase of occurrence of the problem and the growing use of prescription drugs for it—along with increased medication abuse and deaths due to overdose.

When, why, and how does social anxiety develop, and who is prone to suffer from it? Experts during the "decade of anxiety" in the 1980s searched for the answers. Arriving at a lack of self-esteem for an answer, they made valiant efforts to correct for this apparent shortage. Self-esteem was considered to be the solution for social problems. However, as is discussed in this book, the forces operating within the disorder of social anxiety are complex and complicated, requiring exploration deeply beyond the surface.

Many research workers agree that there is no single factor that determines the development of social anxiety; rather there seems to be a multitude of factors. Other experts in the field point to general vulnerabilities as the core of anxiety disorders.

Some experts believe that the roots of social anxiety are to be found in one's childhood, and while this seems to be true in many cases, having passed the childhood years does not mean that one will not develop the difficulty later in response to future events and experiences. There is no vaccination available to prevent its occurrence, but changes in one's brain activities when forming beliefs and developing thoughts regarding certain disturbing situations could lead to resolution and relief.

The author's past training with Albert Ellis, PhD, founder of Rational Emotive Behavior Therapy (REBT), and Maxie C. Maultsby Jr., MD, founder of Rational Behavior Therapy (RBT), has provided an appreciation for research and theory-building but also for the power of people's thoughts and beliefs and the impact those thoughts and deeply entrenched beliefs have on people's quality of life, their happiness, and their distress.

As can be observed from the case histories described in this book, patience and intense focus are required from both the client and the therapist as they delve deeply below the surface in their efforts to reach the core of the impairment and explore the implications for achieving relief and healing.

Acknowledgments

My special thanks are deserved by the brave individuals in the community at large who so graciously consented to disclose their life stories and past experiences to the general public. They were generous with their time and the information they shared; it is greatly appreciated.

My appreciation for the clients who allowed me to incorporate their case histories is limitless. Their stories have become a significant part of this book. For reasons of confidentiality their names have been changed, and some of their circumstances have been disguised. Some of their stories have been combined to form composite characters. Although I cannot disclose their identities, they know who they are, and they know the impact of their generosity on this book.

My deepest gratitude belongs to Debbie Carvalko, Senior Acquisitions Editor, Psychology and Health, not only for her expert professional guidance but for the caring recognition that I needed work to help me adjust to and heal over the biggest loss in my life. Debbie, I treasure the experience of working with you on our previous books, and I am deeply indebted to you for the coming to life of this book.

Finally, I want to dedicate this book to the memory of my husband, H. Gordon Featherstonaugh, PhD, who had so much looked forward to seeing this book's completion. Sadly, my psychologist-colleague and life partner's wish was not granted.

CHAPTER ONE

Overview

"It seems so ridiculous, but the whole idea of going to church suddenly frightens me. This started shortly after my divorce. Last Sunday, as we were getting ready for church, the anxiety became so strong, like something awful was going to happen. My heart was racing, my hands became clammy with cold sweat, and I had difficulty breathing. My oldest son saw me tremble and asked me if I was sick. We decided not to go to church."

Those were the words spoken in a barely audible voice by Gina, a 34-year-old woman, divorced mother of two sons, in her first therapy session. At the end of the session, the preliminary diagnosis in her chart read "social anxiety disorder."

According to the current edition of *The Diagnostic and Statistical Manual of Mental Disorders* (*DSM-5*), the essential feature of social anxiety disorder is a marked, or intense, fear or anxiety of social situations in which the individual may be scrutinized by others. And when exposed to such social situations, the individual fears that he or she will be negatively evaluated. The prevalence estimate for social anxiety disorder in the United States is around 7 percent. In general, rates of the disorder have been higher for females than for males. This gender difference tends to be more pronounced in adolescents and young adults. The median age at onset of social anxiety disorder in the United States is 13 years old; about 75 percent of people with social anxiety experienced an initial onset between the ages of 8 and 15.

Self-medication with substances such as drugs or alcohol is common. But despite the distress associated with social anxiety disorder, only about half of individuals with the disorder in Western societies ever seek treatment, and they tend to do so only after 15–20 years of experiencing symptoms.[1]

Apparently, the term *phobie des situations socials* was first introduced in 1903 by Pierre Janet, a French doctor, practitioner of hypnosis, and mentor of Charcot, who used the concept of a *fixed idea*, suggesting that some people *dissociate* an idea and then this fixed idea operates on its own, independent of the individual's consciousness.[2] Sigmund Freud may have been influenced by the French and their notion of the fixed idea; however, his concept added the psychological explanation of how such ideas develop—as *antitheses to intentions.*[3]

During the first half of the 20th century, Karen Horney raised the notion of the "hostile world" by defining *basic anxiety* as "a feeling of helplessness toward a potentially hostile world."[4] It is understood as a developmental issue in response to situations where a child feels insecure or intimidated.

Returning to the 21st century, for the United States, the 12-month prevalence estimate of social anxiety disorder was reported to be approximately 7 percent by the *DSM-5*. This seems to be higher than in other parts of the world, with a median prevalence of 2.3 percent in Europe. It would be relevant to ask what factors might account for this difference. Could the reason be found in what Eric Luis Uhlmann defined as "American psychological isolationism"—being inwardly focused and lacking regard for others' perspectives while focusing outward in the desire to Americanize the rest of the world? Geography may be a contributing factor, but according to Uhlmann, the main reason for this condition lies within America's Puritan heritage, which is thought to instill a sense of divine mission in its people.[5] Does that mean if America as a country were less psychologically isolated, there would be a reduction in the number of American individuals suffering from social anxiety? This is a heavy question; however, searching for the answer to this question goes beyond the scope of this book.

Returning to Gina's case, what were the factors in her life that justified her fears of the church environment and the diagnosis proposed by her therapist? As she mentioned, her difficulty with anxiety started after her divorce, indicating that she sought help for her difficulty sooner than most people would. Further explorations revealed that she feared being exposed or accused of having committed a crime. Everybody would point the finger at her.

What crime could she have committed that she feared to be chastised for by the people in church? Leaving her marriage and depriving her sons of living with their father was Gina's answer. Since then Gina had attempted to master her fear and attend church the following Sunday. Although her anxiety mounted as she drove closer and closer to the church, she managed to enter the church after dropping off her sons at the children's group. She decided to stay in the back of the church so people would not notice her. But again, the anxiety became overwhelming and she could not remain for the whole service. Trembling, with downcast eyes, she quietly left the church and walked to her car, calming herself down somewhat before collecting her sons. After that ill-fated attempt Gina felt totally defeated.

What could have induced that anxiety to strike her in church of all places? She had attended church all her life and regarded it as a safe place. Never before had she experienced anything like those recent terrors. Then she remembered an incident from her childhood. She had overheard a discussion between her mother and a neighbor of theirs. They were talking about one of the church members, a young, recently divorced mother, attending church with her children. The absence of the previously accompanying husband and father had been obvious to all. Now the neighbor lamented about the shame or even crime it was to deprive those poor children of the daily presence of their father. The reasons for the divorce did not seem to matter; it was the wife's responsibility to hold the family together. In her current recollections, Gina tried to remember what had happened to the divorced woman but could not come up with an answer—the woman might have discontinued her church attendance shortly after that.

Another, more recent memory seemed to connect to this situation from long ago: Gina mentioned how people had reacted when another church member, the father of two little girls, was widowed. His wife had died of cancer, and the whole congregation rallied to his side, especially the women. They all wanted to help and comfort him, and they invited him for dinner with his daughters. After Gina's divorce, nobody tried to comfort her. Did the memories of those two situations combine to give rise to the anxiety and fear of being judged a bad mother that Gina felt bombarded with?

Not surprisingly, Gina reported that rather recently those feelings of discomfort arose with anticipating and attending meetings for school-related events involving her two sons. Apparently, her social anxiety experiences were spreading to other situations that might similarly encompass the possibility of being harshly judged by others.

The Development of Social Identities

Almost two decades before the American Psychiatric Association in 1980 officially recognized social anxiety disorder as a psychiatric disorder, Canadian American sociologist and writer Erving Goffman in his book *Stigma* discussed how society establishes ways of categorizing people and the set of attributes that are thought to be natural for members of these categories to possess. Goffman pioneered the study of face-to-face interactions known as microsociology. Although his considerations occurred more than 50 years ago and the terminology and some of his ideology differ from the more recent thoughts of acknowledged experts on this topic, his writings offer an interesting, relevant, and comprehensible discussion of the subject matter.[6]

According to Goffman, individuals' range of personal attributes includes not only personality characteristics but also external features as well as occupation. All these factors constitute what Goffman called a person's "social identity"—the identity that makes him or her a member of a specific social layer. Being members of any particular social formation enables people to assume that other members' identity will include certain attributes (much like their own) that would be seen as normal for this group. With time, these anticipations have a way of functioning as normative expectations for this social layer, like a prescription for the "virtual social identity" of its members. However, some members' set of attributes may not conform to the expected virtual social identity, and the discrepancies in their "actual social identity" may indicate a "spoiled identity" reflecting a discrediting entity in the set of attributes and bestowing a stigma onto such members' social identity.

As Goffman explained, the term *stigma* originated with the Greeks, referring to bodily signs that were burned into or cut out of individuals' bodies to signify that there was something unusual or bad about the moral status of those individuals. These signs exposed the bearers as slaves, criminals, or traitors—blemished persons with whom contact should be avoided, especially in public places. It does not take much imagination to understand that those special marks, especially when viewed in public, would lead to fear and anxiety in those who had to bear them.

The idea of visible signifiers that assign a given status to individuals and of sorting them into different classes or categories did not die with the ancient Greeks. The demand that Jewish individuals in Germany at the time of the Nazi regime wear the bright yellow Star of David on the outside of their clothing is a more recent example of publicly stigmatizing people. Similarly, making prisoners wear readily recognizable uniforms can be seen as another example. If caught in any public dispute, the "branded" person automatically becomes the guilty one, the one who deserves the blame for whatever is wrong in the situation. By the same token, such visible signifiers as military decorations, fraternity pins, special license plates with decals of the college or university one has attended—prestigious awards in various shapes that can be displayed proudly—are just as commonly used to designate an elite status. Various professional uniforms worn by members of different job categories inform outsiders of their status or affiliation.

It is easily understood that stigmatizing visible signifiers would lead to the rise of varying levels of anxiety; however, even positive signifiers could bring about some degree of anxiety in people who might be afraid of not fulfilling all the required criteria for unquestioned continuing membership or in those who have made their entry on a provisional basis. Thus, no matter how we look at visible signifiers, over time, they may not be as reliable as we expect them to be, but we continue to keep them as our guides on how to navigate social relationships. Furthermore, visible signifiers are not the only kind we become aware of when we meet people whose background we are not familiar with. During verbal interchanges, accents and dialects may help place individuals geographically, and use of language and diction might serve to indicate the social status of the speaker. And it was not that long ago when verbal signifiers were used as selection criteria for exclusion by some business enterprises.

Returning to Goffman's discussion, he pointed out that the term "stigma" conceals a double perspective: In one aspect, the stigmatized individual assumes that his being different, or being of "differentness" as Goffman called it, is known already or is evident on the spot. In the other perspective, the individual might assume that it neither is known by those present nor will it be immediately perceivable by them. This distinction gains importance when considering the individual's behavior in response to the stigma. In the first case, the individual's behavior becomes the plight of the already *discredited*, whereas in the second instance it becomes that of the *discreditable*. The behaviors and foci of anxiety experienced are somewhat different for individuals in these two groups. For the already *discredited*, the behavior may take on a deferential manner while the anxiety is based on shame and the hope for acceptance in spite of the shortcoming, whereas the *discreditable*'s behavior is in the nature of evasiveness or avoidance, and the anxiety is focused more on being able to hide imperfections.

Individuals in the second instance may still assume or hope that by quiet withdrawal from social situations the blemish might be kept from becoming public knowledge. In contrast, those who believe that it is already too late for hiding the blemishes may in turn respond to others with angry behaviors. Sometimes ostracized people become aggressive, seeking revenge for having been victims of such ostracism, and they may actually turn to violence.

Goffman's observations occurred in the 1960s; responses of the 1970s stressed the possibility—or even probability—of assertive behavior being within everybody's reach as a panacea for social anxiety. In the preface of one of the many books available on the topic of assertiveness, *Responsible Assertive Behavior*, the coauthors informed readers that their approach was

based on personal as well as professional perspectives. As they successfully worked on changes in their own behaviors, they felt competent to
conduct assertion training groups. This book, like many others on the topic,
provided a plethora of modeling sequences, review questions, rehearsal
procedures, homework, and exercises.[7]

But it took until the 1980s for anxiety to be discussed in scientific journals as a problem in its own right. The 1980 National Institutes of Mental
Health survey showed that anxiety disorders were the most common psychiatric conditions in the United States. According to the survey, 8.3 percent
of the population suffered from anxiety disorder during any six-month
period.[8] As a result, psychiatric clinicians and researchers came to refer to
the 1980s as the "decade of anxiety."

Looking back on some studies undertaken around that time, we learn
that of all patients seen by their physicians, 11 percent mentioned anxiety
as their chief complaint,[9] and other research reported that 12 to 31 percent
of medical doctors' patients suffered from severe anxiety.[10] How many of
those patients were referred to psychiatric clinicians and how many
remained under the general care of their family physicians is unknown.

Vulnerabilities—The Core of Anxiety Disorders

What accounts for those incapacitating forces of people's vulnerabilities? Where do they come from? Most researchers agree that there is no
single factor that determines the development of social anxiety; rather there
seems to be a multitude of factors, including biochemistry, genetics, and
early-childhood and later-life traumatic experiences. For instance, the bio-
chemical response to stress is relevant in cases where individuals experience overwhelming physical symptoms when socially anxious. Perhaps
some people experience a "dysregulation" of the chemicals that come into
action during stress-provoking situations, chemicals that normally allow
the nervous system to operate in an optimal manner. The traumatized nervous system may then become overly sensitive, going into overdrive at the
slightest threat.[11]

Other experts in the field pointed to general vulnerabilities as the core
of anxiety disorders. These vulnerabilities may have resulted from some
incapacitating forces in the past and prevented individuals from performing activities that seemed just like ordinary tasks that people around them
handled without difficulty and that they themselves might also have been
able to execute in the past. While now engaging in some regular activity,
the individual's cognitive-affective state might sense and transmit threats
or danger signals.[12]

For instance, walking down a flight of stairs, a person may feel a moment's unsteadiness in the descending leg as the foot gets caught on the step. "What if I stumble and fall in a movie theater or other public place where people can observe me? They might think I am drunk or clumsy and don't know how to walk," the individual might think. Although some people would dismiss the situation without another thought, others might remember it whenever they are faced with descending a flight of stairs. What is worse, the perceived possibility that others might witness such an incident will raise the fear level with every repeated occurrence.

Another area of rising vulnerability can be seen in individuals' perception of themselves and their expectancies of their capabilities. Expectancy is the subjectively perceived likelihood or probability of success or failure, the degree to which an individual sees a goal as attainable or out of reach.[13] For instance, individuals believing themselves to possess insufficient social skills to negotiate their way through a social gathering of strangers will feel extremely uncomfortable and find reasons to avoid such situations. Over time, repeated avoidances have a way of increasing the perceived danger in the individual's mind and thus strengthening the avoidance tendency.

Ralph, a graduate student in his early thirties, worked hard toward achieving his professional goals. The years of his late adolescence and early twenties were spent like many of his peers', drinking alcohol and using drugs. Thanks to his high intelligence, he had been able to complete his bachelor degree despite the chemical abuse. However, his graduate study program had to be delayed until after recovery from his addictions. Ralph remained in therapy and devoted himself to his studies, wanting to make up for lost times. Finally, his goal appeared within reach when he achieved the "doctoral candidate" status. At about that time, Ralph attended a professional conference, a new experience for him because he had been avoiding any type of social encounters—to stay focused on his studies, as he told himself.

At the end of the first conference day, during the social part, Ralph panicked at the sight of strangers that seemed ready to involve him in conversations. During all those years of his addiction, Ralph socialized in a state of intoxication, which did not promote any learning of the skills people use in regular social interactions. Now being thrown into this situation without his previous crutch, the drugs and alcohol, he was at a loss on how to behave.

As the terror inside him mounted, he was unable to locate the exits from the big room. Finally, just as one of the conference attendees was about to introduce himself, Ralph caught sight of an exit sign and with a feeble excuse turned away from the young man, almost running out of the room in sheer panic. Outside, in the entry hall Ralph collapsed onto a chair, trying to slow down his rapid breathing so he could walk to his car. It felt like a narrow escape, and Ralph knew that if the avoidance technique would not be workable in a given social situation, his discomfort might escalate into a panic state. Removal from the feared situation becomes the overriding command in the individual's thinking.

For those who struggle with situational anxiety, the book *Situational Anxiety* seemed to promise help and provide assistance in negotiating "calmly and realistically those 'anxiety triggers' that abound in daily life."[14]

While some people respond to similar situations by realistically appraising their skills, individuals that—like Ralph—are prone to social anxiety most likely see themselves as deficient in social skills. Such self-perception turns the possibility of participating in a social event into a dangerous situation that individuals are unable to cope with. In turn, every incoming stimulus in the situation will be evaluated in terms of the perceived danger. The vulnerability mode (low self-esteem in this case) is triggered in those individuals by their perceptions of possessing insufficient coping skills.

Choosing between Self-Compassion and Self-Esteem

Help for the problem of social anxiety was offered with the arrival of books searching for and promising delivery of self-esteem as the answer to people's difficulties. One of the books' cover instructed: "Stop letting your life lead you! Master your own destiny through self-esteem,"[15] to be followed by the authors' renewed offering of a "proven program of cognitive techniques for assessing, improving, and maintaining your self-esteem." The book cover of the third edition boasted that over 550,000 copies had been sold.[16] In a similar vein, the American educational system's mandate of "leaving no child behind" can be understood as an attempt to prevent or at least reduce at an early age the development of individuals' poor self-esteem, which seems to grow like a silent epidemic. In spite of the various treatment approaches, by the end of the 20th century social anxiety disorder had become the third most common psychiatric disorder, and the popular press at that time focused on the increase in medication prescriptions to cope with the problem.[17]

Self-compassion, a construct from Buddhist thought, has been introduced into Western psychology,[18] with initial empirical work indicating that self-compassionate individuals tend to experience greater life satisfaction, social connectedness, emotional intelligence, and happiness, and less anxiety, depression, shame, fear of failure, and burnout.[19] Self-compassion can be understood as having three interrelated components that are experienced during individuals' times of pain and failure. Each of the components consists of two parts, the presence of one construct and the negation of another. The three components have been described as (a) practicing kindness and understanding toward oneself rather than being self-critical, (b) viewing one's fallibility as part of the human experience rather than as isolating oneself from others, and (c) keeping one's painful thoughts and feelings in mindful awareness rather than avoiding them or overidentifying with them.[20]

Kindness to oneself includes forgiveness, sensitivity, empathy, warmth, and patience toward all aspects of one's life.[21] In contrast to that, self-judgment involves being critical, hostile, and demeaning of one's self.[22] Relentless self-judgment causes pain equal to or even exceeding the pain of the eliciting situation.[23]

In times of pain or disappointment, many people feel cut off from others. Because they believe that their failures and shame need to be hidden, they withdraw from others. But common humanity, on the other hand, entails recognizing our connection to others, particularly in our sorrow and imperfections.

The third component of self-compassion, mindfulness, involves awareness and acceptance of and attention to the present moment.[24] Observing and labeling thoughts and feelings rather than reacting to them are parts of mindfulness.[25]

Self-compassion is not synonymous with self-esteem, which historically has been referred to as self-evaluation that is bolstered by attaining goals and threatened by failure.[26] More recently, self-esteem has been divided into two main types—*contingent* or *unstable* self-esteem[27] and *true* or *optimal* self-esteem.[28]

Contingent self-esteem is referred to as the degree to which the self is judged as being competent in important domains of life[29] or as "feelings about oneself that result from—indeed, are dependent on—matching some standard."[30] True self-esteem is viewed as reflecting secure feelings that are not based on one's actions or on living up to some standard; it is unconditional.[31]

The relationship between self-compassion and goal motivation has been a topic of research. A study of 110 undergraduates found that self-compassion was positively related to mastery goals (curiosity, accepting mistakes as part of learning) as well as to intrinsic motivation. A negative correlation was obtained between self-compassion and performance goals.[32] Other studies indicated that self-compassion is positively correlated with a sense of social connectedness.[33]

There have been opportunities for compassionate mind training (CMT) during pilot studies conducted for patients with high self-criticism and shame. The intention was to teach them to produce self-soothing and self-reassuring thought processes.[34] A basic assertion of CMT is that there are two pathways in the brain, one of them being self-judgmental and the other being kind. These two pathways tend to inhibit one another.[35] The focus of CMT is on enhancing the self-kind pathway to achieve a cognitive and affective shift.[36] In addition, therapists assisted patients with examining the function of their self-judgments.[37] However, the findings were not conclusive, indicating the need for controlled clinical trials involving larger samples to determine the effectiveness of CMT over other types of interventions.[38]

Influences of Childhood Experiences

Another topic exploring the development of the disorder focused on the question of whether particular childhood difficulties lead to later social anxiety disorder in the adult individual. Reports on studies done by Canadian researchers in 2001 had revealed high correlations between certain childhood events and the occurrence of social anxiety disorder later in life. The lack of a close relationship with an adult, poor performance in early grades of school, sexual abuse, and moving more than three times during childhood were among the variables associated with social anxiety later on. Surprisingly, social class did not seem connected at all to the development of social anxiety.[39]

Another study, on the importance of vicarious learning, which involved 40 children (25 boys, 15 girls between 9 and 12 years of age), found a significant positive relationship between mothers' and children's fears. An additional relationship was observed between the frequency with which the mothers expressed fear in front of their children and the level of the children's fear. The children of mothers who showed fear more frequently were more fearful; and those mothers who showed moderate fear had children with moderate levels of fearfulness.[40]

Although social anxiety disorder seems to run in families, that does not necessarily mean it is genetically transmitted. It is difficult to sort out what is genetic and what is environmental. Three different theoretical approaches, the neurobiological or evolutionary, the behavioral, and the cognitive, have attempted to explain some of the irrational behaviors associated with social anxiety. As each has its logic and supporting scientific evidence, no strong argument can be made to support one theory over the other two.[41]

Vulnerability and the "Theory of Mind"

As stated earlier, social anxiety, as well as the other anxiety states, has its base in a pervasive sense of vulnerability. This sense of vulnerability may stretch over several different categories or areas of a person's life. It could be based in the aspects of missing some or possessing inadequate skills, lacking some general knowledge, making poor judgments of particular situations, or just having a generally poor concept of self.

A factor significantly increasing the sense of vulnerability is the individual's fear of others' awareness of his or her lack of self-assuredness. From the age of about four years, human beings are capable of thinking about others' beliefs, even when these beliefs are false or differ from their own beliefs.[42] In the field of developmental psychology, this general capacity to consider others' beliefs is called a *theory of mind* because the behaviors of others can only be explained and predicted by making causal inferences about the unobservable mental states that are linked to those behaviors. Thus, the socially anxious individual develops a theory about the observers' thoughts.[43]

Because the same behavior can look different to different observers, behavior cannot be more objective than anything else we perceive. Behavior is a perception because the only way we can experience it is through our senses as we are trying to interpret it.[44] Furthermore, behavior is an ambiguous perception; the same behavior can be viewed in at least two different ways. One perception is that behavior is *caused* by someone or something;[45] the other stresses that behavior is *purposeful* as intended by the person who displays the behavior.[46] From a psychological framework, expectations about how behavior is perceived depend on the theoretical preferences of the observer. In effect, these preferences can be understood to function like different prescriptions for glasses, and the prescriptions influence the way we see and interpret behavior. They may be named *causal theory* prescription and *control theory* prescription, which reflects the theoretical preference to perceive behavior as *purposeful*.[47] But this perceptual ambiguity regarding observed behavior is generally disregarded or overlooked by socially anxious individuals; they are convinced that they *know* the other's behavior constitutes harsh judgment of them.

Much of psychological research involves questioning or interviewing participants about their own experiences, thoughts, or feelings regarding various issues to obtain information directly from the targets of observation. For instance, male and female undergraduate psychology students participating in a study were asked to recall and describe situations in which they had experienced embarrassment.[48] The analysis of the results revealed that each embarrassing situation had occurred in unintended and unexpected interactions with others. The embarrassment emerged following an evaluative moment of insight as the students realized that their observed behavior had been unusual or aberrant.

Furthermore, the students' self-focused evaluation of their unusual behavior was experienced by them as a third person, one who would, justly or unjustly, negatively evaluate the behavior and the person who exhibited it. The students admitted feeling "exposed." While experiencing embarrassment, the participants arrived at an aversive self-conscious awareness through the imaginative projection of the evaluations of those others they had interacted with.

The findings of this study concur with the theory of mind, which introduced a powerful set of social emotions, such as shame, pride, embarrassment, and humiliation, each one being dependent on "feeling" what other people think about us as individuals.[49]

If accepting individuals' sense of vulnerability as the core or basis for social anxiety disorder, a stigma can be the source of vulnerability, and so can lack of assertiveness and poor self-esteem. And just the suspicion that others may be aware of those shortcomings results in *epistemic social anxiety*, the negative affective state associated with someone else knowing about—or threatening to know about—the self's undesirable attributes, which include such issues as moral offenses, questionable intentions, embarrassing foibles, or even physical defects.

This broad spectrum of social anxiety disorder indicates that all the approaches mentioned earlier are relevant to the problem of social anxiety. In addition, equally relevant are other approaches, such as those described in the "complete guide to understanding and overcoming social anxiety disorder,"[50] or the empathic guidance and key strategies from a clinician who struggled with the impairment,[51] or the help of mindfulness and compassion in freeing individuals from social anxiety, fear, and avoidance,[52] as well as the use of cognitive behavioral techniques,[53] or compassion-focused therapy,[54] or even the German program for immediate help to become "simply self-confident!"[55]

Now in the third decade following the "decade of anxiety," what have we learned? When dealing with a disorder in the magnitude of social anxiety disorder, it makes sense to explore different approaches to come to a resolution of the problem. However, it is difficult to declare any one approach more successful than any of the others. Perhaps it is a case of different approaches working for different people.

The Difference between Social Anxiety and Other Anxiety States

Social anxiety differs from other anxieties and phobias in one significant aspect: the feared situation will actually be brought on by the fear. Being afraid of speaking in public will result in the individual's mind going blank. Studies have shown that socially anxious people focus their attention on themselves and their discomfort when interacting with others, which impairs their ability to communicate successfully with those others. Socially anxious individuals are too busy attending to their negative thoughts to the point that they are unable to realistically discern their listeners' responses. And they tend to exaggerate to the degree of irrationality any possible negative impression formed by others in the interaction.[56]

Gina, the woman introduced at the beginning of this chapter, might serve as an example here. When her anxiety spread from church attendance to school conferences for her sons, her focus at such meetings was on what she thought the school personnel thought of her having divorced her sons' father and on being judged harshly for limiting her sons' contact with their father. Being consumed with that aspect of her family situation, she had less energy left to really listen to what the teachers' issues were concerning her sons' adjustment in school. Her assumption that she would be found guilty of preventing her sons' unlimited access to their father numbed her intellectual acuity and kept her from accurately perceiving what the school personnel had meant to discuss with her.

Can the Development of Social Anxiety Be Prevented?

How and when do social anxieties develop in a person's life span? Many patients with social phobia recall an isolated childhood broken up by agonizing episodes of forced interaction with others, and even some parents of patients—when asked—remembered their children's severe shyness and situations of extreme social reticence.[57] But social phobia in children is largely unstudied because it is difficult to distinguish any social abnormalities in the fearfulness or reticence that occurs naturally and for good reason during childhood development. We usually accept the fact that many children are shy. The shyness is expressed in different behaviors or in the absence or lack of some behaviors because of avoidance tendencies. Although the shyness discomfort is experienced at different levels by different children, a system of measurements for the various degrees of shyness has not been developed. Perhaps a closer look at shyness is not considered to be urgent because it is generally hoped that children will outgrow their shyness and that it will not develop into a case of social anxiety disorder or social phobia as the child grows older.

About 40 percent of American adults describe themselves as "shy," but it is not necessarily clear what they mean by the term. They might be referring to normal levels of social anxiety or to a feeling of being sensitive in the presence of others. Or they could be referring to their memory of the normal stage of shyness, which most children pass through, as well as its occasional re-emergence in adulthood. Or they might be referring to feeling a general lack of self-confidence. But it is evident that shyness is more common than social anxiety.[58]

Studies in search of an "anxious gene" that have compared identical twins to fraternal twins or siblings have failed to produce evidence beyond the notion that genetic makeup forms the template for personality (including the tendency to be anxious or shy). An interweaving of nature and nurture determines how individuals confront new circumstances and challenges in general.[59]

Because shyness is linked to self-consciousness, some experts proposed that its earliest emergence can occur at about the age of two years, the time when children become aware of themselves as distinct entities, when they reach the realization of a "sense of self."[60] The picture of that "self" very often is a composite of insidious family messages, which become part of the fabric of our families. These messages die hard, and until we can understand why and how they influence our lives, we continue living according to those messages and pass them on to the next generation.

Many of those family messages affect another variable intimately linked with social anxiety—the developing individual's self-esteem. Studies attempting to measure individuals' levels of self-esteem over periods of their lives have shown different results. For instance, some researchers have reported a decline of self-esteem in people from early preadolescence to middle adolescence, with a reversed trend during middle adolescence with increases through early childhood.[61] On the other hand, examining the development of self-esteem across the life span for a sample of 326,641 participants showed that the mean levels of self-esteem were high in childhood, with decreases during adolescence and increases again throughout adulthood with a marked decrease in old age.[62] Still other research has demonstrated that age has a curvilinear effect on the development of people's self-concept. For females, mean self-esteem increased until 12 years old, then declined until age 17, and increasing again after age 17. For males, mean self-esteem increased until 14 years old, then declined until age 16, and increased again after 16 years of age.[63]

In a meta-analysis of 59 studies providing 130 independent samples, a longitudinal design was used to examine the development of self-esteem. The mean age of the 130 samples at the beginning of the study was 17.78 years old. Across the life span, mean levels of self-esteem increased in childhood, during college years, and in the first decade of young adulthood. The overall pattern of change in self-esteem reflected an increase until 30 years old; no systematic change appeared to occur after age 30.[64] For that reason it would seem advisable for parents and teachers to help young people gain an adequate level of self-esteem early on in life. However, the question remains: What should the self-esteem be based on to be beneficial and meaningful to the individual's life?

An examination of birth cohort differences in self-esteem concluded that in general an increase in self-esteem occurs among adolescents and young adults, seemingly caused by the cultural emphasis on self-worth and perceived increases in competence. However, the authors of the meta-analysis caution that despite these apparent increases in self-esteem, there is little evidence that any of the societal problems allegedly linked to self-esteem have been resolved.[65] The authors' caution underlines the fragility of trying to explain one psychological phenomenon with the existence of another.

The Developmental Psychopathology Approach

Considering the situation that anxiety disorders are among the most prevalent forms of psychopathology affecting children and adolescents, some researchers have adopted a developmental approach to explore this disorder. Furthermore, the finding that in many adults symptoms of anxiety disorders were traced back to their childhood or adolescence seemed to indicate a developmental link to the disorder.[66] The developmental psychopathology approach has emerged as a major organizational framework for studying psychological disorders in childhood.[67]

Several researchers have voiced the opinion that the beginnings of social withdrawal can be found in individuals' dispositional or temperamental traits leading to behavioral inhibition,[68] and studies on adult subjects have supported the notion of a physiological basis underpinning social wariness or anxiety.[69] Other research findings suggested that infants with right frontal EEG asymmetries have a greater tendency to cry at maternal separation and express fear in novel situations.[70] As these findings suggest the involvement of unique patterns of brain electrical activity in individuals' expression of fear and anxiety, it is important to realize, however, that human physiology may be modified by environmental means.[71]

When focusing on social anxiety disorder, one encounters various terms such as "social withdrawal," "social isolation," "inhibition," and "shyness."

Some of these terms can seem to overlap, leading to confusion. To clarify some of the terms according to their characteristics and functions, a set of definitions has been suggested. According to those definitions, inhibition refers to the disposition to be fearful when encountering unfamiliar nonsocial situations, whereas shyness is linked to inhibited responses to unfamiliar social situations. Social withdrawal carries the meaning of isolating oneself *from* the peer group, whereas social isolation refers to isolation *by* the peer group.[72]

Social withdrawal by itself does not constitute a clinical disorder; the central issue reflected by the individual's social withdrawal may be underlying difficulties of a social or emotional nature. Some children have a low motive for social approach without a strong avoidance tendency. They might engage in more object- than person-oriented activity, preferring exploratory or constructive solitude to social activity. Other children may want to interact with peers but are compelled to avoid it.

The Parents of Socially Anxious Children

Parents, when interacting with their socially inhibited young children, often demonstrate overly solicitous and directive behaviors, characteristic of an overprotective parenting pattern.[73] The range of parenting behaviors is wide, and some studies conducted to assess parenting beliefs about children's socially withdrawn behaviors have shown that mothers of anxious-withdrawn children were more likely to endorse the use of high-control strategies (e.g., using directives), compared to low-power strategies (e.g., redirecting the child). These mothers were also more likely to explain their children's consistent display of social withdrawal with dispositional factors, and they expressed more disappointment, anger, embarrassment, and guilt about their children's withdrawal behaviors.[74]

Similarly, earlier studies showed that boys who were perceived by teachers to be socially withdrawn and who remained as spectators among peers had fathers who were highly directive and less playful during father-son interactions.[75]

From a developmental point of view, it is important to remember that "the nature of the bonds that were developed and subsequently modified during the individual's childhood in relationships with members of his primary family" determines the substructure that supports the adult individual's self-esteem, ego ideals, and autonomy.[76]

Do Childhood Attachment Styles Predict Social Anxiety?

Relevant to an understanding of the family dynamics underlying childhood anxiety are the explorations and findings of attachment theory. Based on the extent to which children's relationships to their caregivers confer a sense of security and confidence in the child's transactions with the environment, infants and young children are considered to be securely or insecurely attached. As suggested by Bowlby, many forms of anxiety disorders could ultimately be traced to insecurity about the availability of an attachment figure.[77] Individuals' attachment styles developed and internalized in early childhood are perpetuated throughout the life span. Because the overriding childhood goal is to acquire and maintain security, children develop attachment styles that are particularly suited to the type of parenting they experience.[78] These early-childhood differences in attachment security are thought to lead to broader representations of relationships, the self, and the caregiver in the future, continuing as either secure or insecure in their underlying affective tone.[79]

The extensive research leading to the formulation of attachment theory had as its major concern how caregiver-child relationships influence socioemotional functioning.[80] Within the attachment system, a child's proximity seeking of the caregiver is activated by real or perceived threats in the environment, actual or anticipated separation from the caregiver, and internal distress. Once a sense of attachment security is restored, the child is free to shift attention to other activities, particularly exploration, which often occurs at a distance from the attachment figure.[81]

Various attachment styles used by individuals and their reflective interactions with other people have been grouped into four categories. Securely attached individuals are expected to face discomforting challenges in direct ways. People with preoccupied attachment styles tend to be hypersensitive to threat cues, and having exaggerated negative affect, they respond impulsively to distress in attempts to alleviate distress. Use of a fearful attachment style renders the individual as socially withdrawn. Feelings of vulnerability are kept hidden from observers, and self-disclosure is avoided. On the other hand, people with a dismissive attachment style may initially disclose a difficulty but later on deny the existence of any problems.

Studies have revealed that individuals with a fearful attachment style were the most troubled, with a high prevalence of avoidant, self-defeating, narcissistic, and obsessive-compulsive disorders. Furthermore, individuals with fearful attachment styles also had the highest occurrence of personality disorders that involved some kind of distortion of reality or negativity about others. Those are personality traits often encountered with social anxiety disorder, and as was mentioned earlier, social anxiety has been observed to develop early in childhood. And the behaviors adopted by those children, attempting to somehow cope with their distress, can be understood within the framework of attachment theory.[82]

Eventually, as children mature, the secure base phenomenon shifts from the actual situation to an internal working model.[83] Individuals' mental representations of themselves (including how acceptable or unacceptable they are in the eyes of their attachment figures and of the social world) replace the original secure-base need. Although these models are based on individuals' early experiences of care, they can be revised or modified by later experiences.[84]

Different patterns of insecure attachment have been distinguished by attachment theorists; the most common distinction is between anxious-ambivalent and avoidant styles of insecure attachment.[85] In adulthood, the strategies of anxious-ambivalent individuals are expressed in hyper-activating responses to attachment distress, whereas avoidant individuals' strategies reflect such deactivating responses as denial, suppression, and avoidance of contact.[86] Both of these strategies operate out of underlying concerns about self-worth.[87]

From Internal Working Models to Mapping Out the Future

As young people focus on their future, significant parts of their planning activities are spent in setting goals for themselves, their careers, and their social and family lives. Researchers working within "Goal Orientation Theory" have examined what motivates people to achieve in school and other settings while others tend to give up easily or avoid trying.[88] The findings have led goal orientation theorists to distinguish between *self-validation goals* and *learning goals*.[89]

Self-validation goals (also called "performance" goals) generally focus on seeking to prove one's ability and to defend against judgments of incompetence. Learning goals (also referred to as "mastery" goals), on the other hand, have been found to be more adaptive, particularly following one's failure to perform. The main focus of learning goals is on improving one's ability.[90] In other words, the focus of self-validation goals is on proving and defending, whereas learning goals focus on improving.

Two types of self-validation goals have been identified; the approach and the avoidance forms of performance or self-validation goals.[91] Evidence indicates that performance-avoidance goals have a high likelihood of negative outcomes, such as anxiety, self-handicapping strategies, poor performance, and lack of persistence.[92] Similar negative outcomes can be expected from performance-approach goals following prolonged failure, especially when people experience low perceived competence.[93]

In the process of establishing internal working models and setting goals, individuals may arrive at misconceptions of themselves: "Misconceptions about others and about the external world undoubtedly influence our adjustment, but misconceptions about the self probably play a major role in our enduring maladjustments."[94]

Both attachment theorists and goal orientation theorists stress the importance of an adaptive goal of seeking to learn over a maladaptive goal of seeking to validate self-worth. In addition, attachment theory tends to highlight another adaptive goal, that of seeking proximity and contact with the caregiver. Thus, the goals of learning and proximity/contact seeking are considered to be closely linked to one another.[95] In both theories, defensively focusing on self-validation is considered to be interfering with learning.

The Link between Peer Interaction and Normal Development

The importance of peer interaction for normal social, emotional, and cognitive growth was stressed by Jean Piaget about 90 years ago when he pointed out that young children are egocentric and unaware of the perspectives, intentions, and feelings of others. However, peer interaction provides opportunities to examine conflicting ideas and explanations, to negotiate and discuss various perspectives, as children learn to decide on or reject the notions held by others. Thus, social cognitive maturity is considered to be a function of children's peer interactions.[96]

Previous research has lent support to Piaget's notions when it demonstrated that interactions and conversations among peers produced *intrapersonal* cognitive conflict, which subsequently led to a decline in ego-centered thinking.[97]

There is a cyclical relationship between withdrawal and anxiety. The possibility of expected interactions with peers may raise a child's anxiety to such a level that the child decides to withdraw from the interaction. If the level of anxiety decreases markedly following the avoidant behavior, social avoidance will be reinforced, thereby increasing the probability of recurring withdrawal in the future.[98]

Repeated social avoidance interferes with the normal development of social skills. As the deficiencies in social skills further reinforce social anxiety, they foster negative self-appraisals and negative self-esteem.[99]

Because peer interactions influence children's understanding of the rules, norms, and expectations of their peer subcultures, avoidance of peer interaction will deprive those children of understanding normative performance levels, which, in turn, will impair their ability to evaluate their own competence against the perceived standards of the peer group.[100]

Early Planned Interventions

Karen, the loving grandmother of three-year-old Linda, told her friends about a day so perfect that it would stand out in her memory forever. It was a Thursday during a winter that seemingly did not want to end. Thursdays are special to Karen and Linda because they can spend the whole day together as Karen takes care of her granddaughter on those days. Remembering the time when her son, Linda's father, was Linda's age, Karen, while operating a day-care service in her home, introduced the toddlers and preschoolers to the local public library and its storytelling programs. Karen was delighted to find out that the local library's storytelling was scheduled for Thursdays.

There was reason for apprehension; Linda has to be eased into new situations because large gatherings can be overwhelming to her, even if she knows everyone there. Linda needs time to observe the gathering and get herself comfortable in the situation before she slowly merges into it. But Linda is also a child who loves books and loves to hear stories and poems. So Karen took the chance, thinking that the worst that could happen would be Linda's not wanting to leave Karen's lap or becoming frightened and crying to leave. Karen could handle those scenarios in a way that would make it possible for them to try again in a few months if this attempt did not work out.

That Thursday morning, Karen started by describing to Linda the library and what they would see and do there. But Linda was not excited; she preferred to stay home and play. Karen did not give up. She let Linda play for a while, and shortly before it would have been time to leave for the library, she told Linda again about all the wonderful things that could be seen there, and she mentioned the nice lady who would tell stories. This time Linda did not reject the idea, and the two of them put on their coats. Karen was careful not to hurry Linda because she knew this would be a trigger point for stress in a two-year-old. It took a while to get the little girl into the car seat, but they made it to the library without any incidents.

A moment's hesitation came when on the walk from the parking lot to the library a man passed them. "Who dat?" Linda asked as she stopped walking. Her voice reflected a bit of panic when she stated, "I don't wanna go." This crisis was resolved when shortly thereafter the man came out of the library again, walking toward the parking lot. Karen quickly explained that the man had probably just returned some books and was now on his way home, while she and Linda were going to find the storytelling lady.

The way to the storytelling room led past an aquarium displaying colorful fish and the kids' computer station. With the promise to visit those attractions later, Karen was able to carry Linda into the room and find a place on the floor for them to sit and listen to the stories. Little Linda tensed up when she saw all the other children sitting on the floor in front of her. But holding on to Karen, Linda was able to remain in the room.

There were songs between the stories, and Linda seemed to forget her initial tension. There were books with pictures of animals, and the librarian held up a page with the picture of an animal walking along the edge of the water, asking if anyone knew what the animal was. "It's a raccoon!" Linda shouted without being intimidated by the other children. "Yes, it is a raccoon. Good job!" the storyteller replied. Linda was ecstatic; the librarian's praise was the best and biggest thing that could have happened.

On returning home before afternoon naptime, there were a few more little adventures as well as some tentative danger points that could evoke anxiety in Linda. But with the earlier successes and particularly the storyteller's praise—all possibly building up psychological momentum—Karen was able to gently lead Linda through this eventful day.

It may seem to have taken much patience and thoughtful planning on Karen's part, and it did, but what was accomplished here was to introduce the little girl gently to some parts of the outside world and to strangers without overwhelming her with painful anxiety. Karen's main goal had been to establish in Linda an early positive link to books and libraries, a link free of tension and anxiety, which would allow her to see libraries as a place of refuge that offers learning and satisfaction of curiosity without undue stress.

A couple months after the library adventure, Karen decided to introduce little Linda to the wonders of Eagle Creek Park, a local reservoir with many acres of walking paths and a large indoor nature center. Many years ago Karen had brought her son, Linda's father, here for explorations. Now it was Linda's turn to get acquainted with the wonders of Eagle Creek Park.

The old nature center had grown into a large new building called Earth Discovery Center, large enough to hold some live animals in Plexiglas habitats. The exhibits of live turtles, snakes, salamanders, frogs, mudpuppies, and fish were a delight to Linda, who could not contain her excitement and shared it freely with the attending docents and visitors alike. Finally, it was time to leave this paradise. Karen and Linda walked on the sidewalk toward the parking lot when a flock of geese flew by overhead. At the sight of them little Linda shouted, "Look Grandma, eagles!"

Karen did not think they were eagles and mentioned to Linda that they looked more like geese. But Linda would not hear of it. "No, they are not geese, Grandma. They are eagles because this is Eagle Creek Park!" Karen did not contradict Linda's statement; instead her behavior reflected an attitude of "my mistake; they must have been eagles after all."

Why reduce the child's excitement over all the wonders of nature by pointing out that she was wrong in calling the geese eagles? The fact that she had made a mistake might induce feelings of shame over having been wrong and stifle Linda's free expression of what she had learned and liked to explore further. Besides, there was plenty of time ahead for Linda to learn to recognize the difference between eagles and geese.

Shame may arise in any situation that focuses attention on the self or some aspect of the self that is found to be incorrect or mistaken. This experience can be traumatic in a child that tends to be shy, as is the case with Linda. In the shame-producing situation, the individual is affected by a sudden and intense heightening of awareness of the self. This awareness strongly dominates the individual's consciousness, inhibiting cognitive processes and causing a loss of presence of mind. Inappropriate stammering and clumsy coping behaviors may be immediate responses. Typically, shame occurs in the presence of other people, who somehow play a role in activating the shame.[101]

Karen would not want to be the person associated with the effect of such a shame experience on her beloved granddaughter. Karen's many years of experience in working with young children as a teaching assistant in kindergarten and first-grade classes have provided her with the ability to recognize the importance of patience and with the wisdom of knowing when to confront a child's hesitation and shyness with gently moving forward, minimizing the risk of terror and anxiety arising in the child.

Will Karen's loving care be sufficient to protect Linda from developing social anxiety later on in life? Only time will tell; but since studies have shown that early environment plays a role in predisposing people to social anxiety, Karen's plans and actions present an example of a positive approach to prevention.[102]

CHAPTER TWO

Cultural Institutions: A Breeding Ground for Social Anxiety

As mentioned in chapter 1, the discomfort experienced by individuals suffering from social anxiety arises in situations in which they expect to be observed and judged by others. Examples of these situations include social interactions in which individuals are meeting and expected to engage in conversation with unfamiliar people. In other situations, their behaviors, such as eating or drinking, are being observed by others. Or they might be performing, such as giving a speech, in front of others. In most of these situations, behavioral expectations are generally prescribed by the cultural environment. In other words, the experience of social anxiety and the expression of its symptoms occur as functions of the particular culture in which the individuals suffering from the disorder live.[1]

Different cultures provide different patterns of beliefs and values for their citizens. For example, America, in its symbolic framework for the self, reflects the Delphic oracle's imperative "Know thyself," and this knowledge turns individuals' beliefs, skills, and accomplishments into primary features of their identity. In addition, the emphasis on individuals and their mental state received amplification through the tenets of Christian philosophy, which turned people's private state of faith into essential components of their sense of virtue. Thus, being confused about one's value would render one vulnerable to uncertainty and a compromised sense of potency.[2]

However, societies and their cultures and institutions change over time, and humans have a tendency to worry when social arrangements that have existed over many generations show signs of change. Confronted with the changes, people uncertain about the basis for their personal value develop a new sense of vulnerability. For instance, in rural societies of the early 18th century, children derived a sense of self-esteem or self-worth from the work they performed under their parents' directions on their farms. But later urban populations were not in need of their children's help with chores and learned to rely on other ways to develop their children's sense of self-value. Verbal or physical declarations of love from parents, especially mothers, and academic success in the culture's schools may have fulfilled the function of developing a sense of self-worth, creating "the illusion that underneath their ordinariness they were a young prince or princess."[3]

Cultural rules and habits, as well as their changes, create and determine the types of situations that might appear to contain threats to some people. As members of a given culture become aware of the expectations others may have of them and their behaviors, the mere possibility of failing to fulfill those expectations can give rise to discomfort, self-doubt, and fear.

Approach and Avoidance Goals

Goals bestow direction on our explorations of options and purposes for decision-making processes. Goals prevent us from wandering around aimlessly. Our successful journey will be based on actions that are aimed at goals, and the actions will terminate in reflections and representations of those goals.[4]

Among members of a given culture, expectations give rise to systems of approach and avoidance goals.[5] There are variations from culture to culture as cross-cultural research has indicated, such as East Asians, for example, tending to be more avoidance-oriented and less approach-oriented than Westerners.[6]

At a narrower context than the cultural context, specific environmental goal structures operate that correspond to specific social situations that may prompt individuals to develop or demonstrate competence (approach goal structure) or to avoid experiencing or demonstrating failure or incompetence (avoidance goal structure). Such situations are found in the classrooms of schools[7] or in the climate of sport teams[8] where these environmental goal structures have been adopted by the students or athletes. And in achievement settings like those, the person's competence and self-worth are always salient.

Among the environment goal structures, social comparisons are particularly influential in determining individuals' engagement in approach or avoidance goals. For instance, downward social comparisons tend to activate avoidance motivation in people who are vulnerable to others' misfortune.[9] In people experiencing social anxiety, for example, this vulnerability may take the form of witnessing someone's difficulty and connecting this to themselves with the thought "This could happen to me! If it did, I would die of embarrassment."

In general, examples of unfortunate models are more likely chosen to sustain motivation when one aims to abstain from a potentially deleterious activity—an avoidance behavior—whereas fortunate models are preferred when one considers engaging in a potentially beneficial activity—an approach behavior.[10] The way people define their sense of competence (using self- vs. other-referenced criteria) has a bearing on their level of confidence in a given task, and it will influence the decision on whether they will engage and persist in the task or avoid the challenge.[11]

Early Childhood Experiences: Schools and Families

Being the focus of observation of those around them and perhaps being made to feel unimportant, or worse still, unable to do anything well, some children fail to develop positive self-esteem. Or there might be a competing sibling, who seemingly can do everything well, earning the family's admiration for his or her accomplishments while the less accomplished child quietly stands by, largely unnoticed. Even though some of the "unremarkable" children may grow into competent and accomplished adults, the old feelings of being inferior and worth less than others often remain.

Memories of not receiving praise for accomplishments or even of being made fun of persist and can overshadow later successes. The pain of rejection lingers for a long time, and the person will do anything to avoid experiencing it again. Unlikely to take risks of disclosing feelings and thoughts to others, the person may assume the appearance of being easygoing or of not caring about the opinion of others, just to hide the internal discomfort. And then there are the external features that can't be hidden. Take the girl whose parents came from a different part of the world to make a new life in a new country. Looking different from the rest of her classmates in school is an open invitation for ridicule and bullying. Instead of calling her by her given name, her classmates refer to her as "Latina" as they snicker about her. To make the situation worse and heighten her anxiety, she might also be the one to develop breasts earlier than the rest of the girls her age. For many getting into the teenage years, anxiety becomes a normal part of life.[12]

From the early days in school to daily attendance at jobs, to shopping and living in communities, there are millions of opportunities for competition, leading to exaggerated fears of failing and consequently trying desperately to hide one's real or imagined shortcomings. As can be seen from the case history at the beginning of this book, even churches are not guaranteed safe places anymore.

Although anxiety-producing situations can occur as early as the end of the second year of one's life, for the general population this moment might come about during the early days in school. Imagine a five- or six-year-old child arriving at a building he or she has not been to before, surrounded by some grown-ups and many other children of equal age but otherwise unknown. "Who are all those kids? Are they going to make fun of me? Are they going to beat me up?" Those are questions that might be going through the minds of some of the new first graders.

At this point, the field is wide open for any bully to establish his or her turf. And if the bullying does not make the new child feel unsure and afraid, there is the performance in class, rated by the teacher. Every step of the way, the child is aware of being observed and evaluated, and of possibly being classified as not meeting the standards of the situation. And every observation, it is feared, might end in failing to achieve approval and facing rejection instead.

A 27-year-old high school English teacher recounted in her book, *What You Must Think of Me*: "Whether as a student or a teacher, much of my life—and much of my social anxiety—has revolved around school. I can't say that I ever completely vanquished my fear of being judged in school situations, but I did manage to subdue my anxiety enough to finish my master's degree. To me, that was a major victory."[13]

For many children suffering from social anxiety, speaking out in class is a fear-producing moment. "What if the teacher calls on me with a question and I don't know the answer?" is a thought flashing through the brains of many of them. Or having to give a presentation in front of the class, taking tests, interacting with the other children, and interacting with teachers—all of them present near-panic possibilities in the minds of the fearful children.

If those scenarios are not stressful enough, there are the physical education classes. Every child's performance is observed by the rest of the class and the teacher. And who will be selected for the team sports? Who will be chosen first, who will have to wait to the end to be picked for the team?

For some socially anxious children, the temptation to "play sick" is an opportunity too good to pass up when it comes to avoiding school, whether it is "Bobby," a 15-year-old boy, who had been shy all his life but whose problems really intensified with the beginning of middle school,[14] or Rae, the teenage girl who described herself as "a certified expert at pretending to be sick. I should have a plaque."[15] Pretending to be ill is just one way to avoid feared situations; there are others as the desperate mind searches for possibilities.

Absence from Selection Processes as a Safety Measure

Andrew remembers the scenario of selection for a team sport quite well. He was an awkward kid, seemingly all bones lined up not in the right angles or direction. He didn't aspire to any athletic standing on his own merit, but he very much wanted to be part of a team. The school's softball team seemed like a good place for him to blend in. But as the selection process started, nobody took any notice of Andrew. Observing the process of how others were chosen for the team's positions without his name being mentioned drove his anxiety into high gear. He did not know whether to sit or stand or walk around to hide his nervousness. Finally, he left the situation, mumbling something about having to go to the bathroom. In reality, he could no longer stand the anxiety of having to face the now almost certain likelihood that nobody wanted him and that he would be left sitting or standing there, waiting for nobody to choose him.

When he returned from the bathroom—making sure he had stayed there long enough—all the positions on the team had been filled. Moreover, nobody had missed him, and they then assigned him to a standby/fill-in position. Andrew had known that nobody had wanted him, but by leaving the scene, he could make believe that he was not chosen because he had not been there; he had not been available for the selection process. And that could count as the reason for not having an important position on the team.

It worked, and for many years Andrew used the technique of being absent during selection moments. In his mind it saved him from having to face outright rejection, but it did not help him in becoming more closely involved with any of his classmates or teammates. This thin protection from acknowledging public rejection kept him from forming any meaningful relationships with those around him at the time—a high price to pay.

Andrew's scheme worked in protecting him from acknowledging the truth (as he felt it), and he adopted this strategy for most of his life. It kept questions from others at bay, and it helped him to forget for brief periods why he really was not on anybody's team.

During the school years, there are many occasions for children to be judged as not meeting standards, be they for academic achievements, sports, or just plain social standing in the community. When we think of Andrew, we can imagine him on the sidelines of what was going on during his school years. Not many of the other students would choose him to be their friend; they did not have a chance to know who Andrew really was.

Did he attend his high school prom? You guessed it; no, he did not. He could not ask any girl to be his date unless she would say yes right away, and that was too slim of a chance to take. He envied the position of girls because they were not expected to ask for a date; in our culture, they are expected to be shy and waiting to be asked. If he had asked any of the girls at school to be his date and she had said that she wanted to think about it, that would have meant that he was present for the selection. And she might have chosen another boy, one who seemed more attractive than Andrew, to take her to the prom. But if he did not ask anybody, nobody could turn him down. As in many prior situations, it seemed so much safer to stay out of the whole competitive selection process.

How did Andrew ever manage to get married? would be a natural question to ask because he most likely would have been too afraid to ask a girl for a date. And indeed, he had not progressed in this part of life since his high school prom days. But Andrew filled in as a blind date when one of his male acquaintances juggled too many dates with different girls at the same time. Fortified by the excuse of his friend's inability to appear at the girl's house, Andrew offered to take her out.

Because the friend had chosen to be with another girl at the time, it is likely that this girl's fate was closer to Andrew's—not being the first choice of the young men who knew her. And that was how Andrew got to date and marry a nice but less popular girl, someone very much like Andrew himself in the social popularity ranking.

As Andrew's scheme of not being present for selection processes appeared to work in sparing him the pain of facing outright rejection, he decided to stay with it. Why make changes when you have found something that works for you? Adapting to changes induces stress by itself, so Andrew remained absent for many of life's selection processes.

Adolescence and the Process of Neuroplasticity

A contributing factor to Andrew's sad experience relates to the fact that the time of adolescence is a critical period in brain development that can represent the onset of anxiety and depression. Although by the age of six years the brain has reached nearly its full size, during the process of neuroplasticity, when the brain adapts to internal and external forces as the density and organization of various brain regions and the connections between them shift, changes in the brain's gray matter, white matter, and limbic system occur. In addition, at this time the adolescent system becomes flooded with a deluge of hormones and neurotransmitters.[16]

Attempting to explain all the complicated neurophysiological and hormonal changes that occur in the lives of adolescents at that time goes beyond the scope of this book, but we need to be cognizant of all the changes that evolve and interact at the same time. For instance, there is a transition in the adolescent's life at this time from the parents' position as central social figures to peers fulfilling that role, and concurrently, changes in the brain increase the sensitivity to social cues, rendering this period of adolescence as significant for the development of social understanding. As adolescents start developing a sense of self-consciousness, they perceive social cues differently from children and adults, and they might also misinterpret them. Thus, in general, adolescents are neurologically more sensitive to social rejection and ostracism than are children and adults. A study on adolescents' and adults' perception of facial expressions revealed that adolescent participants perceived emotions incorrectly more frequently than did adults. Furthermore, unlike adults, adolescents had difficulty switching attention between different information in social situations and accessing limbic areas of their brains even when told to focus on nonemotional components of faces, such as structural aspects like nose width. The question of how technology may affect both the brain and behavior of adolescents has not been clearly answered yet, but it was found that tweens who had no access to technology, such as television, computers, and mobile phones, for five days significantly improved their ability to read nonverbal emotion cues compared with peers who had unrestricted access to technology. This finding could be interpreted to indicate that technological interactions absorb a greater potential of adolescents' brain energies than do social interactions.[17]

Another study explored the possibility of compulsive Internet use (CIU) functioning as an antecedent to poor mental health. A longitudinal design was used to track the development of CIU and mental health in grades 8, 9, 10, and 11. The findings revealed that CIU predicted the development of poor mental health across the high school years, but poor mental health did not predict the development of CIU. Comparisons between male and female students showed that female students had higher CIU and worse mental health than male students. Also, female students tended to engage in more social forms than search forms of Internet use.[18]

Although adolescents seem to perceive or evaluate experiences differently, in general one would expect that during further development into adulthood some of the misperceptions of adolescence would yield to the realities of adulthood. But it does not always happen that way.

Adulthood—A Change for the Better?

At age 32, Alex was a success; everybody said so. With his MBA degree, he had climbed to the position of department head in record time. His bosses liked him for his decision-making skills, always quick and relevant to the issues at hand. The people who worked under his supervision were generally proud to be on his team. Being married with two young children, his personal life seemed to be well organized, too.

Tuesday mornings were scheduled for meetings of the different department heads with the firm's CEO to keep everybody informed about the company's activities. Toward the end of one of those meetings, a new department leader asked a question regarding some productivity issue in Alex's department. Alex was surprised and did not have an answer but responded with "I'll check it out and let you know about it," to which the other replied, "Please don't bother; I was just curious about some of the figures in this report." Unfortunately, Alex did not know which part of the report his colleague was referring to, and he thought he detected a smirk on the other man's face. But it was the end of the meeting, and everybody filed out of the conference room.

At the next meeting, Alex felt a slight uneasiness rising in him. He could not explain it, but because it disappeared as soon as the meeting was over, he did not give it much thought. However, he became aware of that uncomfortable feeling again the following Tuesday morning. He realized then that it was connected to that particular Tuesday when he was confronted with a question he could not answer. Week by week his anxiety rose, and he developed several strategies that would allow him to leave a meeting earlier, interrupt his attendance for an important phone call, or join later because of other significant last-minute matters.

Those maneuvers worked for a while until he realized that the interruptions he created reflected on him as a poor manager of his responsibilities because none of the other department heads needed that kind of flexibility in their attendance schedules. He began to spend more time in his office than before. Walking around in the hallways previously provided welcome interruptions when he ran into his colleagues, resulting in a friendly chat. But now this could also lead to an awkward meeting with the colleague who had presented that question in that particular Tuesday meeting. As the weeks went on, the nagging discomfort at having to face inquiries from any of his colleagues increased.

Finally, upon the urging of his wife, who had noticed increased irritability in her husband's behavior, Alex consulted a psychologist to explore the basis for his anxiety related to the business meetings. After the preliminary questions and answers had been exchanged, the psychologist turned the conversation to the event that caused Alex's visit to the psychologist's office.

"Why was the other department head's question so disturbing?" inquired the psychologist.

"Because," Alex admitted, "I did not know the answer to the question."

"Should you have known the answer?" the psychologist asked.

"Yes," Alex responded, "because it was something that occurred in my department that I should have known about."

"If that is the case, were there any special circumstances that prevented you from having the answers?" the psychologist asked in a quiet tone of voice.

Obviously embarrassed, Alex stumbled over his words, "I should have known about it but I had not prepared myself enough for this meeting to have answers for everything that goes on in my department."

"When you say 'for this meeting' do you mean this was just a one-time situation?" the psychologist continued with the inquiry.

There was a long moment of silence before Alex was ready to answer. "I usually don't prepare myself for meetings like the Tuesday meetings because as an intelligent person I should know what is going on without taking a closer look."

"Are you saying that being in a certain position enables you to discern all there is about the position and its workings without looking into the details of its functioning?" the psychologist asked.

"Well, I would not say that all the details are that obvious, but with a certain amount of intelligence one would be able to discern in general what is occurring without having detailed knowledge of it."

The psychologist observed that at every turn of the conversation Alex's responses appeared to increase in vagueness, except for the emphasis he put on the word "intelligence." Realizing that this line of questioning was not leading anywhere, the psychologist changed the subject to inquire what Alex's goals and dreams were as he was growing up.

Alex thought for a moment before responding. "There was a time in high school when I wanted to be a teacher. But my friends made fun of me, saying being a teacher is for dumb kids who have to hold on to their schoolbooks all the time."

After a brief pause, Alex continued: "My friends made fun of one of the boys in class, Bruce, who wanted to become a teacher, and before exams he never had time to play or fool around because he had to study to get a good grade. My friend Pete said that on the most recent test Bruce got only two more points than Pete, and Pete had not studied at all. Another boy added that when you are smart you don't have to study. You get it all in class. That's how you can tell the intelligent ones from the dumb ones. If you have to study before a test, you are not one of the intelligent kids. 'I never open my schoolbooks outside of class,' the boy stated, and the rest of my friends all agreed with him."

"That's an interesting approach to learning," the psychologist responded thoughtfully. "Where did you fit in the group?"

"Oh, I was one of the smart ones; I did not have to study. Even in college and graduate school I didn't have any problems," Alex answered. "Actually, my friends were a bit envious when I got my MBA degree. For one thing, it was what they called the 'money track,' and my friend Pete said, 'That fits; you were always one of the smartest among us and you never had to study. And remember, our IQ scores were pretty high when we were tested back in high school.'"

"It sounds like your friends believed that truly intelligent people do not study or prepare themselves for an exam or any such situation." The psychologist carefully approached the similarity of his school experiences to the work situation Alex was in now.

"At the time I was not thinking much about it; it seemed to be a fact of life that those of a certain level of intelligence knew more than the rest of the people and they did not have to prove themselves by studying."

"You mean that their level of intelligence had established them as members of a special group and their attendance at school was certifying their knowledge or level of intelligence?" the psychologist asked.

"I guess you could explain it that way. I accepted my friends' opinion because it seemed to be true. I did not think much about it; it was like a fact of life," Alex agreed somewhat hesitatingly.

After a brief pause, Alex started talking again: "The way you are talking about it, our reasoning sounds somewhat flawed. We did study; we just did not need to prepare or study extra hard for exams. Talking about it now sounds childish."

"At the time you apparently were successful without putting in the extra effort, but now do you think that your grades might have been even higher if you had used additional preparation for tests and exams?" The psychologist was leading Alex to consider the possibility of enhanced performance through task preparation.

"It's possible; we just did not worry about it at the time," Alex responded. "Why are you asking those questions about the past?"

"Our past is the foundation for the present and the future; past beliefs guide and shape current and future behaviors. For instance, if you believed that studying for an upcoming exam was not necessary, preparing for staff meetings may also appear unnecessary, and in the actual situation you may fail to recall some details," the psychologist offered as an explanation.

"Are you saying that this relates to the Tuesday morning meetings, that I did not prepare myself for the meeting?" Alex inquired.

"It is a possibility, and only you would know how much information about your department's processes was available to you at that meeting. Were there pieces of information you had not checked into? In other words, would the answer to your colleague's question have been available to you if you had looked into that part of your department's processes before the regular Tuesday meeting?" the psychologist probed.

"I think I understand what you are getting at; information about my department's processes, progress, and results should be and is available to me if I check it out as preparation for the Tuesday meetings. And what is keeping me from doing so is my old habit of thinking that truly intelligent people don't have to do that—they just know!" Alex tried to interpret the psychologist's explanation.

"You described it exceptionally well," replied the psychologist. "Your beliefs from long ago kept you from doing what might be best for your professional success now."

"I did not even know I had such a belief, but I admit, I acted as if I believed in the old school thoughts and rituals without knowing why, just as a habit. Is there a way to change this habit? I don't like the discomfort when avoiding certain people," Alex asked somewhat anxiously.

"As you described it, behaviors that are based on long-standing beliefs occur almost automatically; they become habits. Because our beliefs are so firm, we don't have to question their rationality. And there are no warning signals either—we just act on them as if, as you said earlier, they are facts of life that don't need to be questioned or challenged. It will take time and work to undo some of those old maladaptive beliefs and behaviors, but it is certainly possible to do so."

For Alex this was the point of recognition; overcoming his old habits by examining the nature of his underlying beliefs, he made the transition to educating himself about the details of his department's functioning. Alex's story is just one example of how powerful cultural influences during our early lives can be, as was reflected by his classmates and friends in school.

Self-Esteem as a Solution to Social Problems

One of the most prolifically researched topics in modern psychology is the concept of self-esteem, briefly mentioned in chapter 1. What was once a term solely used in scientific literature has evolved into a concept widely recognized among the general public.[19] According to the culture of self-worth model, the notion of self-esteem changes with changing normative social influences or the degree to which it is accepted by society.[20]

Having latched onto the idea that self-esteem is linked to "all matter of positive behaviors and outcomes,"[21] people consider self-esteem as positively related to happiness[22] and to satisfaction in life, especially in individualistic societies.[23] But there is also a negative side to self-esteem, as individuals high in self-esteem generally react defensively when threatened.[24] Another negative result—that of "nonproductive persistence"—can occur when people continue to pursue a task even when it is useless to do so.[25] Those positive and negative aspects of self-esteem have brought about a dichotomy between those who advocate its benefits and those who doubt its usefulness. This dichotomy can be viewed as "evidence that the word *self-esteem* touches a sensitive cultural nerve."[26]

Children and young people have felt the influence of the "culture of self-worth."[27] And although the continued cultural changes in the direction of self-worth may have brought some increases in self-esteem, college students' narcissism scores also increased over the same time period,[28] reflecting that narcissism and self-esteem are positively correlated.[29]

Two models of self-esteem relate to the debate whether self-esteem is a function of competence or whether it is influenced by a culture's emphasis on the self. The *competencies model* states that self-esteem is a product of the individual's proficiency in certain aspects of his or her life; whereas the *culture of self-worth model* suggests that self-esteem increases because of the importance that the culture places on self-liking.[30]

It is interesting to note that scores on the verbal section of the Scholastic Aptitude Test (SAT) did not change between 1995 and 2008 and math scores showed only a slight increase,[31] yet the *perception* of success has increased. Twice as many high school students announced receiving an A average as did in the 1970s, even though fewer reported doing more than 15 hours of homework per week.[32] This raises the question "Did the educational system inflate grades to increase the students' level of self-esteem or to provide students with more free time?" This question may have some relevance to the case of Alex described above.

While American culture has always nurtured the belief that an individual can singularly improve his or her situation, the concept of the "self" did not reach prominence until much later.[33] The importance of self-worth has increased during the last few decades. For example, educational practices during the 1980s and 1990s shifted by incorporating self-esteem into school curricula and, in some cases, obscuring academic goals by discontinuing practices such as graded report cards, competition, and correcting wrong answers. Thus, self-esteem became independent of, rather than a result of, academic competence.[34]

Considering self-esteem a solution to social problems in part contributed to the expansion of the self-esteem movement. In 1990, the California Task Force on Self-Esteem was searching for evidence that would turn self-esteem into a "social vaccine" to substance abuse, teen pregnancy, child abuse, welfare dependency, violent crime, and educational failure.[35] But no causal relationships between self-esteem and any of the social problems have been discovered so far. As the emphasis on self-esteem continues, children and adolescents are being immersed in the culture of self-worth.[36]

Similarly, with self-esteem entering the public consciousness, it has grown in popularity, as is exhibited in magazines, TV, and music. And the Internet has become a rapidly growing medium for self-expression, with websites like Facebook, MySpace, and Twitter providing opportunities to create personal websites listing interests, friends, and status updates reflecting personal successes. With the slogan "Broadcast Yourself," YouTube allows ordinary people to reach millions.[37]

However, there is little evidence that any of the societal difficulties allegedly tied to self-esteem have been resolved. A promising path for change would be if we "as a society can focus our national attention on increasing levels of other psychological/behavioral constructs that might have a great societal pay-off, such as self-control, educational competence, happiness, or positive social functioning."[38]

Considering sources in the relevant literature connecting negative self-regard, low self-esteem,[39,40] negative self-perception,[41] or low self-worth[42] to social anxiety disorder, caution seems indicated—based on the above discussion—in assuming a causal relationship. As mentioned in chapter 1, the core of social anxiety disorder is thought to be the individual's sense of vulnerability with various factors functioning as sources of the vulnerability. For example, stigma, lack of assertiveness, poor self-esteem, and many other causes can contribute to the felt vulnerability, and emphasizing one over the others without supporting evidence can lead to misinterpretations and misattribution.

The Power of Cultural Myths

At the biweekly meeting of a local writers' group, members were critiquing each other's stories. The current discussion focused on a children's story dealing with Christmas, Santa Claus, and gift giving. The story described the main character, a little girl, as she was sitting on Santa's lap (unknown to her, one of her uncles was impersonating Santa). Nodding her head in response to Santa's question if she had been a good little girl, obeyed her parents, and been nice to other people, she was ready to receive a colorfully wrapped package from Santa Claus before he released her from his lap. With a big smile on her face, she thanked him as he left the room. Everybody agreed that it was a delightful story.

However, one of the male group members, while praising the story in general terms, raised the question why we keep this myth about Santa Claus alive in our children. It has nothing to do with reality and may actually lead to disappointments later on when the children realize that there is no Santa Claus.

"But it is so precious to keep our children's innocence alive for as long as we can," one of the female members protested.

"Perhaps it is more for our convenience than for the children's sake that we keep Santa Claus alive," Ellen, another female writer, suggested. Everybody looked at her, some shocked and disbelieving what they had just heard, others looking at her questioningly.

"Put yourself in the place of a child from a poor family, whose gifts from her parents for birthdays and Christmas are low-priced items from the stores, not at all representing the abundance of the other children's gifts. Boasting of the wonderful and sophisticated toys currently on the market, those children appear more valued by those who take care of them. Characterized by her mediocre toys, the poor child appears less valued. It is one thing to receive smaller gifts from one's parents whose poverty the child is familiar with than from another entity outside the family like Santa Claus, who would be expected to treat the children justly for the children's sake, not for their parents' money," Ellen explained her opinion.

She continued after a moment's pause: "While making believe that gifts from Santa Claus are connected to the child's quality as a little person, the people hiding behind Santa Claus deliver a sentence to the child about the child's standing and value in the immediate environment. Thus, a child's perception might be 'if impartial Santa Claus gives me gifts that are less nice than those he gives to my playmates, that must mean that I am less valuable, less lovable than my playmates.' How much do you think that child is looking forward to meeting with his or her playmates after Christmas when everybody is bragging about the wonderful presents they received?"

As it turned out, this was Ellen's own story. As a child from a poor social-economic background she—after an initial run-in with another little girl in her immediate neighborhood—had avoided getting together with her playmates after the Christmas holidays. As she walked out of her parents' apartment, anxiety filled her with every step; she feared running into one of her playmates who might ask her what gifts she had received from Santa Claus. It took years to overcome the feelings of being a second-class citizen. After all, Santa Claus himself had made that pronouncement. Even years later when she knew there was no real Santa Claus, the early-childhood experience left its mark on her emotional being. She continued to avoid social gatherings around the holidays. What we as adults refer to as 'children's innocence' is often a more anxiety-filled experience than we might realize.

"How did you overcome the discomfort about being with people during the holiday season?" asked another female writer.

"The anxiety built up in me as I was confronted with the fact of meeting with people, but after all those years the reason for the anxiety was not that obvious to me. I just did not want to be invited anywhere or be visited by anyone during that time."

"Didn't you live with your family then? You couldn't just walk out at the Christmas season," another member asked Ellen.

"Being with my family was not a problem; it was people outside my family that I felt uncomfortable being with. And for a while I made the excuse to myself that Christmas is a time to be with your family only. I usually did not attend holiday parties at work or anyplace else, trying to avoid the whole gift-giving scene without exactly being aware of why. Then one day our neighbor's little girl proudly showed me her new puppy. It was the Christmas present she liked best, she told me. And then she asked me about my presents and which one I liked best."

Ellen paused for a moment before continuing: "The little girl's question took me right back into my childhood. I was stunned as I realized where all the anxiety about being with people during the holidays originated. I told the little girl that I did not have my favorite present yet, it wasn't quite finished. But I would come over and show it to her as soon as I had it. She said that would be fun and I could look at her other presents, too, if I liked that."

"What did you do?" several of the writers asked at once.

"The next day I went out and bought myself a beautiful sweater. I put it on in the store; then I found a colorful little warm cover for the girl's puppy and went straight to her house, showing off my sweater and giving her the cover for the puppy. Of course, she insisted on putting it on the puppy right away and taking it for a walk. The three of us took a short walk to celebrate. My celebration was about finally being aware of where my anxiety and discomfort had originated. At that time in my childhood, I felt helpless about feeling less fortunate than my playmates, but now I could control how I wanted to enjoy the holidays and let people come closer into my life. I did not have to be afraid anymore that receiving less expensive gifts would turn me into a second-class citizen. The little neighbor girl was the first one I let enter my life at that moment," Ellen ended softly with a smile on her face.

The group members applauded. They thought it was a wonderful and meaningful story, important enough for people to read and learn from. They encouraged Ellen to write it up and submit it to a magazine for publication.

"Facebook Depression"—A Phenomenon of Our Time

As if the pursuit of social interaction with an uninterested target person were not stressful enough, the development of Internet social networks, such as Facebook, Twitter, and others, has added another dimension to the social-anxiety-producing system. Some regard Facebook, which has long eclipsed the other social network sites (SNS), as a forum that habitually elicits in its users feelings of low relative social value because it is a system for impression management, where comparative status is a matter of competition.[43] There is always the possibility that some of a user's "friends" may be doing a better impression management job than the particular user. The term "impression management" was coined by Erving Goffman to describe the strategic behavior individuals use when presenting a favorable image of themselves in the company of others.[44]

The affective result of individuals spending too much time on the social networking site has been defined as "Facebook depression." On Facebook, people invite others to be their friends. But what happens when the invited one does not respond or, even worse, declines the invitation? The person initiating the invitation will undoubtedly feel offended by the rejection, thinking, "Why does Y not want to be a friend? Am I not good enough?" Anger or depression will be the likely result of such an interchange.[45]

Another feature of the Facebook design is that people post accounts of what they have done or thought about lately. Then the friends of the person who posted the story or "status update" will respond by hitting the "like" button or offering a comment. If only a few "like" buttons get pushed, other friends can easily observe that. This is a way to put your life out there to be scrutinized or approved by those who read the postings. Of special interest to many users are the responses of friends of high-status users. In general, users who are high in status will receive more comments and more "likes" for their posts.

As Facebook users are confronted with their friends' overwhelmingly positive status updates, many occasions for negative self-appraisals arise, presenting opportunities to feel like a loser in the competition. The escalating risk for negative self-evaluation can be seen in the user's growth in friends, which increases the number of profiles one can observe in comparison to one's own achievements. According to recent statistics, American users of Facebook have an average of 245 friends.[46] A greater pool of online friends provides more opportunities to compare oneself negatively to others, and the persistent exposure to particular cues on Facebook may trigger feelings of low relative self-worth.[43,47]

Here we meet Lynn, who puts many of her experiences on Facebook for others (her friends) to read. As soon as she has posted the newest experience, she anxiously checks in with her smartphone, computer, or whatever else is available to see the responses to her post. "Oh, only three people 'liked' my story; what about the rest of my friends—are they not checking in with Facebook? Are they not approving of my story? And what about the people who read those meager approval ratings, what do they think of me?"

Doris, a 40-year-old woman who had difficulty making friends and experienced social anxiety all her life, has made changes in her life. She is trying hard to win the friendship of a few women whom she admires but who, unfortunately, remain resistant to her efforts. She ruminates for hours about how to approach them and afterward speculates about what she did wrong. In addition, if her postings on Facebook do not receive a high number of likes, her anxiety increases just thinking of meeting anybody face-to-face who might have read her status updates without responding to them and the meager responses from others. She does not know how many people have seen her status updates without responding to them. How could she face anybody who did not like what she had disclosed about herself? Who approved of it and who did not? With so much uncertainty, Doris found it difficult to face anybody; yet she could not stop either because that would mean giving up the challenge of being liked by everybody—or at least by the special ones, the ones whom she strived to be accepted by.

Of course, this particular type of longing for acceptance has been around since before the invention of Facebook, but technologies that bring about drastic changes that significantly affect the current foundations of cultural social interaction have not only positive but also some detrimental influences, depending on how the members of the current society react to them.

Social Anxiety as an Occupational Hazard

Sometimes social anxiety can find a breeding ground in certain occupational paths. Lisbeth, a young woman, contacted a psychologist's office on an emergency basis. Fortunately, she could be accommodated the same afternoon. The presenting problem was a panic attack, not the first one in her young life. Lisbeth described as the reason for the high anxiety her troubled relationship with Tom, her fiancé. They were in a serious relationship, living together, with the wedding date set for about 10 months from this troubled moment.

There had been difficulties before that the young couple had been able to resolve to some degree. But Lisbeth felt unable to attend to her job the next day. What made this occasion more troublesome in relation to Lisbeth's job? the psychologist wondered. Lisbeth was a dental hygienist, and because she and her colleagues had repeated contact with their patients, over time they get to know each other on a personal level.

Lisbeth was afraid to be confronted by patients asking her about her engagement and the upcoming wedding. How could she handle that without breaking into tears, and how often would she have to repeat the sorry details of her current situation? Lisbeth felt unable to handle the series of confrontations she would have to face the next day. She seriously considered quitting her job, claiming that an illness prevented her from being in close contact with patients.

The psychologist remembered personal conversations in dental offices over the years and decided to ask some questions. The consensus was that dental hygienists, much like hairdressers, felt they had to entertain the customer or patient who was detained in a chair for a certain amount of time. As the hairdresser or dental hygienist works on the customer or patient, there is a silence that needs to be filled to keep the situation from feeling awkward. And as one dental hygienist pointed out, the situation is even more critical for the hygienists because they work on the patients' mouths, rendering them unable to speak.

Contrary to the beautician's job where the customer can engage in the conversation, the dental hygienists carry the major responsibility for their patients' entertainment. So after topics like the weather and current news on TV or the radio have been exhausted, the conversation turns toward more personal aspects. One of the dental hygienists interviewed admitted to periodically having bad dreams about not knowing what to say when being confronted with patients while cleaning their teeth or of not being able to stop pouring out the details of her own life story.

Although they may be exposed to some psychology classes as part of their training, dental hygienist students apparently are not introduced to possible occupational hazards, such as feeling the need to fill the silences with too much self-disclosure in order to avoid an awkward tension between themselves and their patients. What does it say about our culture that silence between people who cannot move away from each other for certain periods of time feels awkward or wrong, like something that needs to be prevented?

What is the sense of talking just to fill the silences that actually could have their own soothing and healing powers if we could accept them as a brief period to contemplate what we really want to say—if anything—instead of frantically filling those moments with idle chatter?

Anxiety about Public Aloneness

Wherever we go, we are reminded that our society places great emphasis on couples, groups, and crowds. The tables in restaurants are arranged to accommodate couples or small groups; only occasionally do we see a small space here or there—mostly in the rear of the room—used to seat a single customer. For many people, aloneness in public places functions as a bad reputation. There has to be something wrong with the single man or single woman that they could not find someone to accompany them. In other words, being alone is seen not as a choice the individual makes but as a destiny determined in some way by the individual's shortcoming or failure to attract others.

Aware of that cultural proscription of attending social or public events as a single person or spectator, what is the individual to think and feel facing a public event by him- or herself? Anxiety will be in high gear just contemplating the possibility.

For the single individual entering a restaurant alone, the hostess or server's question "How many will there be in your party?" immediately raises the anxiety to an uncomfortable level because it includes the assumption that there will be others joining the individual. Thus the question seems to indicate that it is not proper to be alone. After stating that there will be no others coming along, the individual's anxiety rises another notch as the hostess advises another restaurant employee to seat the person at a table for one or the distraught individual is led through the restaurant to a table obviously set for one person. As some of the customers at other tables follow with their eyes, the lonesome person's approach to the designated table becomes hesitant, trying to avoid stumbling or bumping into any of the patrons that might just get up from their chairs and head for the exit.

At the end of this torturous walk, the socially anxious person attempts to make him- or herself comfortable at the table as nonchalantly as possible. Studying the menu, the lonely diner is fully aware that the server would rather serve a table occupied by a group of people than one single diner. And no matter what delicacies the individual selects, the dining experience will be spiced with worries of being awkward and dropping a napkin or what would be worse, a piece of flatware, or tumbling over a glass, spilling its contents across the table. In a state of anxiety, one faces a path filled with hurdles and all kinds of possible disasters.

Much of the anxiety surrounding a situation like this is culturally imposed. And while men suffer their share of apprehension when eating out alone, the cost is not as high to their self-image as it is for women. A woman dining alone in a public place may become the target of men who misconstrue her presence there as an opportunity to make undesired advances.

Millions of Subcultures

Our world is divided into continents and countries, each containing states, provinces, counties—regions with their own cities, towns, villages, and communities. Communities provide meeting places for people seeking spiritual enlightenment within the sanctuaries of various religious denominations and for public-oriented affiliations as well as for many other groups, each one with its own set of directives and guidelines for members to live by. Each group has its social pecking order more or less well established.

Barbara, an attractive, dark-haired woman in her early forties, grew up in a small Midwestern town. Her family was Amish, which isolated her somewhat from the rest of the community because the Amish do not readily mix with non-Amish families. However, Barbara did not feel welcome within the Amish community either because her parents broke some of the Amish rules.

Barbara's father worked for a non-Amish farmer with the benefit of living in one of his employer's houses. This meant that the family had electricity, running water, and a telephone in their home, unlike the rest of the Amish community. Furthermore, Barbara's father drove his employer's automobile to work as well as used tractors in working the fields. This relative comfort came at a price; the family was shunned by the other Amish families, and Barbara felt ashamed when she came face-to-face with any of them.

Just as there were no warm feelings wasted on her family by the community, the atmosphere inside the family was equally cold. Barbara's father was eternally angry and repeatedly threatened to kill his family members and others in the community. Barbara's mother was emotionally distant and never praised her children to avoid turning them into proud people. Barbara was expected to grow into a humble person.

Barbara remembers yearning for a gentle, loving father who would protect her, but that remained an empty dream; instead, she was sexually abused by her older brother. Although her mother knew about the abuse, she did nothing to protect her daughter or punish her son. To Barbara's mother it seemed to have been just a fact of life, and indeed, her mother had also been sexually abused when she was a child. For many years the abuse had been blocked out of Barbara's memory.

The best thing Barbara remembers from her childhood was that her frugal, penny-pinching father decided to give her a bicycle instead of the horse-and-buggy type of transportation customarily provided in Amish families. The bicycle afforded her greater freedom and independence. At least she could get away by herself for periods of time. She hated to tell anybody who her parents were because the Amish community disapproved of them. She felt ashamed, although on the outside she acted as if it did not bother her. With nobody on her side, she sought to prove herself in her schoolwork. She liked school; because of her father's stinginess, Barbara was allowed to go to public school instead of a private school that was attended by many of the Amish children.

Because the family was Amish, her parents did not allow Barbara to participate in sports activities and music or drama lessons. But she excelled in spelling; she worked hard at learning to spell words she could not even pronounce yet. She won the school and the county spelling bee, ready to represent her school at the state spelling bee. What excitement, what an achievement! For a brief moment she dreamed of even making it to Washington, DC. That dream ended abruptly when her teacher called her into the office to tell her that her parents did not give permission for Barbara to travel to the state capital for the spelling competition. It would not be acceptable to the Amish church and the Amish way of living. She could not believe it, but there was no way around it. In a fit of anger, she ran away to a friend's house, but eventually she had to return home.

In addition to the great disappointment over missing out on the spelling bee, there were rumors that she had withdrawn from the competition out of fear of failing. The generally elevated level of anxiety that she experienced when interacting with people rose dramatically, and she withdrew into herself, feeling abandoned and rebelling internally. She had been a straight A student, but after the spelling bee incident, her grades dropped; she did not seem to care anymore. School was soon over for her anyway because Amish children were not allowed to continue schooling beyond the eighth grade.

Barbara was 17 years old when she left home and moved into the little town, sharing a small apartment with another Amish girl. This was freedom! No more angry, yelling father around. She found a job and also worked part-time on weekends. Another opportunity the little town offered was that Barbara could enroll in studies to get her GED. Then she met a young man and fell in love. Their lovemaking brought back the memories of the sexual abuse she had endured as a child. She did not know how to handle it; it affected her marriage. Years of therapy helped her to heal, but the marriage did not survive. Today she works as a registered nurse and lives a calmer and happier life with her new husband and child.[48]

Healing for Barbara meant to resolve her shame, anger, fear, anxiety, and abandonment issues to the point where she could interact with others without fearing their judgment of her. And how remarkable that—relieved of her shame and anxiety—she can now use her strength to help others, nursing them to reduce their pain.

Consequences of Being Raised in a Society

As mentioned earlier, most human beings are born into some form of society, which with its relevant cultural norms regulates the lives of the individuals making up that society. That because human beings are raised in society, they tend to be victims of erroneous ideas is just one of the hypotheses proposed by Rational Emotive Therapy (RET). Being part of society, people keep re-indoctrinating themselves over and over with those fallacious ideas in an unthinking and auto-suggestive manner. As a consequence, those ideas are kept functional in people's overt behavior. According to Albert Ellis, the list of main irrational ideas that people continuously internalize and that inevitably lead to self-defeat includes the following:

1. the idea that it is a dire necessity for an adult human being to be loved and approved by virtually every significant other person in his community;
2. the idea that one should be thoroughly competent, adequate, and achieving in all possible respects if one is to consider oneself worthwhile;
3. the idea that certain people are bad, wicked, or villainous and that they should be severely blamed and punished for their villainy;
4. the idea that it is easier to avoid than to face certain life difficulties and self-responsibilities;
5. the idea that it is awful and catastrophic when things are not the way one would very much like them to be;
6. the idea that human unhappiness is externally caused and that people have little or no ability to control their sorrows and disturbances; and

7. the idea that one's past history is an all-important determiner of one's present behavior and that, because something once strongly affected one's life, it should indefinitely have a similar effect.[49]

Several of these ideas will be encountered in the case histories and discussions within the following chapters of this book.

CHAPTER THREE

Coping Mechanisms—Avoid, Avoid, Avoid

In general, it can be assumed that most people are motivated to develop and maintain identities that help them gain approval from meaningful others and help them achieve entry into groups they would like to be part of. An identity that furthers these two goals of acceptance and inclusion becomes a desirable identity in most people's minds. We can also assume that most people want to maintain a desirable identity both in their own eyes and in the perception of others. Of course, what is considered desirable varies from person to person and may reflect the internalized views of meaningful others.

Those unfortunate individuals who suffer from social anxiety deep down desire the same things: to have a pleasant personality that important people around them would find enjoyable to interact with. Yet tremendous discomfort influences them to do the opposite of being pleasant in the company of others; it pushes them to interact in a reserved, guarded manner or to avoid the presence of those they want to be liked by. The fear of being embarrassed and exhibiting signs of the embarrassment in some behavioral ways, such as blushing, stuttering, or trembling, turns the situation into an unwanted exposure for the socially anxious person; it becomes an event that reveals something the person prefers to keep hidden or concealed.[1] And although some socially anxious individuals want others to be "transparent" in their behaviors, for themselves they insist on remaining obscure to their environment.

The unwanted exposure model interprets the felt embarrassment and resulting anxiety of the individual who wants to avoid being observed and feeling exposed. The safest way to avoid the unwanted exposure is by avoiding the situation. Avoidance thus becomes the main theme and concern of the socially anxious person.

Misinterpretations of Socially Anxious Behaviors

Socially anxious individuals are often the most misunderstood people, and at the same time they greatly misunderstand those around them, the ones they are anxious about. Because of their withdrawal and avoidance tendencies, socially anxious people's behaviors are often interpreted as haughty, as if those around them are not worthy of bothering with. On the other hand, socially anxious individuals regard those around them as criticizing and rejecting them for being not good enough, smart enough, or funny enough.[2] This troublesome condition provides the sufferer with a lopsided view of the world and the people within that world. In fact, one could say that socially anxious individuals do what they suspect others of doing—judging those around them. And because of the strength of their beliefs, they are not easily ready to consider testing their views against reality.

The first, almost automatic response of those who experience the terror of social anxiety is to withdraw from the situation and avoid similar situations in the future. As the areas of threat increase, the individual's circle of life steadily decreases. Socially anxious individuals do not want others to know about them and what makes them so anxious. Disclosure of their vulnerabilities needs to be avoided at any price. They cannot afford close proximity to others, whether it is in their living or work situations. If they and their behaviors are disclosed to others (family, friends, or coworkers), they feel like unprotected organisms, at the mercy of anybody's ill will or wish to humiliate them. It is a dangerous world out there for them.

Losing Trust—Cutting Connections

Trina, married for about five years, had been unable to perform her job as a caseworker for an insurance company, resulting in her receiving disability payments. What was the reason for Trina's disability? She found it impossible to work in the presence of others, such as her coworkers who shared the big office with her. Trina felt that her colleagues observed her every move in order to get to know her thoughts and wishes.

How did this deep distrust of those around her develop? Events occurring in her early-childhood years convinced Trina that she could not allow anybody to know her and to know what she wanted. Because if people knew what she really liked, they would see to it that she did not get it and would give her something else instead.

Trina remembered one Christmas confiding in her mother that she would like to have a particular toy. When it came time to open their presents, Trina observed her sister Nancy unwrap the toy Trina had wanted. Not believing what she saw, she asked her mother if the gifts might have been mixed up. "No," her mother answered, pointing to boxes at Trina's side, "these are your presents, and Nancy is just now looking at hers." Trina was deeply hurt; here she had let her mother know what she wanted only to see it disappear into the hands of her sister.

There were other occasions too when Trina did not receive what she had asked for. At times, her mother inquired what treats the children liked that she could bring home with her food shopping. Trina favored a particular candy bar and told her mother about it. But her mother did not seem to hear her or, what was worse, intentionally brought home other treats.

Over the years Trina grew to distrust everybody; not even her husband knew what she wanted for Christmas, for her birthday, or for their wedding anniversary. Her distrust eventually grew into fear of those around her to the point that she could not tolerate being "exposed" to others.

Trust is a key element in many social interactions. In close relationships, as well as in interactions with strangers, people trust others on many occasions. Spouses and partners trust each other not to cheat; people trust friends with personal problems; and individuals ask strangers for information and directions. People buy secondhand cars, hoping to receive a fair value, and purchase products online without knowing the seller or being able to test the product before buying.[3]

Considering an attribution-based typology of betrayal model, adopting the victim's (truster's) *perspective* and focusing on *interpersonal betrayal*, Trina's distrust developed within the context of the parent-child relationship. Typical responses to betrayal can take the form of retaliation, distrust or suspicion, negative emotions, and withdrawal. At her young age at the time, Trina was probably not in a position to retaliate, but she certainly harbored distrust and negative emotions.[4]

As research has shown, betrayal is so aversive that people are likely to demand harsher punishment for betrayal offenders than for offenders of the same crime who did not betray their victims.[5] In interpersonal betrayals, victims usually attempt to make sense of the betrayal act within their own characteristics and the history of betrayals involving the particular perpetrator. Initially, upon betrayal, the victim engages in an attribution analysis about the underlying cause of the offensive behavior and whether the harmful act constitutes a betrayal.[6] Remembering that Trina's first thought was that her sister received the toy by mistake, her checking with her mother about the status of the toy represents an attribution analysis as much as one could expect at her young age. Did her mother just forget that Trina had desired that toy? Trina did not think so. Later, when her mother neglected to bring home Trina's favorite treats while responding favorably to the requests of Trina's siblings, Trina's suspicions and distrust were confirmed in her mind.

It is interesting to note that Trina never discussed the "betrayal" with her mother or anybody in her family. Being betrayed by her mother and apparently having strong beliefs in motherhood at that early age shocked her to the point that she thought nobody would ever be on her side or take care of her interests and wishes. On the surface, that logical process made sense to her.

Although Trina entered psychotherapy treatment at some point, apparently to focus on the depression she experienced—likely secondary to her high level of anxiety and distrust—she remained strong in her beliefs that there was no hope for change for her. Work situations, shopping, therapy, interactions with the neighbors—even with her family—all constituted unwanted exposure situations for Trina. She refused to take the risk of being caught in situations where others could observe her and gain knowledge of her personal preferences.

The fact that her difficulties in tolerating the presence of others around her ultimately made her eligible for disability payments (her lawyer had argued a case of paranoid personality disorder) confirmed to her that it was dangerous for her to be exposed to anybody's view and knowledge of her. So in the end, the financial assistance she received for having to bear her difficulties strengthened her belief that her impairment was too severe to contemplate working toward improvement, and it thereby strengthened her resistance to even consider the possibility of change.

As individuals avoid painful feelings and frightening situations, they don't learn to tolerate and work with those difficult feelings, and they don't learn the skills for coping with those uncomfortable emotions. Their "distress tolerance" decreases and their anxiety increases, initiating a vicious and cruel cycle where the avoidance actually strengthens the power of anxiety. The more they avoid what makes them anxious, the more powerful their anxiety tends to become.[7]

In summary, avoidance of the anxiety-producing situation leads to increased vulnerability, the very thing the socially anxious person tries to avoid. The degree of vulnerability a person feels signals a lack of psychological hardiness, a resilience that enables individuals to buffer the effects of stress and anxiety.[8] The basic ingredients for psychological hardiness can be found in our beliefs, in the use of certain coping skills, in general health practices, and in our support networks. Belief systems contain several important components, such as *commitment*, which is based on the belief that persistence in working toward our goals will bring meaningful results. Other components are *control*, the belief that we can exert some influence on what is happening around us, and *challenge*, the belief that negative events can be turned around to yield some positive outcomes. Those belief components are exactly the ones most lacking in the minds and lives of socially anxious people.

Beliefs Impairing Psychological Hardiness

Penny, a young schoolteacher, consulted a psychologist for genetic counseling. She and Martin, her husband, were thinking about starting their family, but Penny was concerned about several genetic factors in their family backgrounds. Penny was diligent in doing what research she could through the local university medical center and collecting data about the statistical probability of passing some of those troublesome genes on to her children. With the assistance of her psychologist, Penny compared and evaluated the various genetic influences. Her final decision was that having biological children would be too high a risk for her and Martin to take when seriously considering the welfare of their possible offspring.

Several months after the couple had made the decision about parenthood, Penny called the psychologist to schedule an appointment for her husband. Martin looked emaciated as he entered the psychologist's office. He reported that he had always felt uncomfortable speaking in front of groups, but that was not his presenting problem now. His current difficulty was that he could not eat in front of anybody because of his anxiety that he might spill something or have a choking sensation from the food in his mouth. He was afraid that he might have to cough and inadvertently spit out the food that was already in his mouth.

It had started in a restaurant at lunch with some of his coworkers. As Martin was chewing his food, the waiter stopped in front of him and asked him a question about refilling his soft drink. The shock made him swallow a bigger bite than he had intended because in trying to answer the waiter Martin had to stop chewing. As the piece of food made its way down his esophagus, Martin felt like choking and coughed. One of his colleagues slapped him on the back, laughingly apologizing that he did not know how to apply the Heimlich maneuver. Martin felt so embarrassed that choking to death seemed like the better choice at the moment. But Martin did not die. He finally caught his breath and gained his composure, promising himself never to have lunch with his coworkers again.

Eating his lunch within the confinement of his office worked for a while until one day he heard two of his colleagues walk by his closed door, wondering aloud if he might be at his desk. Although they refrained from knocking on the door and entering his office, the sheer possibility of this happening made Martin realize that it was not even safe to eat in his office. The next solution was to take the lunch Penny lovingly fixed for him and search for a hidden place where nobody expected him or anybody else to be and carefully eat his food there.

The possibility of dinner parties with friends and family members soon engulfed him with anticipatory anxiety. If he had to participate, he looked for mashed potatoes and any pureed foods, professing to prefer them to meat and crunchy vegetables. But even with those selections, his exaggerated swallowing movements made him feel that he was becoming the center of an awkward attention. More often than not, he declined dinner invitations. With the passing of time, his home lost the sense of security because his anxiety grew so overwhelming that he feared eating even in Penny's presence.

Martin's earlier difficulty with speaking in front of a group of people was an indication of social anxiety. As he admitted, it was never resolved; he just avoided situations like that. This tells us that Martin's commitment, his belief in persisting in his goals, was not strong, and neither was his belief that he could bring about a change. His generally defeatist attitude reflected his opinion that things could not be turned around to result in positive outcomes. There was no change in his defeatist attitudes—if anything, they grew stronger in his conviction.

With the psychologist's encouragement, Martin expressed his thoughts, beliefs, and fears. What were Martin's thoughts about eating in the presence of another person?

"I will be too nervous to chew the food adequately, and I will choke on it, spit some of it out for everyone to see. My face will get distorted with the effort to swallow without choking. Everybody will see that I am incapable of just simply eating."

"If you had a choice either to choke on your food and be observed by another person, perhaps one who could call for help, or to choke to death by yourself, which scenario would you choose?"

The psychologist's suspicions were confirmed when Martin answered, "Choke to death by myself." It was an honest answer, but it shocked Martin more than it did the psychologist.

"You would rather give up a life with Penny, the woman you profess to love, than be seen in an awkward situation by people who do not really matter all that much in your life," the psychologist summarized the situation.

"Oh no, that is not what I want at all," Martin stammered, "but how can I get rid of this terrible fear?"

The psychologist explained that Martin's beliefs were the biggest hurdle in overcoming his fear. No matter how often Martin went into a panic with his anticipatory anxiety, if he avoided the feared situation, he did not die and he was not embarrassed. And although not completely logical, Martin's reasoning that it was best to avoid the feared situation was reinforced because he was still alive. Thus, with time the situations became more threatening in his mind, and the relief he felt when avoiding them reinforced his conviction that he had done the right thing. And continuing to do the "right" thing would eventually reduce the space of Martin's life to the confines of his home or even only his bedroom or bathroom.

Martin reported another situation that had remained in his memory. Once in a restaurant, a group of people was settled at a nearby table. Suddenly, one of the men had to sneeze as he was chewing his meal. Because he was unable to hold back the sneeze, pieces of food swished out of his mouth in all directions. Some people in the group started laughing as the poor man tried to apologize for the spectacle he had caused. "I would have died of shame and embarrassment if that had happened to me," Martin ended the story.

"How did the man it happened to react to it?" the psychologist asked.

"He seemed somewhat embarrassed," Martin answered, "but he stayed with the group and continued to eat his food."

"So it might not have been as devastating an experience as some people would think," the psychologist attempted to introduce alternative thoughts to Martin's generally hopeless attitude. And Martin agreed that he would have taken such an incident much more seriously. "In fact," as he admitted, "I kept thinking how easily something like that could happen to me and how awful that would be; what would I do?" With that statement Martin confirmed the psychologist's concern that Martin was ready to accept that bad things would happen to him and that he lacked the second important belief that is a part of psychological hardiness, the belief that he could somehow influence the outcome of the situation.

"What would you say were the man's options at the time he had that sneezing episode?" was the psychologist's next question. Martin hesitated in thought before answering, "He could have died of embarrassment if he had a bad heart, or he could have left the table to go to the bathroom and head for the exit never to come back."

"Without paying his bill? What would the other people at the table have thought of the man? Not to mention the restaurant owner; he might have called the police," the psychologist turned Martin's attention to the consideration of possible consequences of such fleeing behavior.

Martin did not have an answer, so the psychologist continued, "It was a tough situation for the man. He probably realized that he was not in control of his sneezing and emitting the food from his mouth as he did so. However, he might have believed that he had some control about the consequences of the situation. If he did not leave but waited for his sneezing to stop, he could eventually continue with his meal and the people in his company would not have to worry if he was sick in the restroom or who would pay for his food. And most likely, with time the people would forget about the incident and possibly even praise the man for his good behavioral decisions."

Martin's facial expression reflected surprise. "Are you saying that the man felt in control after what had happened to him?" he questioned with disbelief in his voice.

Focusing silently on one of the diagnostic criteria for social anxiety disorder, the point that the fear or anxiety of the socially anxious person is usually out of proportion with the actual threat posed by the situation, the psychologist concluded that the man's behavior as described by Martin did not indicate that the man suffered from social anxiety disorder and that his degree of psychological hardiness might well have been somewhat stronger than Martin's.

"I can't really answer for the man because I don't know him, but from your description it seemed that he might have been aware of some options and decided to follow the one he considered to offer the best consequences or solution," explained the psychologist.

"What do you think is the difference with me? Why can't I be in control?" Martin inquired.

"Because you believe that you are not in control." The psychologist responded in a low but steady tone of voice. "You want to totally control that your food intake process occurs without any disturbances. That type of control most of us do not have all the time. Things do happen that make us cough, sneeze, laugh at an inopportune time, or swallow so that the food seems to go down the wrong way. But most of us can control the consequences of the happening in certain ways—in contrast with those individuals who do not believe that they have *any* control because they did not have the kind of control they wanted to have over the original situation."

"So it's all a matter of beliefs?" Martin's voice sounded incredulous. It was quite obvious that he was not ready to accept the psychologist's explanation.

"Alright, let's change the subject for a moment. When do you normally get up in the mornings during the week?" was the psychologist's next question.

Unsure of where the psychologist was heading with this question, Martin decided to humor the psychologist. "At 6:30 in the morning" was his quick answer.

"Why don't you sleep until 7:30 and then get up?"

Martin had a doubtful look on his face as he replied, "If I waited until 7:30 to get up, I would not be able to make it to my job in time. My work starts at 9:00 a.m.!"

"So you believe that you have to get up at 6:30 a.m. to be at your job by 9:00 a.m.," the psychologist confirmed.

"I know it!" Martin replied somewhat impatiently.

"Yes, you know it because you probably tried several different approaches to getting to work on time from where you live. Those different approaches or test drives are solid evidence for your knowledge or belief that you have to get out of bed at 6:30 a.m. to be on time for work. Here your belief is based on knowledge and evidence." After a moment's pause, the psychologist continued, "What is the evidence that supports your belief or knowledge that you have no control over the consequences of having a problem with swallowing your food—except that if you choke to death, then you have no more control? Incidentally, that is more likely to occur when you eat all by yourself than when other people are around to help."

Martin seemed taken aback by this question. Obviously, he had not considered this aspect. He admitted needing some time to think about it because it was something so foreign to what he had contemplated before. But he did not want to close the door to this, for him, new line of thinking, so he scheduled another appointment for two weeks from this first meeting.

For people who do not distinguish well between beliefs and knowledge, the challenge of being able to turn around some events to result in positive outcomes is extremely difficult to comprehend because their fear and anxiety reduce most situations to the danger-versus-safety level, where the prospect of danger looms so much larger than that of safety. In a seemingly dangerous situation, their immediate and automatic response is "Avoid! This is too dangerous." Their feelings become the evidence for the danger; they believe their feelings. There is no time for contemplating possibly changing the outcome of an event or adopting other coping mechanisms.

The Three Worlds of Human Existence

How does the tendency to avoid affect the individual's life? How does it affect the individual's existence? Swiss existentialist psychiatrist Ludwig Binswanger and other existentialist philosophers recognized some time ago that we live and act in multiple worlds, or spheres, that may appear independent but consistently interact. People shift behavioral patterns as they move from one situation or one world into another. The little-known, or now little-applied, concept of the human existence occurring in three worlds is useful here as it clearly illustrates the effects of avoidance behaviors.

The three worlds in Binswanger's model are the *Eigenwelt* or personal world, constituting the individual's self-world of inner feelings, thoughts, and bodily experiences; the *Mitwelt* or interpersonal world shared with significant others, such as spouses, parents, siblings, children, and close friends; and finally the *Umwelt*, the larger environment, the world around us, including colleagues, neighbors, acquaintances, and both animate and inanimate features of existence. As mentioned earlier, the three worlds can be independent, but they frequently overlap and interact. A healthy balance of the individual's existence in the three worlds is the culmination of a successful, well-adapted human life.[9]

To fully understand the distinctions and meanings Binswanger assigned to the three worlds, it would help to remember that Binswanger tried to comprehend and explain human nature in terms of care and love. In general, the *Umwelt* is the sphere of care, as people care what happens around them; in the *Mitwelt*, however, the emphasis is not on social relations but rather on being together with individuals in a loving way. In Binswanger's opinion these two worlds have different aspects of space. The space of care is bounded all around; it is an exhaustible and finite space. In contrast, the space of love is thought to be boundless, inexhaustible, and endless.

Comprehension of this contrast has to occur on a logical level but also on a phenomenological level. Although the *Dasein* (existence) as care is caring about something in a certain situation—therefore, always being a limited kind of totality—the *Dasein* in the sense of love is seen as existing in a limitless, unrestricted, unconditional being with each other.

It was Binswanger's conception that all phenomena occur within a meaningful matrix; and within this matrix they take on relevance for the *Dasein*. However, when there are only a few dominating themes, the *Dasein* is constricted to one or two world-designs. World-designs are the modes of the individual's perceptions and reactions to the total environment. As the world-designs become fewer, existential anxiety grows until the individual's *Dasein* may exclude all but one world-design, the *Eigenwelt*.

For instance, if the *Mitwelt* and *Eigenwelt* are not compatible, the mounting anxiety will cause the individual to withdraw completely into the *Eigenwelt*. Furthermore, the individual—because of a constricted *Dasein*—may be unable to explore future possibilities. Lack of ability to transcend the circumstances in which the individual is positioned prevents the individual from gaining any sense of achievement. As a result, drifting back—or regression—instead of expanding and growing occurs.

As we can see in Martin's case above, his discomfort and anxiety were first experienced in his *Umwelt*, the area of work and acquaintances. Withdrawing from any food-ingesting situations in the *Umwelt* reduced the interactions between Martin's *Eigenwelt* und *Umwelt* substantially, so that the space for meaningful coexistence in these two worlds became smaller and smaller, allowing superficial contact only.

With progressing anxiety regarding eating in the presence of others, Martin had to eliminate dinner parties with family and close friends, rendering Martin's *Mitwelt* and *Eigenwelt* incompatible when he could not allow himself to eat even in Penny's presence. As outlined in Binswanger's model, Martin's withdrawal into his *Eigenwelt* constricted his existence (*Dasein*) to the point that his sense of failure made him regress and made him unable to think of other options until Penny stepped in with her suggestion that Martin see the psychologist.

The Many Faces of Social Anxiety

Binswanger's idea that the meanings, purposes, and activities of our lives as human beings occur in three interconnected spheres serves as a helpful concept in understanding the various forms and aspects in which the fears of social anxiety are encountered. Although most people think that public speaking ranks very high in raising people's anxiety, there are other anxiety-producing situations that occur in different parts of people's lives.

Although public speaking ranks high on the list, with about one in five people reporting extreme fears about it,[10] there are individuals who become highly anxious at the thought of social gatherings, and others may feel terrorized when being observed in their activities, such as in Martin's story above. Still others are afraid of being rejected by those they want to be loved by. The dating arena might feel like a dangerous minefield to some looking for a partner in life. And even in the intimate sphere of spouses and lovers, some individuals are afraid to be transparent to or completely known by their partners because they fear making themselves vulnerable to rejection if they let themselves be known. In the intimacy of their bedrooms, some try to hide the imperfections of their bodies, although to others nudity appears less disclosing or threatening than letting the other know what they like or desire, as was the case in Trina's story above.

There are many different situations within the three spheres of human existence that can elicit social anxiety, and researchers have found it helpful to classify the varieties of social anxiety by the types of situations that bring on the threat and fear in individuals. For instance, the differentiation into *performance* and *interactional* situations divides individuals' fears into those that occur with public speaking, writing in front of others, eating in front of others (like Martin above), and playing sports (*performance* encounters) and anxiety that arises when socializing with others at parties or meetings, making small talk, asking for help or directions, and speaking to supervisors or colleagues at work (*interactional* encounters).[11]

Me and My Shadow

Ralph, the magician, stood on the stage behind the curtain, ready to begin his act. As the orchestra struck the first notes of "Me and My Shadow," lights came on and reflected Ralph's movements onto the little theater's curtain. The audience seemed stunned for a moment, but then their eyes followed the reflection of Ralph's movements on the curtain. The people recognized the scene of Ralph's shadow and his gestures as he engaged in the opening number of his magic act, and they broke into applause. This was the signal for the curtain to rise and fully reveal Ralph as he continued with his performance.

The people in the audience thought it was a clever beginning to introduce this part of the evening's program. But to Ralph it was more than a clever maneuver to create attention. In his mind it allowed him to remain hidden until he heard the sounds of approval with the audience's applause. And quite different from other magic acts, Ralph's performance left little or no need for verbal interactions with the audience.

As a child Ralph had been painfully shy. Because of his speech defect, he had been the butt of other children's jokes. Speech therapy helped except in an emotionally charged mood when Ralph's speech seemed to relapse into some of his earlier difficulties. Although these relapses did not occur frequently, it was enough of a possibility, and it led Ralph to reduce interactions with others as much as possible. He never felt safe enough to relax in the company of others.

Ralph's school years were not particularly happy. He excelled in mathematics, and his parents wished for him to become a teacher. However, his parents' wish felt like a death sentence to Ralph. Teachers have to address whole classes of students, all ready to make fun of him, and his old speech defect would surely appear again. Instead, Ralph decided to become a cartographer; his math skills came in handy.

In his spare time, he developed an interest in magic acts. The more his skills improved, the more fascinated he became with his new hobby. Concentrating on the many smooth movements of his hands, meant to deceive an onlooker's scrutiny, Ralph felt distracted and relieved from the concerns of his verbal skills. His hands managed to set him free, he thought. But his freedom was an isolated one; he never dated any girls or young women because, as he told himself, how could one romance a female without being sure of one's verbal skills? A stuttered declaration of love is an invitation to be ridiculed.

It is not as rare as one might think to find performers who suffer from social anxiety in their daily lives and who feel more comfortable on a stage because they are able to hide their real personality behind their stage persona. In fact, on the same program as Ralph in the local club was another performer who shied away from social interactions with others. Jonathan, a comedian, became friends with Ralph as they confided in each other about their concerns.

Jonathan, the son of a furniture store owner, felt insecure and incompetent for most of his life, primarily because of his father's ridicule of him. Even Jonathan's girlfriend gave up on him until he attended an ongoing "Taking control of your life" workshop.[12] Jonathan found the workshop helpful and recommended it to Ralph. In fact, Jonathan made use of Ralph's theme song by reasoning with himself that if he could imagine his shadow interacting successfully with others, then Jonathan himself might be able to do the same.

However, as Jonathan, desperate to win back his girlfriend's affection, made progress in overcoming his social anxiety, Ralph was reluctant to give up his "cover" because it had served him well for several years. Even though Jonathan encouraged him, saying that he did not have to change his magic act if he worked on reducing his fear of stuttering in a tense moment, Ralph hesitated to "weaken" his cover by making it less essential to his performance. For the audience, he started as a shadow, and by avoiding any interaction, he remained like a shadow—untouchable, unapproachable.

Comparing Ralph's and Jonathan's lives within Binswanger's existential framework, it appears that Ralph is resigned to continue his existence mainly within the *Eigenwelt* with superficial contacts through his *Umwelt* (largely his work environment and the audiences at the clubs where he performs his magic act). Significant connections in the *Mitwelt* apparently don't exist in Ralph's life. Jonathan, on the other hand, after having lost an important connection in his *Mitwelt*, is willing to face the process of change in order to reestablish that, for him, important link with his girlfriend.

Blaming the Past for Shrinking One's Future

Norman, a lonely man in his late fifties, lives in a continuously shrinking system of his *Dasein* (existence). He is just about to lose Julie, his lady friend, whom he professes to love. However, his love is not strong enough to make important changes in his life. The biggest change required for a happy relationship would be for Norman to work on his slowly but continuously expanding avoidance behavior.

Julie is a caring person; she does not give up easily on those she loves. But Norman has put her patience and goodwill to a test. Because she is a hardworking single mother of two children, her workdays stretch into the evening hours most days of the week. When she can make time available for an evening out, she prefers to have dinner in a good restaurant with an enjoyable atmosphere to perk up her spirits from a long workday. However, most evenings that she appears at Norman's place for their date, instead of selecting one of the fine restaurants in the area, he suggests (or rather insists) that he will drive to the restaurant and collect a takeout meal that both of them can "enjoy" at home. Although Julie doesn't mind eating dinner at home and appreciates the opportunity for takeout food at times, at other times she would prefer to end her long, stressful workday dressed up in her favorite outfits, enjoying a delicious meal in the ambience of a tastefully furnished and decorated restaurant. Refusing to dine with her in a restaurant because he feels uncomfortable, Norman pricks her balloon for that evening. As this scenario has been occurring more and more frequently in the past year, Julie is ready to give up on Norman and his occasional promises to change.

Norman claims that he feels uncomfortable in the local stores and restaurants because he believes that people still remember part of his embarrassing family history. What was so embarrassing that Norman could not bring himself to be seen in the community? Apparently, his parents' marriage had not been the ideal union his mother had dreamed of. Being married did not keep Norman's father from being romantically involved with other women. One of the women, a friend of Norman's mother, became pregnant by his father. That was the last straw for Norman's mother; she ran out of the house into the street screaming hysterically, trying to make her way to the friend's house. A police officer stopped her, and she ended up in the state hospital with a diagnosis of paranoid schizophrenia, which was probably a misdiagnosis because her claims of betrayal had roots in reality. While there, she managed to kill herself.

Norman's father left town after the funeral, and the pregnant young woman followed him after a while. Norman's grandmother raised the boy after his father had deserted him. Perhaps because of her own pain over losing her daughter, Norman's grandmother refused to tell Norman any details about his parents. It might have been his grandmother's silence about his parents that convinced Norman that what had happened was so evil that it could not be faced or discussed. Therefore, he, as a biological extension of his parents, needed to be silenced and hidden, too.

Julie's suggestion for Norman to move out of the area where all these unfortunate events happened does not convince Norman that his troubles would be over if he did move. And he seems to be correct in that prediction because by now his belief that he is being judged by people around him for his parents' past mistakes has shifted to distrust even of people he does not know and who do not know him and his past; now he believes that people everywhere will dislike him. So what's the point in moving? he argues in response to Julie's suggestion. It appears that Norman's beliefs have taken on a paranoid flavor.

The worlds of Norman's existence had been confined to very superficial interactions in his *Umwelt* and one or two links to his *Mitwelt*, which most likely will shrink even further as Julie recognizes the impossibility of building a meaningful intimate relationship with Norman.

Accepting one's parents' misfortune or misbehavior as a stigma of one's own person occurs across and within social classes. On his 16th birthday, Calvin found out that his parents were not his birth parents. He had been adopted as a tiny baby when his young, unmarried birth mother decided that she could not cope with the responsibility of raising a child on her own because she had not even achieved professional standing assuring her financial security.

The shock of finding out about the circumstances of his birth was twofold. The fact that his birth mother had not been married when she conceived Calvin indicated to him that most likely both of his parents were of questionable moral character. In addition, the fact that his mother had been eager to give him away suggested that Calvin was not worth keeping even by his own mother. If a person is not wanted by his or her own mother, that puts a low value on that unfortunate person, Calvin reasoned. And even though the behavior of his friends toward him did not change, Calvin felt vulnerable to all kinds of criticism that might be expressed by those he encountered.

Calvin and Norman, mentioned earlier, based their feelings of inferiority not on something they had done poorly or failed to complete but on events that involved their parents, something they had no control over. And even though Calvin—with the help of his adoptive parents—had already established an acceptable identity, he now chose to focus his own life on those regrettable events of the past. Thus, both men accepted a blemish not of their own making as a reason to be judged for by others.

The Importance of Relationships

It has been argued that human beings have a fundamental *need to belong*[13] Normally when a disturbance in the relationship is introduced, such as rejection or isolation, people respond by seeking more affiliations (quite contrary to the responses of socially anxious individuals). In general, people are very sensitive to cues of rejection and isolation.[14] Information indicating threats of rejection by others may function as a motive for restoring one's sense of relational value.[15,16] As experiments have shown, even minor instances of rejection by strangers have kindled people's desire to establish themselves with new sources of potential affiliation[17] but with greater interpersonal wariness.[18] In addition the "pain" of social rejection and isolation show neurophysiological overlaps with the experience of physical pain.[19] Those observations within the emerging field of social neuroscience suggest that human beings are interdependent creatures programmed for empathy and relationships. Thus, people suffering from social anxiety, who like Norman above and many others avoid meaningful relationships, add to their already painful existence the risk of additional physical and mental health problems.

Avoidance behaviors take various forms; some individuals attempt to refrain from interactions, whereas others might be physically present but mentally and emotionally distant in certain situations, like 79-year-old Dora, who has been widowed for more than five years and is living in a retirement community. Dora has no children and no close relatives. Her apartment is tastefully furnished and reflects a cultivated and elegant prior lifestyle. Dora was her husband's helper in the business he developed. And Dora's purpose in life seemed to have expired with the death of her husband. Although there are many social activities scheduled in the retirement community, Dora rarely takes part in them. She is a regular visitor to the physical exercise room, engaging faithfully in her individual exercises, and her trim figure reflects her dedication to physical fitness. Her other interests, knitting and working crossword puzzles, constitute individual activities in a solitary setting.

At mealtimes, Dora sits at her favorite table—alone. She makes it a point to sit there and eat by herself, always making sure that there are fresh flowers in the little vase on her table, something her mother passed on to her. Although she greets other residents in a polite manner, she remains reserved in all her interactions. Dora admits to being "nervous" in social situations. Being robbed of her previous social standing through her husband's business, she feels vulnerable by herself and hides behind the protective wall of her distancing behavior. The time in her tastefully decorated apartment is spent reading or reminiscing about the past. The paintings, sculptures, photographs, and knickknacks in the rooms all are focal points of her memories, going back to her childhood, parents, and friends during those early days. Later memories contain travels and life with her husband and their business partners and acquaintances.

Dora does not want to be unhappy; her deceased husband would not like her to be depressed. For him, she tries to do her best, but she can only do it within the framework of the past. The present and future don't hold happiness or emotional satisfaction for her. Interactions with other residents distress her to the point of fear and anxiety because they seem foreign to her and threaten to disrupt her equilibrium of living in the past. The antianxiety medication prescribed by her family physician helps in maintaining the equilibrium. Dora is not alone in taking antianxiety medication; in the past 20 years, the prescription and use of antianxiety medication have increased 65 percent.[20]

In clinical settings, social anxiety disorder and social phobia are often diagnosed with avoidant personality disorder because of the large overlap between these disorders. In fact, this overlap may lead to alternative conceptualizations of similar conditions. Although avoidant behaviors or avoidant personality traits are exhibited by many socially anxious individuals, according to the fifth edition of the *Diagnostic and Statistical Manual of Mental Disorders* (*DSM-5*), it is only when these traits are inflexible, persistent, and maladaptive to the point of causing subjective distress or significant functional impairment that a diagnosis of avoidant personality disorder is warranted.[21]

Perfectionism: Make-Believe vs. Reality

If socially anxious people were granted one wish, what would they ask for? To be perfect in their actions and appearance would most likely seem to be the fulfillment of their dreams. But would it really be a dream or might it turn into a nightmare? Some consider the relentless pressure to be perfect as a factor that sets the stage for suicide attempts among vulnerable individuals—especially those whose perfectionism is accompanied by high levels of hopelessness (of ever achieving the perfect stage) and social isolation.[22,23]

Why would anyone wish to experience the unhappiness of perfectionists and their loneliness and sense of isolation when even popular magazines like *Cosmopolitan* warn that "perfectionism is a total confidence killer"?[24] Why would anyone want to subscribe to perfectionists' all-or-none thinking and adopt their tendency to place themselves in no-win situations? Standards so high ensure either that they will fail or that even if they achieve a measure of success, their ability to experience personal satisfaction will be undermined by their stringent self-evaluative criteria. As they strive for unattainable goals, they pay the high price of low self-esteem and poor personal relationships.[25]

Perfectionism is not a simple, one-dimensional concept; in fact, it is a complex construct involving several key elements that may not be immediately apparent to observers. Perfectionism has been conceptualized as a multidimensional construct operating with both interpersonal and intrapersonal characteristics.[26]

Perhaps the best known of the three trait dimensions within the perfectionism construct is self-oriented perfectionism, which is based on intrapersonal characteristics. Individuals set high standards for themselves, supported by tenacious striving for their fulfillment. This striving contributes to rigid thinking styles, representing a specific form of rumination, such as a cognitive preoccupation with not living up to the perfect, ideal self, and fueling the sense of inferiority, deficiency, and hopelessness.[27]

Other-oriented perfectionism is interpersonal in application, as it involves demanding perfection of other people. This type of perfectionism provides an opportunity for some positive feelings. As can be expected, those others usually do not succeed in their perfectionistic attempts, which can be interpreted by other-oriented perfectionists as not trying hard enough and can be followed by the thought "At least I know how important it is to strive for perfection." This affords them the luxury of feeling superior about themselves, at least for a moment.

The third trait dimension is that of socially prescribed perfectionism, which involves the belief that others hold unrealistic expectations of the person. The pressure or demand for perfection in this case comes from society in general. In extreme cases of socially prescribed perfectionism, elements of helplessness and hopelessness are involved because of the individuals' sense that perfect performance will only result in future expectations being raised even higher.

Because of individuals' strong concern about making mistakes and their self-criticizing tendencies, socially prescribed perfectionism is often included in a higher-order construct, commonly referred to as "evaluative concerns perfectionism" or "self-critical perfectionism."[28]

A study of children and adolescents who were psychiatric outpatients showed that both socially prescribed perfectionism and perfectionistic self-presentation were associated with a measure of suicide potential. Suicide here can be equated to the ultimate withdrawal from involvement with others.[29]

Some perfectionists have adapted a strategy of self-concealment, a maladaptive interpersonal style known as perfectionistic self-presentation. This type of self-concealment becomes deeply ingrained and is shrouded in emotional perfectionism and concerns about stigma.[30] These perfectionists experience a need to appear as being in control of their emotions because they believe that even people who are fallible should be strong; they cannot afford to be weak.[31]

Barbara, a 75-year-old resident of a retirement community, is getting a lot of physical exercise upholding her perfectionistic self-presentation. Barbara appears to know everything. Whatever topic might be mentioned, she knows all about it and does not hesitate to inform others about her degree of knowledge of the subject. But the other residents cannot test her knowledge because they cannot keep up with her pace. She hardly ever sits down—at least not in the presence of others. Most of Barbara's conversations occur while she swiftly walks down the halls of the building, leaving any inquiries regarding her knowledge way behind.

Because many distressed perfectionists have a disclosure phobia, their access to social support is seriously limited, and they may experience great psychological distress and hopelessness. Their negative views about the future leave them with a sense of inability to do anything about it.[32] In general, long-term interventions are often needed to address perfectionism's core themes of the self and personal identity issues.[33]

Even in cases showing some success, interventions may reduce but not completely resolve the problems inherent in perfectionism.[34] Furthermore, it seems that the pernicious negative influences of higher initial levels of perfectionism tend to result in lasting vulnerabilities.[35]

Expectations of Self-Related Feedback: Consequences

Although most people in Western cultures believe themselves to be optimistic most of the time, studies reveal that people show significant declines in optimism when they expect self-relevant feedback. For instance, students estimated on four occasions the score they would receive on an exam. The four occasions were one month prior to the exam (Time 1), the day of the exam (Time 2), 50 minutes before the grades were returned (Time 3), and moments before the exams were handed back (Time 4).

The students' optimism led them to rate their scores exceedingly highly at Time 1, but they revised their initial outlook to become more realistic at Time 2 and even more so at Time 3. At Time 4 the students' outlook turned pessimistic, and their predictions fell not only below their earlier predictions but also significantly below their actual scores.[36]

The shift in predictions when self-relevant feedback is expected occurs in other areas of life as well. In general, people shift their predictions in response to new information, and they do so when they brace themselves for undesired outcomes. Both of the shifts serve the common need of preparing people to respond to uncertainty.

The most important among the moderators of shifts in predictions seems to be the temporal proximity of behavior and information that could culminate in potential bad news. For instance, an invitation for a social get-together when received a month or two in advance may elicit a positive response even in a socially anxious person. But as time passes and the event appears closer in reality, images of possible difficulties or negative reception may invade the thinking until the event assumes the characteristics of a punishing ordeal that has to be avoided at all costs.

Evidence suggests that people generally are more likely to change their predictions for outcomes that have the potential for strong negative consequences. But people are less likely to forsake their initial optimism when they perceive that they can control either the outcome or its consequences. But people who lack psychological hardiness don't perceive themselves as having any control to change the outcome of a situation that may not be favorable to them. Therefore, any sense of optimism is discarded early on.

Adjusting one's predictions in anticipation of feedback, especially negative feedback, can be understood as a type of control. Instead of attempting to control the outcome, some people attempt to control the emotional impact of feedback.

As some studies suggest, people with low self-esteem scale down their optimism more readily than those with high self-esteem.[37] This lower tendency for people with low self-esteem to reduce their predictions in anticipation of feedback may be linked to their chronic uncertainty about their self-conceptions.[38] It has been suggested that people with low self-esteem regulate their affect through advance anticipation and preparation for the possibility of negative outcomes.[39]

It can be concluded that people who lower their personal predictions regarding the outcome of a self-related future event do so as an attempt to brace for negative or undesired outcomes. Reasons for bracing may include the avoidance of disappointment or regret or making it a tool for magical thinking to avoid "jinxing" personal outcomes. Bracing may also function as a cognitive strategy of defensive pessimism.[40]

Bracing for disappointment, people may develop more mental simulations of undesirable scenarios as the event or performance draws near, generating increases in anxiety over the prospect of disappointment. On the other hand, anxiety over the impending outcome may generate mental simulations of undesirable scenarios. In this case, the anxiety does not bring information about the outcome; instead, the anxiety spontaneously generates mood-congruent cognitions, prompting people to think of ways in which the outcome may be poor.[41]

All Is Social—What's to Avoid?

The argument has been made that most of what people do is social, and even for those who for various reasons shy away from social interactions, their behaviors are socially controlled. Even such activities as thinking, feeling, and other ways of acting alone can be thought of as social behavior.[42] And when one is alone, the contexts for one's actions are almost all provided by other people.

Starting in childhood, actions and behaviors develop with a "social scaffolding" of consequences, which continues into adulthood. "Social scaffolding," a term used by developmental psychologists, refers to the way children's behaviors are shaped with parental social behaviors as consequences. In other words, children explore and act while glancing back at their parents to understand the effects or consequences of their actions as reflected by the parents' behavior toward the children.[43]

These patterns of glancing or looking seem to be socially constructed rather than a physiological given. While the audience changes from parents to significant others, the social scaffolding of behavior itself remains, and the "glancing back to the parents" turns into rehearsals of stories to relate to others.[44]

Major skills of thinking and cognition are learned and maintained through social scaffolding or social control. Similarly, language is learned as it has been developed by and taught to us by others. Thus, language is something that only works with people. Even when one is alone, language in thought and action enlarges the scope of social control of human activity. And the act of thinking, even when in physical isolation, depends on the use of language developed by others. Furthermore, language, including the meaning of individual words, is changed in its use over time by others. This changed meaning, however, influences others in how they think about a particular word (see, for instance, the use of the word "challenge" as discussed in chapter 7). Thinking and language are also socially controlled because most of what we think is about what we will say to others.

Most of the things we think and say are stories or reasons explaining our actions after we have performed them. The functioning of these explanations is shaped by preventing social punishment or through social reinforcement. Therefore, thinking is typically focused on people: ourselves and others.[45] Whatever our actions may be, people will inquire about them, potentially with such punishing consequences as being laughed at. Because of this potential possibility of punishment, we learn to engage in ongoing self-dialogues, rehearsing what we say to others, explaining our actions.[46]

Presenting a good story about one's actions or the logic behind them may increase one's status or reputation (generalized social consequences), or at least it may prevent criticism and other generalized social punishments.

From the foregoing, the case can be made that no matter how much socially anxious people avoid others and withdraw into their self-prescribed isolation, they cannot escape the influences of others because they carry those influences and concerns with them into their own inner sanctums. A logical conclusion might be to explore the meaning of the anxiety and question the validity of the underlying beliefs, leading to a different, more benevolent view of others and the self, finally opening the doors to a new outlook on life.

CHAPTER FOUR

Technology Obscuring the Problem

With our modern conveniences, a person can physically survive a solitary existence. But that existence is probably not a happy one because the choice of a solitary existence was made out of fear or anxiety, not really being a free choice. Despite a long history of natural selection among humans, being rejected is still painful, although modern technological developments seem intent on easing that pain.

The ancient notion that good relationships are central to both physical and mental well-being has found support in research studies. Health risks ranging from the common cold to stroke and many psychopathologies are reduced through involvement in meaningful relationships.[1] And good relationships are associated with greater happiness, resilience, quality of life, and even cognitive capacity. Furthermore, analyses of the various domains of life have suggested that quality of life is determined by the domain of intimacy. In general, people with overt psychopathology experience a lower quality of life, particularly in the domain of intimacy.[2]

Declining Quantity and Quality of Relationships

Even though relationships are of great importance to individual and collective well-being, the number and the quality of intimate relationships seem to be declining. The health risk of social isolation has been compared to the risks of smoking, high blood pressure, and obesity, whereas "participation in group life can be like an inoculation against threats to mental and physical health."[3] Studies have shown that a lack of social support adversely affects the body's healing function. For instance, stress and negative emotions brought on by a lack of social support seem to prolong infection and inflammation in many conditions, such as cardiovascular disease, osteoporosis, and type 2 diabetes. On the other hand, close personal relationships appear to have a positive impact on the immune and endocrine systems, diminishing susceptibility to infection and inflammation.[4]

Although the human organism is able to function as a separate unit by itself, it cannot operate effectively in isolation, especially early in life. But throughout life as well, without the input of caring others, the individual's protective capacity is undermined. In other words, as in "self-protection," the self is hardly possible without other selves.[5] Notwithstanding those insights, compared with American people in previous decades, individuals now spend less time with friends and family, have fewer intimate friends, and are less socially involved in groups and communities.[6] This observation may have given rise to the debate on whether Internet social networking exacerbates or compensates for the reduction in direct personal contact.[7]

The technology of a given culture has far-reaching effects on its people's psychology and lifestyles.[8] Modern technology affects our psychology, biology, society, and lifestyles in many ways we may only begin to comprehend. Furthermore, technological innovations and their effects on lifestyles may change faster than we know how to change ourselves.[9] According to Roger Walsh, at the University of California, Irvine College of Medicine, many medical and psychological complications of contemporary pathogenic lifestyles may be reduced or modified with the use of individual therapeutic lifestyle changes (TLC).[10]

Technological Advances Eliminating Face-to-Face Contact

Neighborhood stores once required social interaction, but people now shop mostly in large supermarkets, silently filling their shopping carts and heading for the checkout line that is served not by a person but by machines. And "curbside pickup" is offered by some pharmacies and stores to eliminate the need for people to enter the store. Using their smartphones, customers can call in their orders and receive them at curbside while remaining seated in their cars. The many available apps on one's phone make it possible to order all kinds of merchandise, foods, and meals without ever having to utter a word; everything will be ready for pickup at curbside or in front of the store. No actual verbal interaction is required. If that still presents too much "exposure" in having to face people briefly, online shopping presents a solution. As mentioned on June 9, 2016, by Jane Kingseed, better known as Jane King, during her daily TV broadcast report *Business Headlines* from the NASDAQ MarketSite, consumers can now buy more online than in stores and apparently did so for the first time that year.

Service stations and banks have made great strides in reducing or eliminating face-to-face contact. Most people communicate through computers; even telephones, once developed for verbal communication, enable people to avoid speaking by inviting them to text instead. Little attention is given to the fact that by texting a whole level of information is lost in the interchange. By eliminating the voice, the emotional state often reflected in a person's speech is lost to the recipient of the message. If the message had been spoken, would the voice reflect the speaker's surprise, amusement, anger, or perhaps even love? That additional information through sound is lost in the letters of the message.

Distance learning is replacing classroom meetings and students' social interactions, and they don't even have to wait for distance learning until they get to be college age. Television commercials inform the public of tuition-free online academies for grades K–12, such as the Indiana Connections Academy. The list is ever growing.

Learning about all these new technological wonders might make one think that technology has set its goal to ease the lives of those who suffer from social anxiety—a noble mission, indeed. And as one former child actor explained, "I'm actually shy. There are women I wouldn't go up to in a club. But I'll e-mail them on MySpace. For some reason you get on there and all the barriers come down. Girls will say things they'd never say to you in public."[11]

MySpace, launched in January 2004, became an Internet phenomenon, with 24.5 million unique visitors reported in November 2004 and 170,000 new members signing up each day. Just "in two years, MySpace has become the most popular social-networking site on the Web, a virtual city of sex and youth culture, with its own celebrities, Casanovas, and con artists."[12] But as usual, there are two sides to this situation as well. Not only do these technical innovations help socially anxious people avoid feared situations, but they also strengthen the belief that there is something dangerous about interacting with others (why else would society come up with all those technological remedies to allow the avoidance of contact with others?).

Online dating sites like Match.com, Chemistry.com, eHarmony and others certainly seem to have their share of customers looking for soul mates, and according to the *International Herald Tribune*, 97 million seekers visited Internet dating sites in 2007, but apparently not everyone wants to work through millions of online profiles, being disappointed when their picks turn out to be different in person from their description in the profiles. Professional matchmakers have come to the rescue, using "their intuition and extensive social databases, to set you up with your true love."[13] Fees for such personalized services can amount to $25,000 and up to $500,000 a year for some of these matchmakers. And one of the more successful ones claims responsibility for more than 800 weddings.

Not everyone in need can afford those fees, and many searchers for happiness will continue to rely on online dating systems. Unfortunately, socially anxious people without great financial resources are not the only ones to make use of those technical innovations. More and more crime reports are about gas pump skimmers, criminals tampering with gas pumps, inserting devices that can skim customers' credit cards and make the card number available to the skimmer. These thieves always seem to be a step ahead and are difficult to catch because the equipment they use cannot be traced because they mostly purchase it online. While the race between technology and crime goes on, many people have decided to pay for gasoline with cash in face-to-face interaction with store owners.

But to be in possession of cash, Helena, a 62-year-old widow, had to visit the bank. It was a rainy afternoon, and because of her anxiety when interacting with the bank tellers, she decided to use the external ATM as she had done several times in the past. Occupied with her transactions, she did not pay close attention to the car that had pulled in close to where she had parked her car. As she received the requested amount of money from the machine, she stuffed it into an envelope and turned around, intending to get to her car. Helena was faced by a strong-looking woman, who immediately grabbed the envelope out of Helena's hand, pushed Helena against the wall of the bank building, and jumped into her car. The engine was idling and the woman drove off in a hurry. All Helena could see was what looked like a black SUV. She did not get the license plate number, nor could she be sure about the make of the car. Helena had heard of similar attacks before, but in weighing the fear of her discomfort in interacting with the bank's personnel inside, she decided to risk the possibility of being robbed while conducting her business with the external ATM. In the race of technology and crime, Helena had lost when she let her anxiety override the risk of being robbed.

Andrew, first encountered in chapter 2, sadly grew into a young man whose childhood awkwardness remained in adulthood. His long-boned body just wasn't made to move smoothly. Of course, Andrew was very much aware of that and hated to enter stores or restaurants with open spaces that people moved through to the counters or tables. For Andrew, banks were the worst places to navigate. As he entered the bank's lobby, he could feel all the tellers lined up at their stations stare at him. It seemed unfair as they were sitting behind the glass windows, with their lower body parts hidden behind the long counter. He imagined that they all stared at him while he awkwardly, almost stumbling, made his way to the nearest unoccupied teller. Even the teller's friendly "hello" did not relax him because he knew that as soon as his business was completed, he had to turn around and walk all the way back to the entry under the scrutiny of each teller's eyes.

For Andrew, life took on a bit of fairness when machines were installed that could be operated from the outside, and especially when banks installed drive-through lanes where the bank tellers conducted the business through a window while the customer was sitting in his or her car. Securely covered in his car, Andrew finally felt equal to the teller helping him; his car provided as much coverage as the bank tellers had at their stations. Andrew was much relieved; finally, some technological genius had come up with a solution that would make life a little easier to bear for Andrew.

Some technological developments are likely to be regarded as a blessing by those who seemingly benefit by them. For instance, the growth of computer and information technology that has become such a big part of our lives has opened up night-shift jobs for many in the technological workforce. To avoid slowdown in their daily work activities, hospitals, universities, and big companies are served by installation, maintenance, and repair work on their computers at night. This arrangement creates perfect jobs for the socially anxious computer expert. Face-to-face interactions are virtually eliminated as the lonely technician enters the quiet workplace shrouded in dimmed lights, waiting for him to perform his magic with the sophisticated machines so that at the brink of dawn the workflow can resume smoothly. A few helpful notes instructing the operators what to do in case such and such happens may be the only evidence of the technician's nighttime appearance at the workplace.

Technology Accommodating Obesity

At a recent authors' fair where the upcoming arrival of a book on understanding social anxiety was announced, a young woman inquired about the publication date for the book because she was most eager to buy it. She volunteered that her job duties were online work situations because she could not handle face-to-face contact with others. She added, almost as an afterthought, "And I am not sure how long I can even perform this job because I become more anxious with every interchange with anybody even online."

Another visitor to the authors' fair stood close by, listening to the brief interchange. She was also interested in the arrival of the book because she thought it might help her sister Emily. Fifty-eight-year-old Emily was never very socially active, but her anxiety problems really grew with the growth of Emily's weight. As she continued to gain weight, her withdrawal from social contacts increased. The thought of going out in public terrified her; only close family members were allowed to come and visit. Her employer made it possible for Emily to work from home, a tiny apartment on the ground floor.

Emily knows how to drive and has an automobile, but because of her obesity she now finds it too difficult to walk from her apartment door to the parking place assigned to her apartment. Grocery shopping has been greatly reduced to the few times she is able to walk to her car after having ordered her purchases with her smartphone, to be picked up at curbside. When the walk to her car becomes too troublesome, Emily calls in her order to the nearest supermarket for delivery. However, she prefers not to interact with the person who handles the delivery. The shame of being observed by others is too painful. Earlier in her life, she loved to go to the movies; now she rents movies that are delivered to and picked up at the mailbox at her door.

Emily's life has become a vicious cycle: the more she eats, the less she moves, and the less she moves, the more she weighs, which then raises her anxiety level to the point that she indulges in her favorite foods again. When and how will this cycle end? Emily's sister is worried—and with good reason; the family physician frequently expresses the need for Emily to lose weight because her bones will not be able to carry all that weight, and her heart will be too weak to keep pumping in this deadly race.

Cyberbullying: Graduation from Playground to Internet

For people who seek information about topics they are too embarrassed to talk about or those experiencing social anxiety when searching for answers, the relative anonymity of the Internet may be appreciated as a beneficial tool. However, the same anonymity provides cover for those who aim to inflict fear, anxiety, and depression on others. Whether people are threatened by abusive comments or malicious rumors posted on Facebook or by "doxing," the public release of personal information, anyone can become a victim of cyberbullying. However, children and teenagers are particularly vulnerable victims as the playgrounds and school yards are replaced by email, texting, instant messaging, social media, or any other digital form of communication or information dissemination. In addition, although traditional bullying was restricted to daytime hours on school days, victims of cyberbullying can be tormented at all hours of the day or night. There is no safe time to relax.[14]

No matter what the reasons for bullying are, for the target the effects are not only painful but also isolating because the target might withdraw in shame from social contact. In addition, bullied victims often have to refer to or rely on adults to resolve the issue, which instills a sense of help-lessness in the target.[15]

Many students now spend their nonschool time communicating with others through social media. Threatening messages can be received any time the individual enters the world of social media, and the impact of those threats can lead to reduced self-esteem and declining grades in addition to the fear and anxiety experienced during the bullying.

Professionals approached for help, such as school counselors, have suggested that victims of cyberbullying identify and associate a color with the emotions they feel at home, at school, and online, resulting in different categories in which to explore their feelings as well as behaviors to deal with the situations.[16]

It is interesting to note how one of the school counselors defined the students' three worlds as home, school, and online, with the online world apparently growing continuously in time spent there as well as in influencing power. It might even be disturbing to realize the ultimate power of technology. What might have originally been conceived of as tools for human beings to utilize for their needs has exerted wide-ranging influences in creating a "can't wait" generation of people. The immediacy of social media provides knowledge as well as feedback at any moment, and this immediacy reinforces people's lack of patience, providing instant gratification of whatever the individual wants to know or is afraid to know at the moment. Instead of turning on the tool when it is in the person's will and interest, the tool commands the person's immediate and almost constant attention.

Designing and Presenting One's Perfect Image

Another fertile ground for the application of social media or digital communication systems is provided by some individuals' obsession with attaining and presenting their "perfect" image. From such websites as Am I Hot or Not? to entire social media platforms, such as the popular site Instagram, which is like Facebook for photos, these enterprises display all kinds of pictures supplied by individuals. The technology available allows users to present a dream version of themselves to the world. Instead of using their own criteria for establishing a sense of their person, these individuals incorporate into their identity the reactions and likes of those observing the idealized pictures. The object of the photo makes him- or herself vulnerable to the effects of those responses, which can range from very complimentary to highly critical and humiliating, a vulnerability few can afford.[17]

From Dating to Computer Mating

While some technological developments might be regarded as a blessing, other technological innovations, apparently developed to help people, have a way of creating their own problems.

As some of the socializing institutions of the past—in step with technological developments—have given way to distance learning experiences, people have fewer chances to meet and get to know each other. Although college campuses were not meant to function as a dating ground for students (at least not primarily), young people were provided opportunities to meet in their classes, to observe each other, and even to express their liking for one another.

Today much of the dating scene is based in computer dating or other distance dating services. In the mid-1990s, Web-based dating services made their initial appearance; now they have become a $2 billion industry. As of December 2013, such services as Match.com (the largest and one of the oldest dating services on the Web), Plenty of Fish, and eHarmony had been used by 1 out of 10 American adults.[18] MySpace, mentioned earlier, has changed the way young people especially share, relate to, and absorb one another. Apparently, about one fourth of MySpace users are under age 18.

For students who grew up with social media, utilizing social media in developing romantic relationships seems like a natural thing to do. As the partners communicate through Facebook messages, they can take their time to fine-tune their answers before actually sending them, rather than having to answer immediately as they would feel they have to do in phone communications or in face-to-face meetings. This allows them greater control in how they present themselves to their partners. Once a romantic relationship has developed, it is not "official" until a person's status on Facebook is declared "in a relationship," as described in studies conducted by a faculty member of the University of St. Joseph in West Hartford, Connecticut. Having announced one's personal romantic status to friends on Facebook, one may find a breakup painful because of public involvement. Some students feel disappointment and sadness to the point that they experience anxiety in contemplating facing their friends, and they may decide to skip classes, miss work, and avoid social gatherings.[19]

Among those looking for their soul mates, who could resist an invitation to join the "Online Dating Fairy Godmother" Bela Gandhi, CEO of Smart Dating Academy, who uses her magic wand to demystify the process of meeting one's soul mate online? E-mail invitations sent by Arielle and Claire at Art of Love stress the fact that one does not even have to leave the living room to find out the time-tested relationship secrets of the more than 25 leading love relationship experts associated with this enterprise. There are online programs, summits, seminars, and workshops with special upgrade packages available in downloadable format. For instance, the Gold Soulmate Package, valued at $2,938, can be purchased for only $97 (special event price). For the Platinum Soulmate Package, valued at $7,632, one has to spend $197. Bargains like these are available through the efforts of our modern technology.[20]

The Ease and Risks of Online Dating

This online-dating boom has opened the door to fraud and misrepresentation. According to the Federal Trade Commission (FTC), complaints about impostors in romance scams more than doubled between 2013 and 2014.[21] How do the targets of these scams become victims? When things sound so good that they want them to be true, the targets may convince themselves that fate has brought an incredibly romantic person their way, turning the online service into destiny's tool and investing the power of their blind beliefs in the con artist's game.

Even in the absence of any scam, online dating involves risks. On a superficial level, individuals get to know each other from a distance, more or less relying on what the other person is willing to disclose. Quite often, communicating partners don't live in the same area and can rarely observe the other's behavior to draw some conclusions about his or her personality.

When two people, being introduced distantly, finally come together face-to-face, their meeting can be expected to be much more awkward than when two college classmates meet for a date. Any person feeling anxious about meeting new people can easily experience a panic attack just thinking about meeting a stranger with whom they might expect to embark on a romantic relationship. For men, the difficulty might be in deciding whether and after how many meetings they are expected to seduce their female partner, and if so, whether the degree of desire will be reflected in the nature of their erection at the decisive moment.

For the female partners in situations like these, the decision is not much easier. Should they disrobe of their own accord or let the man struggle with getting rid of those intricate garments? How should they disclose the intimacy of their body? How to hide from scrutiny the less than perfect parts of their anatomy? With all those concerns occurring simultaneously, how could they relax sufficiently to focus on pleasure?

Probably because of her obesity, Cynthia never had a romantic date in her almost 30 years of life. Following the advice of her friends, she was introduced to a shy ("socially anxious" would be a more accurate term) man through an online dating system. Harold was about eight years older than Cynthia, and his dating history was, like Cynthia's, essentially nonexistent. Because they did not live in the same town, their meetings were restricted to some weekends. After a couple months, Harold proposed marriage. Cynthia was elated; now she would not have to die a spinster with her virginity still intact.

On the evening of their engagement, Cynthia was ready to try sexual intercourse. But Harold stalled; sex was messy, and in his opinion it seemed more meaningful for them to wait for sex until their wedding night. Their wedding night came and went; they fumbled around awkwardly. Cynthia did not quite know what to expect, but she was not prepared for what she did not get—sexual intercourse. Harold was extremely anxious and anything but happy. He was clumsy in kissing Cynthia and caressing her various body parts. He never achieved a full erection, and they finally gave up for the night. The following nights and days proved to be equally unsuccessful.

Harold, in his extreme fear of being in an intimate situation with another person, had never engaged in sexual activities except for masturbating while watching pornography. He never had to worry that he did not do the right things in pleasuring and satisfying another person. By himself, he could not do wrong, and he did not have to worry about having an erection at the appropriate time. He did not have to worry about contracting a sexually transmitted disease or running out of condoms either.

Why after all those years of taking care of his own needs did he decide to get married? His older brothers and his colleagues at work teased him. They had never seen him in the company of a woman. Finally, they suspected Harold to be gay. Harold's father confronted him about that suspicion, adding that Harold brought shame to the family name. Their small rural town was not ready to accept that one of its citizens was leading a homosexual lifestyle.

How to throw out all those suspicions? Getting married to a woman appeared to be the answer. It was Harold's ticket out of an uncomfortable situation. But what about Cynthia, the woman he married with the help of the dating service, and her expectations? one might ask. Did she deserve what was happening to her? Nobody asked her if she would agree to a sexless marriage. Divorce was an option she was not ready to accept when the ink on their marriage certificate was hardly dry yet. How was she going to deal with the fact that on the very day her dreams of love and marriage seemed to come true, she had to bury them? Did she wonder whether her marriage would ever be affirmed by a true sexual union of two partners?

It was not only the sexual part of their marriage that was missing; when two socially anxious individuals decide to live together, that does not necessarily render them less socially anxious. Just as they had not learned to relate to others before their marriage, they did not know how to do it within their marriage. Cynthia realized the hurdle they had to overcome to have a happier relationship, and she embarked on psychotherapy as a learning path. Harold, on the other hand, was not willing to share that learning experience.

In the meantime, Cynthia has made great strides on her own, working on overcoming her anxiety about meeting people. She has shed a lot of weight and is participating in many health-focused activities and public events. She is starting to construct a life for herself that is meaningful and enjoyable, allowing space and time to explore and express her creative talents. Will it be enough, or will she look for more in another relationship? Time will tell.

Until Our Beliefs Do Us Part

Waiting for the wedding night as the first opportunity to engage in sexual intercourse might be rare in modern times. But it does happen, and often it comes as a part of the couple's religious beliefs. When Annette and Bob were dating after finding each other through an online dating service that emphasized Christian values, they kissed and touched and felt each other's desire. Annette was ready to have intercourse, but Bob stopped their lovemaking prior to that point, saying it would be a sin for them to complete the sexual act without being married. He would be ashamed going through the wedding ceremony with that sin on his soul and body. The wedding itself would then be meaningless.

Annette was stunned, and at the same time she felt the sting of being judged. Because she had been willing to continue their sex play into intercourse, this made her appear more open to sin and shame than Bob. Their equal standing in the relationship was now somewhat unhinged in Annette's mind.

They did get married as planned, but Annette did not allow herself a second failure. She was thinking of her perfectionist father, who was always right and did not hesitate to point out others' mistakes to them. Growing up, Annette had felt like she was on probation. Her father's criticisms of her behaviors came down swiftly and clearly. Even as an adult, Annette hardly ever displayed her true self in her father's presence.

Now she felt toward Bob like he were her father. She could not reveal herself to her husband, especially sexually; she had to be on her guard. If she became aroused by his touch, she would not let herself express it. Her fear of being caught in another sexual failure made her want to complete the sex act quickly, without talking, and without emotions. Participating as little as possible in sexual intercourse was Annette's idea of avoiding mistakes and failures. As she said: "Quick and to the point. Then I have done what I'm supposed to do and I can go on to the next thing."

Many marriages are unions of "intimate strangers"—two people who at times are involved in intimate physical activities but emotionally do not know one another. It is interesting to note that some people are more trusting with their bodies than with their emotions. Low self-esteem induces thoughts like "If he/she knew how I really am, my spouse or lover would leave me." Thoughts like those lead individuals to hide their emotions and the innermost parts of themselves from their significant others.

Annette's insistence on not disclosing herself to anyone is reminiscent of Trina, mentioned in chapter 3, who could not risk letting anyone know what she desired because, as she believed, they would then prevent her from getting what she wished for. And Trina also could not let her husband know what would please her sexually. It amounts to a sad life to settle for. By hiding their wishes either because they thought their wishes were unacceptable or that others out of malice would want to deprive them of getting what they wanted, both Annette and Trina made sure they would not receive what they desired out of life.

Disappointments are usually suffered silently, especially by socially anxious individuals. Rather than letting the other person know what would please the disappointed individual, further tightening of any emotional disclosure is the next step. This, in turn, results in further withdrawal from the significant other. In doing so, the individual makes several assumptions: the other person has no shortcomings and furthermore will be as rejecting as others in the individual's past might have appeared to be. Both Trina and Annette followed that line of reasoning.

In Annette's marriage, Bob apparently wished for a more emotionally based experience and found it in a friendship with another woman. Although they did exchange thoughts, ideas, and feelings, the relationship did not become a sexual involvement. For a while Bob and Annette separated. During that time Annette engaged in a "sex-only" relationship with another man. She never dated him; she left him as soon as the sex act was completed, and she did not allow any intimacy to develop with him or anybody else. This was her secret, just sex, "quick and dirty"—nobody would ever know about it.

After a little more than a year, Bob decided to get back with Annette for the sake of their two children, who had been living with Annette during the couple's separation. Bob missed being with his children on a daily basis, and he was willing to do whatever necessary to have them all live like a family again. Annette realized that she had some work ahead of her and called a psychologist to make an appointment for the first available opening.

Annette seemed surprised at herself when in her initial session with the psychologist the first thing that came into her mind was the memory of being flooded with anxiety on her wedding day. As she was about to put on her wedding gown, the gown she later cut up in little strips and pieces in a fit of anger, she felt a strong wave of anxiety overwhelm her. Her body was shaking, and she had difficulty getting into the gown without tearing it.

"What thoughts or memories troubled you when you were about to put on your wedding gown?" the psychologist asked, noticing how Annette suddenly stiffened in the chair facing the psychologist.

"At the time, it occurred to me that my wedding was the occasion for two men that were important in my life to judge me and find me lacking or even unworthy," Annette answered in a low tone of voice.

"Was your new husband one of them?" the psychologist asked, concerned what this question would reveal.

"Yes, my husband was one of them because he had earlier in our relationship refused to have sex with me, saying that it would be a sin to have sexual intercourse before marriage. Since I had been willing to try it, I was the sinful one, the one who needed to be ashamed. I could never live that down, even though technically I was entitled to wear that white gown of virginity."

"Who was the other man who judged you?" the psychologist inquired.

"My father," was the quick answer. "My father refused to dance with me at my wedding. He told me beforehand to inform the DJ not to announce the father-daughter dance."

"Why did your father refuse to dance with you?" the psychologist wanted to know.

"My father does not dance, and he did not want to make a fool of himself trying to dance with his daughter. I was not worth taking that chance of dancing a few steps with or perhaps even taking a lesson from a dance instructor on how to do that at his daughter's wedding. So I ended up dancing with my father-in-law instead of with my father." Annette sounded pretty much discouraged as she finished the account of her wedding day.

"Your father-in-law taking on your father's role might have seemed like a double-edged blessing," the psychologist mentioned in trying to help Annette open up about this aspect of her marriage.

"My father-in-law was nice enough about it. I could not find any fault with him." Annette continued her story, describing her feelings at the time of her marriage: "The fact that made it difficult for me was that there seemed to be no support for me in my family, and I was handed over to my husband's family without any support from my family, like I was ready to be discarded and picked up by anyone passing by and feeling sorry for me. I, by myself, it seemed that I had little value."

"As you explained it, you felt unsupported by your family. You are not mentioning your mother; what role did she play in your life and in your wedding?" the psychologist tried to expand on the family background.

"My mother, in my mind, has been a 'nonperson' parent. She always agreed with my father, no matter what the issue was. She never took my side. Her greatest responsibility was to have everything at home run smoothly and quietly. My father could not tolerate noise. It was always uncomfortable to bring any of my friends to our home, which happened rarely enough because I was not popular with my schoolmates. My mother did not encourage them to talk or play. She seemed anxious to have them gone before my father returned from work," was Annette's reply.

Although Annette did not mention anything about her mother at the wedding, the psychologist did not pursue the issue. Annette's description of her relationship with her mother was sufficient for the moment. Instead the psychologist turned the discussion to Annette's parents-in-law. "You mentioned that your father-in-law danced with you at the wedding. How would you describe your relationship with your husband's parents?"

"It's all right; my mother-in-law and I get along when we are visiting. They don't live close by, so we don't see each other all that often. There is some emotional distance between my father-in-law and me. That is probably my doing; I am holding back. In general, I am uncomfortable with people, and in particular, I have a fear of men. It is not a sexual fear. But male physicians, employers, therapists, even dentists intimidate me. I fear that they will think I am stupid or weak and unimportant."

"Does that fear include your husband because he is a man and because of not having intercourse before being married to you?" the psychologist wondered.

Annette nodded her head, "That's why I can't be intimate with him. I cannot let my guard down and let him know me."

At this point the psychologist was confronted with two issues. What was Annette's picture of herself? But it also seemed important to know whether Annette's husband was aware of her feelings and their origin. Annette admitted that she had mentioned it once early in their marriage, but her husband's answer did not resolve her anxiety.

"What was your husband's response, do you remember it?" the psychologist asked.

"He said it did not matter what went on before because now that we were married, everything was all right," Annette responded.

"But it was not all right for you; you did not agree with him," the psychologist correctly guessed Annette's thoughts, as was indicated by Annette's nodding her head in agreement.

How could this difficult and painful situation be resolved? It was not sufficient to educate Annette's husband about her feelings regarding his refusal to have sex before being married—although at that point, the psychologist had no way of knowing how the husband would respond.

The more complicated issue was to help Annette understand that not everybody was judging her in a negative way, and what was even more important than her willingness to try sexual intercourse before marriage was not necessarily designating her moral standards as inferior to those of her husband. In fact, couples in similar situations may well consider it prudent to check their relationships for sexual compatibility before entering a lifetime commitment.

As might be expected, Annette was not ready to accept the fact that her opinion could have been an acceptable one, considering her own value system. The biggest hurdle by far was Annette's deeply entrenched belief that most people did not like her and that men actually disapproved of her. This belief had been a stumbling block in her early life and in her dating history, finally leading her to turn to a dating service to find the right partner, as Annette admitted.

While working through this issue, an unexpected ally appeared on the scene. Annette's mother, after hearing that her daughter was considering reuniting with her husband, called Annette, first apologizing for not having been much of an emotional support to her daughter in the past and then cautioning her to make sure that returning to the marriage was truly in Annette's best interest. For all the years her mother had lived under her husband's rule, she had paid dearly, not only by losing any self-esteem she might have had but also by abandoning her daughter when not supporting her in confrontations with the overpowering father.

Her mother's support at this crucial time was probably the major turning point in Annette's struggle with overcoming the fear of letting anybody, and especially a man, know about her innermost thoughts and feelings. As she stated, "It was my mother's courage, admitting to me her failure in supporting me that helped me get a different perspective on my father and on myself. Keeping people at a distance emotionally was his way of hiding his imperfections. It did not evolve out of power or strength but out of fear, I finally realized. What was there to learn from? Perfect isolation does not guarantee freedom from fear."

All those years Annette's mother had outwardly agreed with and supported the father's ideas and behaviors—was it out of love for him or out of fear of him? Annette did not have to ask anymore; she knew it had been fear that kept her mother silent, a fear not unlike Annette's fear that kept her from revealing herself and her innermost thoughts and desires. The newly blossoming mother-daughter relationship greatly enriched both of their lives.

What happened to the marriage? Had Bob and Annette met within their community or a circle of friends, taking more time getting to know each other, they would have been able to observe the difference in opinions regarding premarital sex, they might have decided not to marry each other, or perhaps Annette might have been less open about her sexual attitudes, realizing Bob's stance on the issue. In that case she might not have been as vulnerable to losing her self-esteem. It is difficult to say how the marriage would have turned out under different circumstances.

Dealing with the situation as it had developed to this point, the psychologist in their next session decided to focus on Annette's opinion. "If you or someone else in your position had not been so vulnerable to criticism because of your father's behavior, how do you think that person might have looked at your husband's statement about sex before marriage being a sin, even though he had engaged in kissing and caressing you, just short of the penis-in-vagina moment?"

Annette thought for a while, finally mumbling, "It seems nitpicking the way you describe it, hanging the idea of sin on a small technical difference, almost an artificial borderline."

"So if you had been able to be open-minded enough to trust your own judgment, you might not have accepted your husband's opinion without some reservations," the therapist suggested. "You might have taken the time to explore in your mind what sin is and where to draw the line. But because of your built-in sense of not being correct, of being flawed in some way, you automatically accepted your husband's opinion as correct and your own as wrong because it was different from his, the man in the situation."

Annette did not reply, apparently thinking about the psychologist's statement. After a brief pause the psychologist continued. "In our first session you described your mother as a nonperson parent, one who does not express her own opinion and silently accepts her husband's judgment. In a way, when you accepted your husband's opinion of sin without considering its basis in morality and in regard to your beliefs, wasn't there a similarity to your mother's behavior?" the psychologist asked gently.

"You are saying I am judging my mother for behaving the same way I do . . ." Annette's voice trailed off, but continued after a moment's thought, "So, has my mother taught me how to behave or has my father taught me how to be?"

"Probably both in their own way," was the psychologist's response. "But how do you decide what to learn and take from the things they teach? Do you swallow everything, or do you select some items to learn from and leave others unnoticed?"

"I never thought about that," Annette's voice sounded surprised. "Somehow things just become established in a person's mind."

"Let me go back again to our first session," the psychologist began. "You mentioned that you had a fear of men, that they would think you are stupid or weak or unimportant. Where did that fear originate, do you remember?"

"I think it stems from my father. He did not hesitate to express his low opinion of women in general," Annette responded.

"And you thought that if you did not let him know you, he would not judge you in the same way? And you are applying that kind of thinking to other men in your life. But what is the evidence that you are stupid or weak? You earned your college degree, you have a good job that you perform to your employer's satisfaction, and you carry the major responsibility for your two children. I don't think many, if any, people would agree with your opinion of yourself."

"It must be so, or I wouldn't feel that way," was Annette's quick response. Obviously, she was not ready yet to investigate the foundation of her unrealistic beliefs. With those beliefs firmly intact, Annette would not consider revealing herself to others. How could she work on improving her marriage without building intimacy into her relationship with her husband?

Sometime later the psychologist received a surprise phone call from Annette's mother. The woman asked the psychologist for a meeting to express her concerns about her daughter's situation. After the psychologist's explanation that the mother's visit would not be confidential as far as Annette, the client, was concerned, they scheduled an appointment.

The psychologist was totally unprepared for the kind of woman who entered the office. Unassuming in outward appearance, it soon became clear that she had definite goals in mind. Mildred, Annette's mother, started out by saying that she did not think returning to her husband would be a happy solution to Annette's life. When the psychologist wondered about the mother's reasons for this idea she readily replied that in her opinion, her son-in-law wanted a reunion of the family because he believed divorce was a sin and the children needed a solid family life. Mildred expressed her opinion that the wish for reuniting the family was more her son-in-law's preoccupation with moral concerns and the community's opinion than a loving desire to be reunited with his wife. Mildred wanted more for her daughter.

The psychologist, surprised by this turn of events, asked what the woman based her opinion on. Without hesitation she mentioned that Annette's use of an online dating service to find an eligible partner had been one of the very few occasions when she as a mother did not agree with her late husband's opinion. When Annette had told them of her contact with a prospective husband through a dating service, Mildred had expressed her concerns that those situations might not allow for sufficient opportunities to observe and gain in-depth knowledge about the other person. However, her husband had brushed her concern aside by stating that it was time for Annette to be out of her parents' house and starting a family of her own.

Annette had listened to her father and got married. It was too late to change the impact of a lifetime's influences. When the psychologist asked why her daughter might have listened to her father and not her mother's advice, Mildred admitted that her daughter might have learned from and followed her own behaviors. Mildred herself had grown up with a fear of male dominance. Mildred's father would not allow her, the only daughter in a family with three sons, to go to college even though her grades had been promising enough. Her father believed it was a waste of money to invest in college education for a young woman, who would be expected to get married soon and have to raise children. Mildred was afraid of her father and her grandfather, who lived with the family at the time. There was no physical abuse, but it was obvious that her father thought she was a mistake; she should have been another boy.

To escape that situation, Mildred married early; Annette's father was a man much like Mildred's father. Mildred readily admitted that Annette could have picked up the fear and anxiety about men's disapproval from her mother. "For so many years my husband blamed me for not giving him sons." And when the psychologist seemed ready to say something, Mildred assured him that she had read somewhere that only the man in his sperm could contribute the male genes for the conception of a son, but her husband would not listen to her explanation or educate himself on the matter. He refused to let any new knowledge creep in and erode his beliefs.

The psychologist was impressed with Mildred's honest attempts to help her daughter to find happiness, but the path to it seemed a complicated one. Mildred had just explained her husband's reluctance to change his beliefs, even in the face of scientific evidence contradicting his belief. People refuse to accept any evidence that might contradict their beliefs because if they give up their beliefs, they have to make changes in their behaviors. And the need for change presents a threat to many people.

Considering Mildred's description of her husband, he might have been plagued by social anxiety, hiding it behind his judgmental and rejecting attitude and behavior. In her own way, Annette became his extension to the next generation.

In the following months, Annette tried hard to overcome her tendency to keep her innermost thoughts and feelings hidden; she even opened up discussions with her husband about her thoughts of intimacy and her fear of being judged by those she trusted with herself. And although her husband seemed to listen, they never reached common ground. Finally, Annette felt that what once seemed to have been love for her husband had died. Reconciliation did not work for her in this relationship. It was time for a new beginning.

Technology's Constant Presence

Technology has expanded the dating world from a limited geographical area of one's living base into a global market. Through social media and online dating sites, the number of possible partners has grown exponentially. However, the combination of "improved" self-portraits of the candidates and the wishful expectations of the lonely searchers for happiness has a way of shrouding the other's characteristics into an ambiguous proposition. The stories of Cynthia and Harold's marriage and Annette's sad story above raise the question of whether those soul-mate searchers will allow sufficient time to really get to know each other well enough to build a compatible basis for the future or whether they will jump into a shaky marriage.

On the other hand, breaking up is easy to do; a long-distance romance can be extinguished when one partner returns to claiming "single" status on Facebook or similar media: "In such instances, the ease of technology can deny individuals the growth opportunities that result from the discomfort of breaking up in a sensitive fashion."[22]

Technology also has expanded the ways we communicate and obtain information compared with previous times. When before we had to physically visit, write letters to send through the postal system, or make phone calls to remain in contact with friends or relatives, now it can all be done immediately using Twitter, Facebook, Instagram, Skype, blogs, and other media services. All these options for immediate contact with others apparently have not changed or reduced the loneliness people feel. In fact, some professional counselors have mentioned an increase of clients struggling with feeling lonely. Professional journals are reporting on AARP surveys indicating that loneliness has become a common issue among adults older than 45, with about 35 percent of the respondents admitting to being lonely. Other research articles have stated that up to 80 percent of individuals under the age of 18 have felt lonely at least sometimes.

Although periodic experiences of loneliness can happen to most people occasionally, chronic loneliness poses a great health risk, perhaps as much or even more dangerous than the risks linked to smoking and obesity, as shown by research conducted over the past few decades.[23]

Technology also has increased incidents of inappropriate communication, according to a poll done in April 2015. The poll included more than 150 college students and reported that many college students send or receive text messages at very inappropriate times. While attending a funeral or a religious service, being in the shower or on a date—even while engaging in sexual activities—they text their messages and check for answers. Even though they are aware that these behaviors are inappropriate, students said they just could not help themselves. Many of them admitted to sending 100 text messages per day and checking for messages almost 16 times per hour.[24] Texting while at work was admitted by 75 percent, and 8 out of 10 students said they texted while in class. Another 70 percent texted while at the movies. The study polled students from a mid-sized university in the northeastern United States. Almost 60 percent of the respondents were female students with an average age of just under 20 years.

One might wonder how much the students comprehend of the lessons in class when they distract themselves by texting and for those who work, how valuable their work performance is when it is interrupted repeatedly by texting. Why pay the price for a movie and popcorn when it does not provide enough stimulation and has to be supplemented by texting? The question comes to mind, Is it compulsive behavior that these young people are afflicted with, or is it the immediacy of contact that is so addictive, or is it a combination of both?

The question of whether all the Internet and online activity has contributed to modern-day loneliness has been raised by several sources, with varying answers. Some professionals interviewed about this topic mentioned that with social media communication, people are not really connecting anymore even if they meet with others at a restaurant; they can be seen sharing the same table and the same meal while looking at their smartphones. For some people, media communication feels emotionally safer than face-to-face communication. Furthermore, social media use may cause some individuals to start on a cognitive comparing process of their own and others' lives with the outcome of feeling like failures, eventually seeking greater emotional and physical distance.

Those cognitive comparison processes may also lead to an increased need for perfection and to a fear of failure, eventually resulting in low self-esteem, more social isolation, and loneliness.[25] Many of those characteristics mark the lives of socially anxious individuals.

CHAPTER FIVE

Self-Help Remedies—
Medication, Alcohol, Street
Drugs, Food, and More

For those who cannot completely avoid social situations, the first attempt of calming down might be aided by a hearty alcoholic drink. Nonalcoholic aids can be found in street drugs or even in prescription medication. And, indeed, the number of filled prescriptions for benzodiazepines has increased significantly in the 21st century.[1] More often than not, these self-help remedies, while promising a calming effect, include a secondary function—adding the problem of addiction to the already painful experience of anxiety.

More than individuals with any other anxiety disorder, social anxiety sufferers admit to using alcohol and certain drugs to relieve their anxiety. Because marijuana seems to discourage social interaction, and psychedelics tend to confuse it, the drugs most favored when individuals face unavoidable contact with others are those with sedative or inhibitory effects, such as barbiturates and other prescription "downers" used as street drugs.[2]

Published reviews of the research literature have shown that among patients in treatment for alcohol problems, about 68.7 percent have anxiety problems as well. Other studies have found that about 50 percent of inpatients in treatment for alcoholism were also socially phobic.[3]

Alcohol Keeping the Lid on Anxiety

Ben's story is an example of a socially anxious person seeking relief in alcohol. As the only child of an overprotective mother and a frequently absent father, Ben was extremely shy all through his school years and afraid to talk to any girls. He was even too timid to decide on a professional path, unable to make a decision because nothing seemed possible to him. Finally, he was drafted into the army. He discovered that ingesting alcohol would take some of the tension away to the point that he could at least interact and converse with other men in his environment.

Not surprisingly, Ben became addicted to alcohol. Although after many years he finally overcame his addiction, he remained socially isolated and lonely for a long time. Feeling awkward about talking to people, Ben turned to drawing as an outlet for his thought processes. However, his artistic expressions had an edge to them, turning them into social commentaries that illustrated the bitterness he harbored about his social insecurities and bemoaned his lack of success in life. Although willing to undergo treatment for his alcohol problem, Ben did not entertain the possibility of seeking help for his social anxiety. Even in his AA meetings and the art classes he had joined, Ben remained socially on the periphery of the interactions, disclosing little of his innermost thoughts to anybody, hiding behind the characters of his drawings.

Should it be a surprise that many socially anxious individuals seek relief through the use of drugs and alcohol? Drinking in the evenings or at the end of the week to relax from the stress and demands of one's work, to "loosen up," has become an approved ingredient of our culture. As alcohol use generally promotes superficial social interaction, some socially anxious individuals seem to seek the opposite type of "cure"—marijuana, which, as mentioned earlier, tends to discourage social interaction as well as reduce ambition and striving for goals.

Marijuana, the Ultimate Relaxant

Randolph's destiny seemed to be that of a follower. As the younger one of fraternal twins, he struggled for the attention his sister forcefully demanded. Lois was stronger and faster than her brother and used every opportunity to outshine him in the affection of family and friends. Believing he could not win in the competition for popularity, Randolph turned to the family pets for affection. The family's dogs and cats doted on him. Both children made good grades in school, although Lois had to work harder for her achievements than Randolph. But she made up in social activities with those classmates whose parents were of important standing in their community.

When it came time to apply to colleges, their parents suggested that Lois and Randolph look for different institutions, hoping that Randolph would find it easier to adjust to a new environment without his sister being a part of it. Randolph, not surprisingly, dreamed of becoming a veterinarian, while Lois considered medical school for her future.

Scholastically, Randolph was a success during his college years; however, socially, he remained on the periphery of college life. He experienced increasing anxiety when it came to social interactions. As he once admitted to one friend, Randolph always heard his sister's voice in his mind taking over any conversation she and he were involved in. Those strong memories from his childhood prevented him from expressing his ideas and feelings. Randolph graduated with honors and had no difficulty being accepted at the veterinary school of his choice. With a slightly less stellar performance record, Lois was admitted to a medical school in a different state.

During his senior year in college, Randolph had started to experiment with marijuana. At first he thought it did not affect him because he did not feel different, but with elapsing time he noticed that his anxiety levels appeared lower during school exams and interactions with his classmates. His newly found peace of mind felt like a miracle. At the time, Randolph did not realize that the ease he felt during social interactions was due more to his not caring so much about the people around him than to any increasing social skills on his part. He was grateful for this new experience without questioning it. At this point he also entered into a romantic relationship with Susan, a young employee in the college's administration offices.

Before Randolph departed for veterinary school, there was a small wedding ceremony; Susan and Randolph were expecting their first child. Susan applied for an office position at the veterinary school, ready to move upon acceptance. Meanwhile Randolph started his studies, living alone for the time being. He had found a small apartment to accommodate his new little family. Getting settled in a new environment was not easy; besides, Randolph felt lonely for Susan. Marijuana helped him over the rough spots, he thought. It seemed to work; he felt less anxious when he studied for his classes. But then during an exam in one of his classes, he had difficulty remembering what he had studied in preparation for this test. This had never happened before, even when he was anxious, and Randolph explained it to himself, reasoning that this was because he had to get more used to the new school and its professors' teaching and ways of writing the exams. It seemed to make sense on a superficial level.

It was a happy day when Susan finally joined her husband. They set up housekeeping together and prepared for the arrival of the baby. Randolph continued his marijuana use even though Susan was not in favor of it. This first semester was a busy time for the young couple; it ended for Randolph with being placed on academic probation because he received a grade of D minus in one of his classes. It was a shock; how could something like this happen to Randolph, who had always excelled in his academic pursuits? Susan blamed Randolph's marijuana use for his academic failure; he denied it, and the couple now argued frequently. The birth of their daughter Nicole did not improve the situation; if anything, Randolph blamed the baby's crying for his difficulty concentrating on his studies.

During his second semester, Randolph's grades took another dive; he ended up with one F, two Bs and three Cs—unacceptable grades for veterinary school—and he dropped out, not only from school but from the world in general. He refused to leave the house and avoided seeing anyone outside his little family. Susan became disenchanted with her marriage and moved back to seek refuge with Nicole in her parent's home. In the meantime, Randolph's father had died of a heart attack, and his mother had a difficult time making ends meet, but she invited Randolph to come and live with her. After an initial refusal, Randolph decided to accept his mother's offer, something she later regretted because Randolph became a financial burden to her.

With his once brilliant academic prospects turning to failure, Randolph's initial social anxiety increased dramatically. He could not bring himself to apply for any regular jobs after he had left two job interviews in a state of panic. Odd jobs provided a way to make some money for a while, but whenever someone asked him about his past, he left. He never made enough money to make child support payments for Nicole, his little daughter.

In the meantime, Lois succeeded in her medical training to become a forensic psychiatrist. Naturally, her mother was proud of her daughter's achievements and told all her friends and neighbors about it. A few years later, Lois married a doctor of veterinary medicine. When the couple expressed their plans to move close to their original community, Randolph panicked and left his mother's home without telling her. One day, early in the morning, when his mother attended aerobic class at the nearby YMCA, he left, leaving a note behind, telling his mother that he could not stay with her any longer. The humiliation of seeing his sister not only having achieved her professional goal but in addition being married to a man, who had succeeded in a profession in which Randolph had failed, was too much for him to face.

What became of Randolph? He moved to another state, living a marginal life, supported by odd jobs and food stamps. He made no friends; acquaintances knew him by the sarcasm he expressed about society and politics. They recognized his significant degree of intelligence, but his bitterness made them retreat from him, something he did not seem to mind at all. Years later, after Lois and her husband had moved to another state to enhance their careers, Randolph returned to his mother's house to take care of the now-fragile woman. After her death, Randolph survived by leasing out part of his mother's house, which she had willed to him.

In the meantime, Nicole had made it her task to find and meet her father. With her mother's permission, she stayed with him for a while to get to know him but left when it became time for her to return home for school. Although he had stopped his marijuana use years ago, mainly for financial reasons, Randolph did not attempt to deal with his social anxiety disorder. The envy that had started during childhood in competition with his sister increased in severity as he had failed in his academic endeavors. The relationship between him and Lois did not improve over time, mainly because of the arguments surrounding the still-unresolved division of their mother's estate.

Social anxiety's intimate link with the threat to the individual's self-esteem activates the fear of being found out, which then floods the person's thinking and feeling, leading to extreme measures to try to hide any shortcomings. Randolph had once been proud of his intellectual capabilities, and even though he feared the competition with his twin sister in social situations, he had been able to tell himself that he would outshine his sister if it came to an intellectual duel. The fact that he failed in his veterinary studies pulled the basis for his self-enhancing rationalizing out from under his feet. Not only did he have to admit to being a failure; he also knew deep down that he was a fraud or fake as he from time to time attempted to flaunt his intellectual talents.

How could he have resolved his anxiety states? After he had stopped his marijuana use, he could have embarked on another professional goal following treatment for his social anxiety disorder. But Randolph firmly believed that he could never overcome his anxiety because he could not prevent others in his environment from observing and judging him. If he had wanted those others to see him in a different light, he could have modified his behavior toward them to yield a different opinion of his personality. But according to his beliefs, he did not have the power to change their thinking about him. With beliefs like those firmly entrenched, he did not entertain the possibility that his assumptions might be incorrect. The strength of his beliefs did not permit the possibility of change, which might have opened a door to a different, less disappointing path.

Self-Help Remedies versus Professional Guidance

Why do people rely on self-help remedies to cope with their difficulties rather than seek the guidance and assistance of a professional trained in their specific type of impairment? One reason might be financial costs associated with professional help. Another reason might involve the individual's reluctance to admit that outside help is necessary. Although alcohol and drugs cost some money, individuals who choose that path can make themselves believe that they are handling their difficulties without having to resort to outside help. This false sense of security or competence strengthens their shaky belief in their independence.

When considering self-remedies, we usually think about alcohol, prescription or street drugs, and in certain cases sexual activities of a hyperactive and compulsive nature. However, for some anxious people, food intake serves the function of a self-help remedy, calming down their worrying. In "emotional eating," the digestive processes not only keep the individual from performing other activities, they provide the body with a physical state of relaxation, which may cross over into the person's mental and emotional systems.

Chewing Down Anxiety

Through most of her childhood and adolescence, Irene had been overweight. What had started as a cute but chubby little girl, with a round face framed by blond curls and supported by an equally round body, had grown into an obese teenage girl, who endured the jokes and snickering of her classmates during gym classes as well as in the school's hallways. Irene's beginning at school was frightening for her. Her family lived on the outskirts of her little town, and Irene did not know many children of her own age. Her first days of school were filled with terror as she was confronted by all the children she did not know. Her shyness was not lost on the other kids as they immediately made Irene the target of their teasing.

Every morning before having to leave for school, Irene was seized by waves of anxiety, and every afternoon when returning from school, she was exhausted from the fear of being helpless in confrontations with her classmates. As soon as she arrived home, her worries about the next day started to haunt her. Was it a coincidence when Irene noticed that the act of eating and chewing made her anxiety subside? Irene's portions at breakfast and dinner grew larger and larger. Eating even seemed to help her cope with the anxiety over tests and exams at school. Although her increasing weight added fuel to the jokes of her classmates, Irene's appetite grew.

Perhaps the only area in which Irene received positive attention was art classes in school. Her talents in drawing and painting became evident in her early school years. During her high school years, Irene was often chosen for community projects designed to draw attention to the school's efforts to produce student achievements worthy of community support for the school. Irene produced her share of applause-worthy art projects, but her initial excitement fizzled when she realized that the main objective of these projects was to make the school and its teachers look accomplished in bringing out the best in their students, so that supporting the school financially seemed a good investment for the community. Heaping glory on the students for their talents and achievements seemed to be of secondary importance, as expressed in the brief acknowledgments bestowed on them.

Irene did what she was asked to do in using her talents to glorify the school and the teachers. Her relationships with other students did not improve; she remained reserved and rather timid in her interactions with them. A disappointing shopping trip for an appropriate dress for a school dance was followed by a painful "wallflower" experience at the dance itself. In the future, Irene avoided this type of torture by abstaining from such social events.

At the same time, she was introduced to marijuana by some of her classmates. Marijuana proved to hold the magic that made it possible for Irene to emotionally distance herself from the disappointments that had been part of her young life. Simultaneously, as she later explained, marijuana use made everything around her more vividly colorful than seeing the same surroundings without the influence of the drug. Irene's addiction to marijuana was immediate and powerful.

One of the side effects of marijuana use, individuals' reduced need for achievement, observed in a few cases, was largely unnoticed at that time. People who used marijuana generally pronounced that it made them feel at peace in an expanded, almost spiritual way.

Irene's social anxiety felt less incapacitating to her because with the aid of marijuana—in addition to her ever-increasing food intake—her social isolation did not seem as troublesome or as real as before. In fact, spending most of her time by herself seemed like a natural and sensible way to live her life. When graduation from high school appeared on the horizon, Irene did not consider future educational or professional avenues. She remained physically and mentally where she was without feeling the need for any further thresholds to cross. Following graduation, she picked one of the low-paying menial jobs available in her small hometown while her classmates went off to college or jumped into early marriage.

While at work during the day, Irene did not dare use marijuana, and her past anxiety about interacting with people resurfaced on an almost daily level. Her family physician prescribed antianxiety medication to help with her difficulty. In her free time, Irene continued to paint, but without professional guidance she floundered around in finding her own style of expression. Furthermore, under the influence of marijuana, she seemed to experience her artwork quite different from the way others saw it. She was less sensitive to imperfections in her paintings than the general public was. This meant that she had lost touch with what other people liked or wanted. Irene's response to the situation was increased social isolation. Where she formerly had dreaded social interactions because of her poor self-esteem, which was due to her obesity, she now did not even entertain the possibility of social interaction beyond superficial involvement with customers while performing her job duties.

Irene's prescription-drug and marijuana use increased as her social interactions and concern about her work activities decreased. Finally, she woke up in the emergency room of the local hospital. From there she was transferred to the inpatient unit for chemical dependency. Following discharge from the inpatient unit after a lengthy stay, Irene was referred to the local mental health center for outpatient therapy.

It was not Irene's desire to be involved in therapy; she did not want to talk about her life. She just wanted to be left alone, but she did not have the financial resources to live in a way she desired. Because she was on social assistance, psychotherapy was dictated by the social support system—no therapy, no food stamps. Reluctantly, Irene gave in and showed up for therapy appointments. Getting her to talk was another challenge. Her therapist's patience was put to the test as Irene's one-syllable responses made up her part of the interaction. With marijuana taken out of her life—at least for the time being—Irene just did not seem to have any interest in anything except eating.

Finally, the therapist tried to engage Irene's attention by asking about her artwork, suggesting that Irene's talents might be strong enough to function as a link to a more satisfying life. Irene exploded, "Everybody is telling me to paint and to take lessons. Just because I have this talent, that does not mean that I have to be grateful for it and work at it. I am tired of people telling me what to do."

Recovering from the surprise and learning a lesson, the therapist agreed that people probably should not tell Irene what to do. But because she did not find anything else worth her attention, people with suggestions to help Irene usually came up with the most obvious or most promising strength or talents. It was certainly Irene's choice what she wanted to do as long as she did something to help herself.

At her next session, Irene brought a small drawing to the therapist's office to show her renewed attempt at artwork. The following week, Irene came in with a watercolor painting of a sunset, framed and ready to hang. The therapist admired Irene's work, and Irene requested that the therapist keep it safely away from Irene because she was afraid that she might at some point be tempted to sell the painting to obtain marijuana. Together they selected a fitting space on a wall in the therapist's office as the therapist assured Irene that her work would be safe where they both could appreciate it. And it could be a help for Irene in learning to find her way back into the reality of life. Seeing the painting during her sessions could serve as encouragement and inspiration to appreciate her talents, to exchange the isolation of her social fears and the marijuana use for a few new steps toward involvement with those around her.

Irene's therapist made it a point to tell her whenever someone had admired the painting in the therapist's office. Apparently, it provided a helpful link because Irene increased the focus on her art. Unfortunately, she could not afford art lessons, and because she had outgrown in age any financial aid available through the public school system, she was left to her own way of practicing and defining her style and techniques with the help of the local public library's books on painters and art.

Very slowly, Irene made friends with one or two other clients of the agency. She never felt comfortable relating to her former friends and classmates and avoided coming face-to-face with them, partly because she was still obese and partly because she was one of the town's failures. In spite of her talent, she did not amount to anything in the eyes of those still living in the little town. This was what Irene told herself, but it was also difficult to challenge this opinion because it was too close to reality—not many people were eager to associate with Irene on a more than superficial basis. Even her parents had difficulty accepting that their once so talented little girl did not make good on her promises.

At about this time, her therapist moved to another town some distance away, leaving Irene to continue with another therapist. About five years later, the previous therapist received a phone call from Irene. Irene said she had to come to the town for a medical appointment and wondered if it would be possible to visit with her previous therapist. Irene's call was an opportunity the therapist greatly appreciated, and she looked forward to learning more about Irene's current situation.

It was a good meeting; they had no problem reconnecting. Sadly, Irene was still overweight, but she smiled more than the therapist remembered. Irene's first question was "Do you still have the painting I gave you for your office?"

"Oh, yes," the therapist responded. "It is hanging in my office here on a wall opposite my desk, so I can see it a lot. And just like in [the little town where they had met], people often ask me about the painting and the artist. Perhaps on your next visit you can come up to my office and see it."

It was an emotionally charged moment for both of them when Irene softly said, "When you displayed my painting in your office for everybody to see, that was such a meaningful thing. There was somebody who believed in me, and at every session in your office it was such an encouragement to see my work on your wall."

What had happened in Irene's life during those five years? As she reported, she had moved to another town where people did not know much about her past. She had made a good friend, who became her companion, and together they enjoyed a small circle of friends. Irene had a job in an office, and she continued to paint in her free time. And she had remained drug free all this time.

Irene did not have the opportunity to visit with her painting in the therapist's office. The years of drug use and obesity had taken a toll. Before she was able to return to the city for another visit, she became seriously ill and had to be hospitalized. Sometime later, the therapist received a letter from Irene's companion, reporting that Irene had died. But the letter also stated that while Irene's life had not been as happy as one would have wished, she had been able to accept her position in life without being intent to hide from others as she had done in the past. Her life had become more peaceful; she enjoyed the warmth of relating to the small circle of friends who liked her and admired the artworks she had been able to produce over the years. The bitterness she had felt in her earlier years had slowly given way to a more peaceful mood.

For a therapist to find out that a former client has died years after termination of the therapy process is a situation of questioning oneself. Were the therapeutic insights the client gained sufficient to last those years between the end of therapy and the client's death? Was the knowledge gained strong enough to render the client free from the impact of the symptoms of the presenting problem long ago? Was the client able to find or mobilize resources providing encouragement in times of need? At times, therapists are fortunate enough to hear from close friends or family members of deceased former clients that the learning and hard work associated with the therapy process had lasting positive effects on the client's further life, as in Irene's case. But those precious moments are rare, indeed.

Rewards Becoming the Source for Anxiety

Returning to the topic of overeating, within the population of socially anxious individuals, a significant number appear to be overweight. Of course, it is not surprising that obesity relates positively to social anxiety because it is an easily observed blemish in a weight-conscious culture. What is intriguing in a way is that for these unfortunate people, the anxiety-reducing activity (eating) is at the same time the anxiety-increasing agent in the felt discomfort when meeting and interacting with others.

Myrna grew up on a small farm in New England. Life was not easy, and everybody in the family worked hard. The parents considered their offspring more helping hands than children, and Myrna never felt special in any way. The usual reward for hard work was to be able to eat while watching TV. Myrna managed to become a successful professional but somehow never met among the men she was dating any that would be husband material. Her single status made her different from most of her female friends, and she felt awkward in social situations. More and more, she refused to participate in the social events of those she knew. Having more free time on her hands, she spent most of it eating in front of the TV. It did not matter much what the TV program was all about. It served as justification for her to sit and eat while watching it.

The Anxiety-Relief-Anxiety Cycle

As would be expected, this regime of increased food intake combined with reduced physical activity led to significant increases in Myrna's body weight, which, in turn, led to increased anxiety when meeting friends and acquaintances because they noticed her weight gain. It was easier to squelch the anxiety over people noticing her increased body weight by staying away from them, treating herself at home to a high-calorie meal in front of the TV.

What a vicious cycle it had become: the discomfort of the anxiety over how she appeared in the eyes of others made her increase the very thing that led to the anxiety in the first place. With every bite she swallowed to calm her fears, she gave rise to an even higher level of anxiety that would plague her when she met her colleagues at work, knowing that she had gained another pound or two. The resurfacing anxiety then, in turn, would prompt her to eat even more to calm herself down.

The following is an example of the path of Myrna's vicious anxiety-relief-anxiety cycle: Myrna returned home at the end of a tough day at work. She had been scheduled to give a presentation about her current project. As she dressed for work the next morning, she noticed that the skirt of her suit was tighter than she remembered it. But it was too late to change into another outfit. On the way to work she worried that her coworkers would notice the tightness of her skirt, associating it with weight gain. All through the presentation, Myrna was hyperconscious of the tight skirt and tried to stand or move in such a way that it would be less obvious to her audience. This, in turn, impaired her concentration on the topic of her presentation, and she experienced difficulties relating to the audience's questions. As a result, her anxiety increased, and by the end of the day she was ready to collapse, which she did in front of the TV at home after serving herself an extra-large portion of her favorite foods.

"I deserve a treat; I had a really tough day today," she told herself. After several bites, she remembered the tightness of her skirt. Having spent a few fleeting moments in thought about the need to lose weight, she calmed herself down with a few more bites, thinking, "It's too late; I already ate more than I should have, so I might as well continue eating. I won't need to wear that suit again for a while, and until then there will be plenty of time to go on a diet."

With those thoughts, Myrna felt relieved and ate some more before going to bed for a good night's sleep. The next morning, she felt sluggish and wondered if she might have come down with a cold. She could not afford getting sick because she had already used up her sick leave for the year. Looking in the mirror as she got dressed, she seemed to look heavier than expected; she must have gained more than just a couple pounds. She felt her anxiety build up as she stepped on the scale. Reading the numbers on the scale resulted in a panic attack. She felt out of control. "How could I have done this to myself?" she cried out, facing her reflection in the mirror. "The scale must not be working right." She tried to calm herself down, but in vain, because she remembered how tight that skirt had been on her body the day before and how much food her "treat" had contained the previous evening. A wave of helplessness and fear engulfed her. She was shaking and had to sit down. A look at her watch told Myrna that it was time for breakfast before heading out to work.

When Myrna decided to treat herself for a hard day with a sumptuous dinner, did she think that her "treat" would actually bring on a wave of anxiety? Of course not; she did not consider the resulting painful anxiety and the fear of being out of control as treats. However, in her thought process questioning the reality, her "treat" had been camouflaged as deserved rewards.

The dynamics that operate in social anxiety disorder are not much different from the dynamics found in other anxiety disorders. Consider, for instance, obsessive-compulsive disorder (OCD). The obsession part consists of thoughts or images that cannot be controlled by the individual. Compulsions are repetitive or ritualistic behaviors that are uncontrollable. Whereas the obsessions provoke anxiety, compulsions actually reduce anxiety through the actions or behaviors dictated by the compulsion.

Thus, if Myrna feels punished or stressed or worn out by anxiety about her performance at work or in social settings, her mind wants to quit the struggle and find a reward, which is eating in front of the TV. This behavior absolves her from any further contemplations or responsibility; she has earned her reward, and behaving according to that logic will bring her relief, the reduction of anxiety—at least for a short while.

In anxiety disorders, the individuals' thoughts and contemplations are the triggers for the rising anxiety, and the behaviors—actual behaviors or abstaining from activities related to the anxiety-arousing core—function to bring about a measure of relief. Therefore, deciding and doing something, at least for the moment, will bring relief from the anxiety.

Anxiety Outlasting the Cure

As early as age five, Cynthia, previously introduced in chapter 4, remembered being chubby; people did not consider her "cute" like some of her age mates. Cynthia was already feeling the isolation stemming from worry over what people were saying about her. If she had been picked even once to be on the kickball team at recess, she would have been happier. She longed to be able to fit into pretty clothes like the other girls her age wore. To be able to run, to play sports, to have her hand held by a boy, to have her first kiss, and to be invited to parties, those were dreams that never came true for her.

Those unfulfilled dreams created a sadness and loneliness that found temporary relief and distraction in the activity of eating. But the relief was never of long duration; intense emotional pain filled most of her days. In fact, even after much later finally losing the excess weight, the pain, anxiety, disappointment, and lack of self-confidence remained with her. The possibility of someone laughing at her or whispering that she was ugly was a frequent fear-arousing thought. In many cases, even after the excess pounds have been shed, the memory of those pounds lingers on and on.

Diets, bariatric surgeries, and other approaches used to shed extra pounds do not deal with the residual deeper roots of the original problem. Those roots tend to remain for a long time in the life of the socially anxious person, long after the weight loss when the skin has already adjusted to the smaller body volume.

Cross-Dressing—An Unusual Self-Help Remedy

An issue not necessarily focused on in discussions of social anxiety is that of gender, and this discussion will focus not on whether one sex is more vulnerable to the development of social anxiety than the other but on whether gender might function in some cases as a developmental factor of social anxiety as well as a comforting self-help element.

Clarence, a man in his mid-thirties, entered therapy with a sex therapist for his desire to cross-dress, which was a point of contention in his marriage. His wife did not like it when Clarence tried to dress in a frilly nightgown during their sexual activities. She wanted a man in her bed, not another woman.

At the beginning of the therapy process, for clarification, Clarence was asked if he had any plans or desire for sex reassignment. Clarence denied any such plans and explained that he engaged in cross-dressing mainly to reach a state of peaceful relaxation. The sex therapist was somewhat surprised by Clarence's response and asked him to elaborate on his statement. According to his report, Clarence liked to dress in women's clothing because he felt less stressed out when wearing feminine garments.

What about the female garments gave him those feelings? inquired the therapist. Was it the dress, stockings, undergarments, or perhaps some jewelry? The therapist could not imagine that wearing women's high-heeled shoes would contribute to relaxed feelings in anyone—men or women. Clarence hesitated before answering, "It is more the idea of being a woman and having fewer responsibilities to face on a daily basis than a man."

Although Clarence's wife, the mother of their two children, was employed on a full-time basis, the therapist did not raise the question of who carried the larger burden of responsibilities because the important issue at the moment was to explore Clarence's perception of what exactly brought him the sense of lowered stress when wearing women's clothes, or what contributed to his distress when dressed in his regular male clothing.

During the course of therapy, Clarence's story unfolded. He grew up as the oldest child in a middle-class family, living in the suburbs of a major city. His father was a partner in a small automobile dealership, and his mother stayed at home to take care of Clarence and his younger sister and brother. Later, when the youngest child was in school, Clarence's mother took on a part-time job, which required Clarence to look after his younger siblings some afternoons.

The sex therapist asked Clarence how he liked taking care of his younger siblings. "Oh, it was all right, but I wasn't able to be with my friends at those times. I would have preferred playing with my friends, but my mother told me she needed me to watch Laura and Danny."

There was no hint of any traumatic events in his childhood history as related by Clarence. His grades in school were acceptable, although he did not seem to be competitive in any area of his educational activities. In college he majored in business administration, and his father had hoped that Clarence would follow in his footsteps in the automobile business, a path that his younger brother Danny later made a successful career in.

Clarence started to work in a large computer factory where he was able to attain a supervisory position after some time. When asked what he found most stressful during his young adulthood, Clarence responded that his early dating history was marked by anxiety because he was worried about how to ask a girl for a date and what to do with her once she agreed to go out with him. He remembered thinking how easy it was for girls; all they had to do was be there. In addition, he admitted that work situations had always been and still were stressful because most of his male colleagues were competitive and tried to advance in their careers as fast as they could. That, in his opinion, was the reason for his slower promotions.

Although Clarence did not think he was less knowledgeable than his more rapidly advancing colleagues, he thoroughly disliked the competitive atmosphere. This discomfort spread into his relationships with his friends because many of them were focused on getting ahead, and their discussions often focused on how to reach their lofty goals. Clarence felt like an outsider and thought that his friends disapproved of him and his more laid-back temperament. He envied his wife's relationships with her friends; their interactions seemed to be much more relaxing and enjoyable. However, when Clarence and his wife, Christina, met with Christina's friends and their husbands, Clarence felt anxious and tried to stay out of conversations with them. Clarence added that in general he felt uncomfortable with other males.

Perhaps that type of gender comparison led to the fascination with female clothing. During his first few attempts at cross-dressing, Clarence felt excited but also somewhat apprehensive about how to move when wearing unfamiliar garments, but then he was able to relax. It felt like a weight had lifted off his shoulders. The garments seemed to give him permission not to do anything, to just remain in a positive and peaceful mood.

The pleasant mental-emotional mood rewarded his subsequent cross-dressing activities. Soon he used this activity to cope with the stresses and anxiety at the end of a difficult day. He even found the additional time needed for cosmetic modifications of his body, such as shaving his legs and other body parts, a peace-inducing endeavor as he focused intensely on those activities, which were brought to the finish by applying makeup to his face.

Since they were parents, Christina insisted that Clarence refrain from his cross-dressing activities while their children were at home. It would be a most traumatic experience for children to see their father in female clothing. That demand did not leave him much time to indulge in his relaxing activities unless he rented a hotel room somewhere, which at times he reluctantly resorted to.

One year Clarence persuaded Christina to go on a short vacation with him, leaving their children with Christina's parents. Clarence's reason for the vacation was that he wanted to attempt to pass in public as a woman, which seemed easier to do in an environment where neither Clarence nor Christina were known. As soon as they were sequestered in their hotel room, Clarence, with Christina's help, changed into his female clothing. His legs had been shaven at home before they left, but his face needed some additional work. Finally, they were ready to go down to the street to take a walk together like two female friends. They even managed to enter a bookstore together, looking around and purchasing a book before leaving the store.

Back in their hotel room, Clarence felt that he had won a victory. Although this adventure had not been without anxiety for him, the fact that he had been able to pass as a woman meant that he could change the distressing parts of his life. Clarence set his goal for the next day as having dinner in a restaurant as a woman, again enlisting Christina's help. That was the last time Christina helped him with his disguise; she insisted on returning home the day after.

After a few weeks, Christina gave Clarence an ultimatum: either he would work seriously in his therapy on resolving his cross-dressing desires, or she would file for divorce. She would allow Clarence about one year to resolve his issues and become a "normal man" again.

Clarence was furious; he insisted he was still the same person; he just wanted to use female clothing to help him recover from the daily stress of a man's life. He had no intentions of turning into a woman looking for a male partner, he said.

Christina became disenchanted with Clarence and their marriage. When Clarence did not agree to her conditions, she filed for divorce. A former colleague and friend, Linda, came to Clarence's rescue, and they started an affair. For a while, Linda accepted Clarence in his female clothes, but then she too had trouble being passionate in lovemaking with someone who insisted on looking like another female. Clarence was desperate. Why wouldn't anyone allow him to do what he thought he needed in order to relax and recover from the daily stresses of living and competing in a man's world with all its responsibilities?

In his therapy sessions, Clarence refused to consider ways to cope with stress and discomfort in interactions with his male coworkers. He firmly believed that he had discovered the perfect way of dealing with his anxiety. Finally, he approached his therapist with the notion of sex-reassignment surgery. The sex therapist reminded Clarence that at the beginning of their work together, Clarence had denied any such desire. If, however, he had changed his mind about that issue, he would have to live totally as a woman for two years before any surgery could be contemplated. Those were the regulations regarding the issue at that time. Clarence was furious about what he called a waste of time, having to wait two years for what he wanted now. He refused to consider the seriousness and consequences of such surgery and left the therapist's office never to return.

A few weeks later, a social worker contacted the sex therapist, asking for a signature on a petition to proceed with Clarence's sex-reassignment surgery. The sex therapist refused the request and never heard about Clarence and his future life. Was this a case in which cross-dressing had been a self-help remedy to reduce the anxiety of being a man among other men, or did Clarence aspire to become a woman to escape what he saw as men's responsibilities in life? By undergoing sex-reassignment surgery, did he want to be able to claim his rights to live as a woman? Apparently, he did not desire a sexual relationship with another man; more likely, Clarence might have felt comfortable as a woman in a sexual relationship with other women, but the premature termination of the therapy process does not provide a clear answer to this question.

The Gin and Xanax Cocktail

Robert and Mark had been lovers for a few years, but they kept their relationship a secret, which was not difficult to do because they lived in different towns. Once or twice a year they planned trips together, traveling to Europe, Morocco, China, and many other places, where they could enjoy their relationship without fear of being found out. Whether it was a bullfight in Ronda, Spain, or a visit to the Great Wall in China, Egypt's pyramids, or any other of the world's wonders, they always treasured their time together.

Several years into their relationship, Robert, who lived in their state's capital, had made many friends and decided to "come out"—stop hiding his homosexuality. He persuaded Mark to apply for a job in the capital city and move in with him. Mark hesitated; he had not told his parents, siblings, relatives, and friends about his sexual orientation. He had been on antianxiety medication for some time to help him cope with the anxiety he experienced in his place of work. Living openly with Robert was tempting, but he feared the backlash of disclosing his secret. In the end, his feelings for Robert convinced him to make the move. Living in another town might not force him to divulge his secret to those at home, he reasoned.

They enjoyed a brief honeymoon; life was pleasant for a while. However, when they were invited to some of Robert's friends' homes, Mark panicked and at first refused to accept the invitations. Because Robert was open about being gay, Mark, by attending the social events as his companion, would automatically be assumed to be gay. Although their relationship did not seem to bother Robert's friends, Mark did not like to be on—as he termed it—uneven ground. In addition, he was afraid that somehow people from his hometown would find out about his present lifestyle. The chances of that happening were extremely slim, Robert told him. Mark was unable to relax and enjoy their social gatherings even when doubling the doses of his prescribed medication. The addition of alcohol helped, and there was no lack of alcohol at their social gatherings.

As Mark was numbing his thinking and his senses with the mixture of medication and alcohol on a frequent basis, he, as might be expected, developed a chemical dependency. He was caught driving while under the influence of alcohol, and soon thereafter he lost his job. Mark started blaming Robert for his misfortune, and their once-loving relationship deteriorated into nagging confrontations, which served as excuses for Mark to calm himself down with another drink.

Finally, Robert convinced Mark to enter a residential treatment program for chemical dependency at Robert's expense. Following discharge from the program, Mark returned to his hometown to seek shelter with his parents.

Mark's sad story is a reminder of how stressful it can be to live on the fringes of one's social-cultural environment. Similar effects have been reported in the literature. For instance, a study examining the effects of the cumulative victimization on mental disorders experienced by lesbian, gay, bisexual, and transgender youths recruited 248 participants from the Chicago, Illinois, area with a mean age of 18.7 years at time of enrollment in a four-year data collection process. Levels of victimization were sorted into four classes starting with low decreasing, moderate increasing, high steady, to high decreasing victimization. It was found that youths who experienced high steady or increasing levels of victimization from adolescence to early adulthood were at a higher risk for depression and posttraumatic stress disorder.[4]

As discussed in chapters 1 and 2, for those who believe they are stigmatized or negatively judged, life can be distressing to the point of wanting to withdraw to varying degrees from interactions with those who share the same environment. The firm belief of being helpless in the situation prevents the individual from exploring and perceiving alternatives. The apparent lack of psychological hardiness can be as sad and as harsh as a death sentence.

Social Comparisons—Consequences

Leon Festinger's social comparison theory,[5] which was based on the belief that people have a basic desire to evaluate their opinions and abilities against reality, has broadened over time to include all those processes in which individuals compare and relate their own characteristics to those of other people.[6] The need for self-evaluation is not the only reason for social comparison to exist; the need for self-improvement and self-enhancement and claiming a social identity are additional motivational factors.[7] However, comparisons with peers are not always appreciated, particularly in instances in which the discovery of one's standing on a given skill or ability relative to others' does not tend to enhance one's self-esteem. This is especially distressing when the ability in question is one that is central to one's self-concept.

Therefore, it seems to make sense to select comparison persons who are less accomplished than oneself when the goal is to feel better about oneself.[8] Such "downward" comparisons serve a self-enhancing function, and, in fact, people are likely to pursue comparisons with others whom they regard as being less accomplished in the skill domains where they themselves feel threatened.[9]

Such downward social comparisons lead to emotional responses. If in comparisons with others people feel they are coming out on top, most likely they experience pride, especially when they believe that their advantage is due to their own internal strength and ability.[10]

Another possible emotional consequence of downward comparison might be contempt. When the individual's focus shifts from the self (the focus of pride) to the inferior-comparison person, the individual may feel contempt or scorn for the other. Possessing lower level abilities, the scorned comparison person now is viewed as inferior in abilities as well as in social standing. Contact with this inferior person needs to be avoided for the self-righteous (and socially anxious or intimidated) individual's own good.

In summary, downward comparisons have to be unflattering to the comparison person, otherwise they miss their purpose in flattering the comparer because the chief motivator of downward comparison is self-enhancement.[11]

Another path to self-improvement is to compare oneself with people who are perceived to be superior in some way to the comparer.[12] Like in comparisons with similar others, there is nothing inherently negative about comparisons with superior others, but there is a flavor of ambition when comparing oneself to higher-ups for the purpose of self-improvement or self-enhancement.

As in the case with downward comparisons, there are emotional consequences likely developing in upward comparisons. Initial admiration might turn to resentment when the comparer concludes that the superior other's advantaged position is not justified because it was bestowed on that person without being deserved through personally performed great deeds. Conclusions like that arouse contempt, masked as socially justified, especially when those advantages are not available to the comparer.[13] The feelings of resentment in cases like that are almost always directed toward the advantaged person, not toward the self. The "unfair" advantage becomes the advantaged person's fault.[14]

Another emotion likely to arise through upward social comparisons is that of envy.[15] Envy, unlike resentment, does not only emphasize the other's advantage; it stresses at the same time the recognition of the comparer's own disadvantage. Personal feelings of disadvantage, however, may not reach the level of legitimate injustice in the eyes of others and may need to be disguised when expressing them to others. Undisguised envy implicates the envious person in ways that make his or her motives transparent and may prevent the receipt of emotional support from others.

Jealousy is another possible consequence of upward comparison; the basis here is the comparer's perception of the comparison person as a rival, a person who threatens to steal a valued (self-esteem-relevant) entity (possession, relationship, or advantage) from the comparing person.[16] Although envy and jealousy develop from different realizations, both involve threats to the comparer's self. To experience these emotions, the individual must believe that he or she will be outdone by a rival, who is either already in possession of something desired (envy) or positioned to take away the desired entity (jealousy). Either case is undesirable because it is unflattering to the self and embarrassing to admit publicly.

In summary, it can be learned that people are interested in and engage in social comparisons because of the desire for self-evaluation, self-improvement, and self-enhancement, and for the establishment of a social identity.

Engaging in Social Comparison

Bruni remembers feeling uncomfortable around others for most of her life. It started in school when she was asked to say her name. "Brunhilde!" one of the boys in the class burst out laughing. The teacher had tried to save the moment by saying, "That is a rare but strong name; it sounds like one of the characters' name in an opera by the German composer Richard Wagner from long ago. Are you aware of that?" It made the situation worse when Bruni admitted that her mother had given her that name because she had wanted to be an opera singer. To avoid further teasing, Bruni had insisted on being called Bruni instead of Brunhilde, but she never forgot the embarrassment she felt on that day, and neither did some of her classmates.

Inwardly she thought if she were as rare and special as her name, the other children would have to like her. But how could she become special? What achievements were needed? For years she tried to figure that out, but there did not seem to be any particular talent she could use to give her a special standing. She had not inherited her mother's voice or musical ambitions. In interactions with others, she felt anxious and awkward, always fearing that someone would ask her about her interests and goals. She could not very well say that her goal was to be special.

Over the years, Bruni developed skills in doing crafts, like making collages, sewing special items, and doing some leather work, custom jewelry, and various gift items. The arts and crafts area seemed limitless as long as one's imagination was stretchable. As the mother of three children, Bruni appreciated her skills because they were valuable in teaching her children and keeping them occupied. Bruni's husband was proud of her. But was that sufficient to assure a special status? Bruni silently doubted that; greater admiration was needed to achieve that.

Some women in her neighborhood through their children heard about Bruni's creative activities; apparently, Bruni's children had told them about the wonderful things their mother made for them. A few of the neighbor women approached her, and Bruni's initial nervousness about meeting with them eased when she realized that they did not have her skills and their social standing was somewhat below her family's level. She would not have to worry about not measuring up to their standards; in fact, she was better off than they were socially and financially.

For a while, Bruni appeared satisfied with her life, at least until she joined a group of female volunteers at the local art museum. The volunteers' social standing was at or mostly above Bruni's level, and, even worse, they did not accept crafts as an art form; they focused strictly on the fine arts. Bruni was impressed and depressed at the same time—depressed because she had nothing special to show for her own person. Obviously, what had earned her the admiration of the neighborhood women would not pave her way with this group. Her anxiety flared up again. If the museum volunteers found out about her crafts activities, they might not approve of her, Bruni reasoned in her mind. But being part of this group would enhance Bruni's standing in the community. Bruni learned that the husband of one of the women volunteers served on the school board of the school that Bruni's children attended. A closer connection to this person might be of benefit to her children. Shifting alignment from the neighborhood women to the museum volunteers appeared to be the correct move. After all, the neighborhood women did not seem to have any ambitions for the future; they were just settling for what they had.

Will Bruni follow the path of the social comparison's consequences as outlined above? Will she develop additional negative feelings toward the neighborhood women as she courts the museum volunteers only to be disenchanted with them in the end, too? The answers to these questions are unavailable because further contact with Bruni was lost. We can only guess.

CHAPTER SIX

Approaching the Possibility of Change: Medical versus Mental Health

After as many as 15 to 20 years of struggling with the terror of social anxiety, individuals may on their own, or through encouraging suggestions from well-meaning friends or family members, entertain the possibility of seeking help. Ultimately, only the sufferers can decide whether the intensity of their social discomfort is strong enough to warrant the time, cost, and effort involved in treatment. Should they disclose what they fear will appear to be a "silly" problem to a stranger?

Primary care physicians are usually the first to be consulted by patients with anxiety. As surveys have shown, general practitioners prescribe about 80 percent of all SSRIs; however, they tend to not recognize and to undertreat social anxiety and social phobia.[1] The process of finding the best combination of medications for a particular patient can be frustrating, indeed. Then, when the medications work well, the edge of the patient's discomfort may be taken off, but with that sometimes goes the motivation for working on the problem. There may be little incentive left to seek psychotherapy for exploring the underlying maladaptive cognitions and behavior. While the patient feels better, the core of the problem remains unresolved.

Furthermore, there are situations in which anxiety disorders in general are misdiagnosed, and this is true in particular of social phobia and social anxiety. Some treating professionals who trained before 1980, when the diagnosis of social phobia was first published in the *DSM-III*, might not be familiar with this diagnosis. Instead, they might consider anxiety a non-specific "neurotic" condition. Another reason for the misdiagnosis of social anxiety is that it may be obscured by other anxiety disorders. In other instances, depressive disorder or a personality disorder might appear to be the problem on the surface.[2]

Pharmacological or Psychological Treatment?

Making a decision whether to use medications is based on a risk-benefit appraisal, involving careful assessment by both patient and physician, regarding the impact of the anxiety on the patient's life compared to the medications' risks. In general, however, for most psychiatric conditions that respond to drug therapy, integrating a pharmacological treatment with a psychological one may be most effective.[3]

As reported in the *New York Daily News* of May 26, 2015, in their continuous search for solutions, researchers have turned to MDMA, an ingredient in Ecstasy, for a possible way to treat social anxiety in adults with autism. They want to explore whether MDMA, considered to be a "heart-opening" drug, might reduce the fear of interacting with people. Apparently, MDMA has been effective in boosting confidence, heightening bonding, and increasing understanding of social cues—all qualities that could ease social anxiety.

The MDMA used in the study is a pure form, not the contaminated substance found in the street drug. Over the last century, MDMA's effects were explored in 1,133 people in various studies. But MDMA is still a long way from being prescribed as a treatment for social anxiety; the current study focuses mainly on the feasibility and safety of MDMA.[4]

The risks involved in some medications were addressed in a *New York Times* article of February 25, 2016, reporting a sharp increase of fatal prescription-drug overdoses in the United States. Reading or hearing about that, our attention may jump to prescription painkiller drugs like oxycodone. But the overdose deaths the article focused on involved anti-anxiety drugs, benzodiazepines like Valium and Xanax, used to treat anxiety, panic disorder, and insomnia. Apparently, the rate of overdose deaths involving these drugs increased more than fourfold from 1996 to 2013. Benzodiazepine prescriptions filled by American adults in 2013 amounted to 13.5 million or 5.6 percent of all prescriptions, compared with 8.1 million or 4.1 percent in 1996. And benzodiazepines were involved in 6,973 overdose deaths, which is about 30 percent of the overall prescription-drug overdoses for that year. The other 16,235 deaths were due to use of opioids.[5]

Seventy-two-year-old Elaine was at a loss to understand her feelings of dread about upcoming social situations. This was a new development for her. Her life had been a rich and rewarding one; she had married the man of her dreams and made his professional goals her own. Raising three children was considered an additional blessing. There was some tragedy, though; her oldest daughter and the daughter's husband were killed in an automobile accident, leaving their son Bertram behind. Bertram had been diagnosed as autistic. Elaine and her husband did not hesitate to adopt Bertram as their son and raised him.

Elaine's life was busy; working with her husband, raising Bertram, and entertaining their friends made her feel fulfilled. Then her husband died. Suddenly the work she had done by his side stopped. She still had Bertram to care for and was involved in activities benefiting the cause of learning more about autism and how to help those afflicted with the difficulty. Elaine first noticed her discomfort in social situations several months after her husband's death. As she was meeting with friends and acquaintances, she found herself at a loss for what to say; it seemed all the things worth talking about were events that had occurred in the past. She remained silent, listening to what her friends had to say, until one day one of her friends asked her, "Elaine, you have been so quiet lately; is anything wrong?" Elaine did not have an answer beyond "No, I am all right. I guess I am just a bit tired."

But she worried about it and developed an anticipatory anxiety regarding upcoming social events. She tried to explain to herself that she was just still too emotionally involved in the loss of her husband. Perhaps it was too early for socializing. While Bertram was at his supervised workplace, Elaine spent more time sitting quietly by herself, wrapped in one of her husband's sweaters or jackets, remembering the past. When with the passage of time her condition did not improve, Elaine confided in her family physician, who explained that Elaine was depressed over her husband's death and prescribed antidepressant medication for her. The physician's explanation sounded logical, and the medication seemed to take the edge off Elaine's discomfort.

However, when more than two years had elapsed without any change in Elaine's condition, one of her daughters suggested that her mother might benefit from talking to a social worker or psychologist. Elaine gave in, and they found a psychologist not too far from where Elaine lived. Elaine talked freely about her past life and the fulfillment she had found within her family and her husband's work. In contrast, her current life was empty, except for the care she provided for Bertram. But even that would be much reduced in the future because Bertram was planning to marry his girlfriend, a young woman who suffered from some developmental difficulties.

After carefully listening to Elaine's report, the psychologist wondered about any interests or personal passions in Elaine's life. Her answer came quickly: "I did not need an interest of my own. I was fortunate to share my husband's excitement for his profession, and I felt rewarded being able to help him with that. And my children and family provided additional involvement."

Elaine has reached a difficult point in her life; from one moment to the next her life's meaning had been taken from her, and it had left her without knowing what to replace it with. What is even more disturbing is that she does not understand why she now needs to do what probably should have occurred in her youth—building her own personal passion that will sustain her even after the loss of her "leader," as she called her husband.

Both Elaine and Dora, the woman introduced in chapter 3, described their marriages and previous lives as happy and fulfilled. Now they try to hide in silence the emptiness and despair that overwhelm them from time to time. As young girls and young women, they could not imagine needing to develop a meaning of life for themselves, independent of others. Finding their happiness in the love of those significant others was wonderful and rewarding, but it left them empty and vulnerable because they did not feel comfortable relating to others in their new environment without their previous partners at their side. How many Elaines and Doras are there, quietly hiding their despair? Can medication soothe the discomfort, or could psychotherapy build a bridge from the past to the future?

Is It Depression or Anxiety or Both?

Depression and phobias at times overlap, and this interplay can occur on different levels. On the most basic level, phobias and depression may be considered two different manifestations of the same biological illness. On another level, depression may be present as a psychological reaction to the phobia state, responding to phobia-connected losses. On a third level, depression-prone individuals who also happen to be phobic may experience increased depression over the discomfort associated with the particular phobia they suffer from.[6]

Because approximately 10 percent of depressed patients report experiencing panic attacks, this situation might be conceptualized as an affective illness being the main core illness and the phobia being one of possible ensuing complications. Another explanatory path suggests that because panic responses have been linked to separation anxiety and because separation and loss are precipitants of depression, the brain centers for panic and generalized depression are contiguous. This would indicate the likelihood that some patients give the appearance of pure depression, while others show a pure panic picture, and some patients express parts of both. One medical source reported that 20 to 25 percent of phobic patients suffered coexisting endogenous depression.[7]

Based on the foregoing explanations, combined psychological and pharmacological treatment approaches would appear to be the answer. But it has been suggested to recognize the existence of two different types of panic attacks. In the first type, patients experience panic attacks "out of the blue," called "spontaneous" panics by professionals. As a result of experiencing those panic attacks more than once, patients develop a fear of them and of the situations in which they felt the panic, which leads to patients' developing anticipatory anxiety. In contrast to the "spontaneous" attacks, other panic attacks only in particular situations, like in simple phobias. For patients with spontaneous panic attacks, tricyclic antidepressant drugs in combination with psychological therapy have been effective in blocking or preventing the panic, whereas for patients who do not experience spontaneous attacks, various psychological therapies alone are beneficial.[8]

The above recommendations were made some time ago, and, in fact, the following two case histories in their beginnings date back to that time. But, as mentioned in chapter 1, many individuals suffering from anxiety initially became patients of medical doctors, such as their family physicians, and it is not known how many of them were referred to psychiatric or psychological clinicians.

She Could Have Been Cinderella

Betty Lou's story is one that makes her life look like Cinderella's—on the surface at least. The treating psychiatrist decided on a diagnosis of "depression with histrionic personality traits" upon referral from her primary family physician. Apparently, the psychiatrist was unaware of or unimpressed by her fear and discomfort in social situations.

Betty Lou had been the prettiest girl in her small southern town, growing up in a poor family. Petite, with wavy brown hair framing a pear-shaped face and bright blue eyes that lit up with occasional smiles, she looked like she could have been the happiest child, but the rare frequency of her smiles indicated otherwise. Being the only child in a poor family, she was not befriended by her classmates despite—or perhaps because of—her prettiness. Her father had been ill for a long time, forcing her mother to work as a practical nurse to feed her small family. Thus, Betty Lou's social status did not entitle her to invitations from her upper-class contemporaries.

Intellectually, Betty Lou would have been able to achieve acceptance to college, and she briefly considered that possibility. But in her last year of high school, she achieved a sudden, double-edged popularity when the son of one of the wealthiest families in town courted her. Now she received invitations from her snobbish female classmates—partly because they wanted to be on good terms with Bill, Betty Lou's beau, and partly to diffuse the danger of competition from Betty Lou's attractiveness by removing her from the dating scene as Bill's steady girlfriend.

Her mother approved of and encouraged Betty Lou's budding romance with Bill. As his wife, her daughter would have a better fate than attending college and facing an uncertain future. Betty Lou listened and did not voice disagreement. It would not have occurred to her to disagree with her mother or any person of authority. Soon after their graduation from high school, everybody who was somebody got ready for a big wedding. In her gorgeous bridal gown, Betty Lou was able to hide signs of her pregnancy. But she was painfully aware of the fact that she had lost her virginity prior to her wedding, something she had always promised herself she would not let happen. At the same time, it also established a position of reduced power in her new marriage; now she had to marry Bill and be grateful if he actually did so. This was the beginning of her married life.

Even the birth of two children did not bring great happiness to Betty Lou's life. Overall, the children's fate was decided by the family. Betty Lou always felt uncomfortable in the presence of her new family and their friends and acquaintances. Her social and personal insecurities were increased by her mother-in-law's decisions regarding the location and type of housing appropriate for her son and his family. Her mother-in-law selected (and paid for) the couple's new home and all its furnishings, as well as the maid who would take care of all this. Even the couple's annual vacations were planned by Bill's mother and other family members. One could not go against those regulations without incurring the punishment of increased isolation from other outside influences.

The only decisions Betty Lou was trusted to make on her own—with occasional suggestions—were personal purchases, such as her wardrobe and jewelry. And there were sufficient financial resources for that at her disposal. While everybody around her envied her, Betty Lou's emotional and mental loneliness increased. There were no strong friendships she could feel secure in, and at all the family's social events she felt like an outcast. She prepared herself for those social events that she had to attend with ever-growing medications, generously prescribed for her by a psychiatrist located in the next, larger town. She would drive there for her early-afternoon therapy session, have dinner with the psychiatrist, then stay the night at a hotel before returning home the next morning. At least the medication kept her from shaking, blushing, and stuttering during the required social interactions.

The only places Betty Lou felt comfortable were in her expensive foreign cars and in the stores she frequented for her personal purchases. Parking attendants, service station personnel, and shopkeepers experienced a smiling Betty Lou who took the time to politely inquire about their lives and their families. Bill did not pay much attention to his wife's discomfort; he developed his own forms of entertainment, especially since he spent some time traveling on behalf of the family business.

Not surprisingly, the steadily increased use of prescription medication led to a hospitalization in the mental health department of the hospital that was served by her psychiatrist. Following her discharge from the hospital, the psychiatrist also discharged Betty Lou from his care and referred her to psychiatric services in her hometown. Soon thereafter her life took another turn. Bill had lost a sizeable part of his inheritance, and a genetic health problem mandated his retirement from the family business. Their scale of life became greatly reduced. They sold their estate and some of their art treasures, said goodbye to the maid, and settled in a smaller home. Eventually, Betty Lou went to work in one of the fashionable stores she had previously visited as a customer. Overall she felt more at ease in her new surroundings, although more work in the upkeep of the home was required of her, and Bill had become more demanding of her now that he was not able to travel anymore.

For a couple years, she felt safe as a member of a therapy group, disclosing to the group members more than she ever had to anybody else. Here she was not being judged and found lacking in some skills or talents. For the first time, she felt accepted by those few around her, but by now it did not produce enough strength for her to venture out and make a new life for herself. Her husband's family still exerted power over her, Bill's, and the children's life. Even after Bill's death she remained under the umbrella of his family and finally agreed to be moved into a retirement home of their choice, where she lost her few remaining outside contacts and died as lonely as she had been for most of her life.

Would her life have been happier if psychotherapy had been added earlier to the prescribed medication? In hindsight it is difficult to determine, even though there was a definite improvement in her mental state when she participated in individual and group therapy following her discharge from the hospital.

Even if people suffering from social anxiety are willing to seek psychotherapy, there are many different theoretical orientations that might prove it difficult to find the right type of therapy for the right client. Not all psychological treatments are equally effective, and it is difficult to judge the effectiveness of a given treatment approach by the experience or the credentials of the therapist providing it. And even though socially anxious clients might be horrified at the mere mention of group therapy, the major advantage of group therapy is that it allows people to develop both confidence and coping skills in a real-life but safe social setting.[9]

Self-help treatments in the form of reading and following exercises suggested in self-help books may be another treatment approach preferred by some socially anxious individuals. Although many of those books or recorded materials can be beneficial by reducing the initial anxiety the individual might experience when talking to a therapist, there are no guarantees that the individual will follow the course, and there are no devices that encourage deeper exploration into some fear or avoidance behaviors. In other words, a socially anxious person may follow the prescribed course of action in a superficial rather than a deeper, more meaningful way because there are no checkpoints other than brief question-and-answer tests provided in the books.

A Case of Surface Repair

Helen's story is another case in which the first reach for help occurred in her family doctor's office. During her early teenage years, Helen's facial deformity (a weak, receding chin) made her afraid of being with people, and her fear was especially paralyzing when she had to meet new people. As she told herself, people who had known her for a long time had become used to her face, but a new person, seeing her for the first time, would be appalled to look at her.

It did not help that her mother was critical of her and often reminded her, "Hurry up, Helen, hurry up." Helen took that to mean that she was not only physically but also mentally slow. Even after she had undergone corrective surgery and her face looked as normal as anyone's, she was not able to overcome her low self-confidence. She was not able to assert herself in the choice of a career, and when her mother insisted she become a teacher, Helen dropped out of college and went to work in a local office. Her wish had been to study music, and with the self-consciousness she struggled with on a daily basis, she could not imagine herself as a teacher in front of a room full of children, who would probably make fun of her.

After a while, Helen found employment in another town. It felt good to get away from her critical mother. In her new environment, she met a young man, whom she fell in love with, and they got married secretly. Helen did not want her mother to criticize her new husband, and the groom was afraid to introduce his bride to his parents because of their different religion. The two young people were happy for a short period of time and looked forward to the birth of their first child. Then Helen's husband was killed in an accident, and her pregnancy ended in a miscarriage. The first words she uttered after hearing of the dead fetus were "I could not even be a mother to our child. I can do nothing right."

After that tragedy, Helen returned to her hometown to help her mother, who had become widowed. Helen had taken back her maiden name and never told her mother about her marriage, the dead husband, or the dead child. She never dated any other men because she firmly believed that she was not good for anyone. Although she was able to interact with her coworkers on a superficial level, she withdrew from more personal social contact with anyone and instead turned her affection and care to her cat.

In spite of the prescribed medication, Helen's depression mounted until suicide seemed to be the only answer. But before she acted on that plan, she had her cat put to sleep because nobody would pamper her cat the way Helen had done. It would not be fair to leave the cat behind. The suicide attempt that should have worked failed because of an unpredictable event. Helen's fate was to wake up in the hospital's emergency room with the knowledge that her beloved cat was dead. "She could not even do it right when she tried to kill herself! What was left for her?" Helen's words sounded like a challenge directed at her new therapist.

The first thing the therapist requested of Helen was to promise not to attempt another suicide while she was in therapy. Helen reluctantly agreed. Then the therapist suggested that Helen might try to give living another, meaningful chance. "Living did not work for me," Helen retorted angrily. Instead of arguing with Helen, the therapist just said calmly, "Well, let's try it again." It was a power struggle; Helen, although reluctant to go along with the therapist's suggestions, did not want to openly rebel because she believed that this therapist was one of the best, and she was also afraid that no other therapist would be willing to work with her.

Because Helen was now entirely financially dependent on her mother after losing her job because of her suicide attempt, searching for a new job was an important next step. Helen could not see herself applying for a job; not surprisingly, her suicide attempt had increased her social anxiety. She was afraid of anyone asking her why her previous job had ended. Who would want to hire her, thinking that she might again consider suicide to be the solution for future problems? As the therapy sessions dealt with Helen's reason for wanting to die, slowly changing the focus to why she might be able to live, a reasonable explanation for prospective employers emerged, and Helen finally applied for a position advertised in the local newspaper.

In response to her application, Helen was invited to an interview. Although her level of anxiety was so high that she did not remember much of the interview, she was offered the position. Shocked about this unexpected turn of events, Helen declined the offer, stating that she needed to take care of her aging mother. Although she wanted to run away, Helen knew that she had to tell her therapist. The therapist listened to Helen's stammering explanation over the phone and told her to immediately come to the office for a session exploring Helen's thinking and reasoning in the job interview.

Although Helen could not remember many details of the interview because of the high level of anxiety she experienced, she must have done quite well, or she would not have been offered the job right there on the spot. Why did she decline the offer?

"The anxiety I felt while interacting with the two people in the interview was so strong that I could not imagine being in a work situation with even more people around me, observing me. I panicked at the thought and could not get out of there fast enough," Helen explained.

"Have you considered working from home?" the therapist inquired.

"Yes, I have thought of it but could not find anything I could do at home by myself other than telephone work, but I am afraid to talk much on the phone; I tend to have difficulty understanding because of my anxiety, and then I start to stutter and lose it," Helen replied.

At this point, the therapist decided to refer Helen to an ongoing therapy group in addition to the individual therapy. At first Helen balked at the thought of being part of a group. But the therapist promised her that if after six group sessions she still felt so negative about it, Helen could drop out.

"Six sessions!" Helen cried out. "That's too much."

"In fact, that is very little because in the first two or three sessions you might not even get to know what's going on because of your high level of anxiety. If we are lucky, by session four you might be calmed down just enough to get to know a bit about your fellow group members."

"And if I still don't like it, I don't have to continue with the group?" Helen wanted to make sure, and the therapist confirmed.

Helen made it through the first group session, not saying much except the most superficial information about herself. But she was able to listen to the interactions of the other group members, and the overall atmosphere of acceptance seemed to set her mind at ease—at least to a small degree. She was still worried about how the other members were judging her, and she admitted that to the therapist during her individual session.

In the third group session, the therapist suggested that group members pair up in teams for a social exercise in getting to know each other. Helen looked at the therapist as if she could not believe what she had just heard. "An open invitation to judge and reject poor, defenseless Helen! Who would want to pair up with her?" she thought, trying to slide back into the chair as far as possible to make herself less visible. To her surprise, two other group members wanted to be her partner. Not knowing which one to choose, Helen looked questioningly at the therapist, who nodded and suggested that Helen work with both of them because the group members present on this day made up an odd number, which would leave one of the women without a partner.

Both women who had selected Helen as a partner seemed intrigued by her. As one of them said, "You have a pleasant voice and I like your smile, even though we haven't heard you say much. We would like to know more about you." Helen could not believe her ears. A small, tentative smile crossed her face as she thanked the women for their attention. Her initial apprehension seemed to lessen somewhat, although she was still far from being relaxed.

During their next individual session, the therapist processed this particular group meeting with Helen. "I thought you looked uncomfortable at the beginning of the group meeting," the therapist started.

"Actually, I was petrified when you announced that we would work in pairs on the exercise," Helen responded.

"What about it frightened you? Was it that you were not sure which of the other group members you would like as a partner?"

Helen answered, "I was afraid that nobody would want me and I would sit there alone, for everybody to see. I was also afraid that if I were to be paired up with another group member that she would criticize me in her mind or tell others how stupid I acted."

"From what you are saying now and have shared with me previously, you seem to be concerned that people will criticize you. Where does that come from? How many people have criticized you—who were they?" The therapist tried to keep Helen focused on this central issue.

Helen thought for a moment, "Well, my mother used to criticize me all the time. I was never fast enough or never did things well enough."

"Who else criticized you?" the therapist asked.

"I can't think of anybody else right now. I am sure there were others," Helen said in a slightly defensive voice.

"It is certainly painful enough to learn that your own mother did not believe in you and your abilities. But it seems that you may have transferred your mother's attitude about you onto other people in your environment." The therapist continued to probe Helen's reasons for her suspicion of other people around her. "Why would other people who might not even know you well enough be judging and criticizing you? What is so unusual about you that people would take an immediate dislike to you?"

"I used to have a misshapen chin. The other children made fun of me, and some grownups felt sorry for me and asked me if I had been in an accident. I could tell that people who saw me for the first time were taken aback by the sight of my face," Helen stated in a tearful voice.

"Since you had corrective surgery done on your face, how many people have behaved toward you in the way you just described?" the therapist asked.

Helen appeared stunned. "Not anybody that I can remember," she answered, adding after a moment's pause, "Isn't it bad enough that I had to go through all that when I was a child?"

"Certainly it was a bad and painful experience," the therapist agreed, continuing after a brief pause, "What was the reason for the corrective surgery as you remember it?"

Helen had an incredulous look on her face as she answered, "To look normal, of course!"

"And would you say that the surgery was successful?" the therapist inquired.

"I think so," Helen replied.

"So you went through the pain and discomfort of the surgery to look 'normal,' and you admit that the surgery was successful in making you look normal, yet you continue to carry the deformity that has been removed from the outside by pushing it onto the inside of you?" the therapist summarized. "Why won't you let go of the thing that no longer exists in reality?"

Helen sat in silence, stunned by the therapist's speech. But she was not ready to give up yet. "It is a reminder that people are ready to make fun of you. I don't want to leave myself open and vulnerable to ridicule by trusting others too much."

"How very sad," the therapist replied in a low voice. "It appears that the surgery that had been successful, medically speaking, turned out to be a waste."

"What do you mean, 'a waste'?" Helen questioned the therapist.

"Well, as I said earlier, you seem to hold on to that old deformity on the inside of you."

When Helen did not answer, the therapist continued, "You said that you wanted to remain aware of being vulnerable to people making fun of you. Could it be that you are distrusting people and at the same time judging them, just because you might be afraid that other people are as critical as your mother? How many of the people around you have you asked what they think of you?"

Helen's facial expression looked as if she was ready to doubt her therapist's sanity. "Ask people what they think of me?"

"Why not ask them? Aren't you ready to pass judgment on people without real evidence? You might as well give them a chance to answer for themselves."

Obviously, Helen had not thought about her own behavior being so similar to what she accused others of doing to her. Stunned, she did not have an answer when her eyes met the therapist's gaze. "I have to think about this" was all she could say.

"Yes, think about it. That's a good plan," the therapist agreed.

And Helen did think about it. Her behavior in group therapy changed; slowly, she became less guarded in interactions and at times disclosed more of herself. The other group members enjoyed Helen's dry sense of humor, which she finally allowed herself to express. Then one day in her individual session, the therapist asked, "Helen, have you thought about looking for a job again? It's been some time since your last application, and you have grown so much in the meantime, I thought you might reconsider ways of becoming independent of your mother."

"Yes, you are correct; it's time to think of my independence again. I feel stronger now, and just two days ago, I applied for a position as switchboard operator at the local hospital. I hope they will seriously consider me. Of course, I am nervous about an interview, but I don't think I will panic like I did before. I have had a lot of time and opportunities to think about my fears."

Helen got the job. She was well liked in her job because she was considerate of the feelings of people she interacted with. Her salary allowed her to rent a small apartment when her mother moved into a retirement home. Helen worked in her job until it was time for her own retirement. She made some good friends, remained close and loyal to her group members, and finally allowed herself to take in a stray cat to share her life. This cat would not be threatened by any suicide attempts of its owner; life had become meaningful once again—or perhaps for the first time ever. During her retirement years, Helen kept in touch with her friends and former group members. When she died of natural causes, one of her friends adopted Helen's cat.

In retrospect we know that both Betty Lou and Helen had years of medical treatment for depression. And certainly both had been depressed for a long time. But in both their lives, it had been the anxiety they experienced when interacting with others that had caused their low self-esteem and most of their depression. As they realized that they could not do what others seemed to have no difficulty with, they became depressed as a reaction to their fear of others' judgment of them. In other words, the medical treatment was aimed at the symptom, not the cause of the problem.

Which Psychological Treatment to Choose?

When deciding on psychological treatment for social anxiety, there are many different kinds of psychotherapy to choose from. Cognitive-Behavioral Therapy (CBT) apparently has the widest scientific support for addressing anxiety disorders; especially for anxious children and adolescents, CBT has been recognized as the leader in psychosocial treatment for this young population. However, according to some voices, there seems to be a disparity between those in need of services and accessibility of qualified therapists capable of delivering empirically supported treatments.[10]

Other available approaches prospective clients might want to explore and investigate include Interpersonal Psychotherapy (IPT), Supportive Psychotherapy, Virtual Reality Therapy (VRT), psychoanalysis, and Analytically Oriented Psychotherapy, among others.[11] Mindfulness and compassion-focused therapy are newer approaches dealing with anxieties and phobias, among other difficulties. For many sufferers of social anxiety, involvement in group therapy can provide a valuable framework. As was seen in Helen's case described earlier in this chapter, although at first the mention of participation in group therapy may elicit additional initial anxiety, it provides a safe and valuable practice environment for its participants.

Despite the growing list of available psychotherapies, concerns have been expressed about economic and institutional pressures pushing therapists toward briefer interventions. Psychiatrists seem to be particularly pressured to provide less psychotherapy and prescribe more medication. There seems to be a pharmacological emphasis within the mental health system. At the cost of psychotherapeutic, social, and other therapeutic approaches, this pharmaceutical bias has been heavily promoted by the pharmaceutical industry. This pharmaceutical bias might suggest to medical doctors and their patients that there is a drug to alleviate every ailment and discontent.[12]

Reaching Below the Surface of Social Anxiety

Social anxiety has many cognitive elements, such as thoughts, beliefs, and cognitive ruminations, as its foundation, which in turn are accompanied by bodily sensations, such as perspiring, shaking or trembling, stuttering, shortness of breath, and so on, which indicate that more than medical relief is needed to treat the whole picture of the impairment—both physically and mentally. Some physical improvement can be reached with the help of breathing techniques and relaxation; for others, carefully dosed medication may serve the need.

Jason reported a history of social anxiety dating back to his years in elementary school. He suffered the teasing of his schoolmates about his speech defect. When he complained to his parents, his father called him a "sissy" and told him to develop his muscles so the other children would become afraid of his physical strength and would not dare to tease him again. With that, he took Jason to the local YMCA and had him started on a physical exercise regime that ensured growing muscle power. It helped; the teasing stopped, and speech lessons turned Jason into a seemingly normal boy all through his high school years until the second part of his senior year.

As his classmates discussed their plans following graduation and applying to different colleges, Jason's anxiety returned. He became moody and defensive and withdrew from his friends to the point that his teachers noticed the change and suggested Jason talk to the school counselor. A few sessions with the counselor and some antianxiety medication prescribed by the family physician seemed to help; Jason calmed down and acted in his usual manner.

However, when it came time to apply for college, Jason refused to consider any colleges away from his hometown. He was afraid of having to spend all his time with others, not only in the classrooms but also in a dormitory room with other students. He applied to the two colleges near his hometown so he could continue living at home and commute to the college that accepted him. To his parents Jason explained his decision as being based on financial reasons; there would not be the higher out-of-state tuition costs and no need for dormitory living expenses.

Unaware of Jason's true reason for this decision, his parents praised him for his common sense and frugality. His college years passed uneventfully except for frequent absences in his speech class (the professor favored the assignment of impromptu speeches). Jason achieved generally satisfactory grades in his classes and got along with his teachers and other students on a superficial basis. He did not form any close relationships with his new classmates, and the friends from his high school days were either working or away at out-of-state colleges.

Finally, as graduation approached, Jason could not decide whether to apply to graduate schools or to consider looking for a job in his major area of study. His anxiety brought him to a standstill. The family physician handed him another prescription for a tranquilizer and suggested a period of rest after all the studying and turmoil over graduation and what to plan for the future. The doctor's advice suited Jason; it was a good reason (or perfect excuse) to avoid the feared discomfort of facing an unknown situation with unknown people. It also saved him from making a decision about his relationship with Marla, the pretty girl he had been dating for the past two years.

After Jason had spent most of the summer recovering from his anxiety attacks, except for the time he spent mowing his neighbors' lawns for some spending money, his parents approached him with questions about his plans for the future. In response, Jason's anxiety flared up again, and they left him alone for a bit. Then Jason's father took the initiative again by talking to their insurance agent. Jason's major in college had been business administration, and it seemed reasonable that Jason could obtain an entry-level position in a local business firm. Fortunately, there was an opening available at the insurance company, and Jason seemed to be a good candidate; he was hired.

Armed with a generous supply of tranquilizers, Jason started his new job. After an initial period of insecurity, Jason seemed to adapt to the duties of his working days as long as he could stay in the office. Difficulties arose when it came time for him to approach prospective new clients for the company. The mere thought of making cold calls filled him with terror. What should he say to those strangers? How could he convince them to buy insurance from the company he worked for? How should he address them? What would they think of him? What if he started to stutter? He remembered his speech defect from long ago.

The fear of those possibilities overwhelmed and paralyzed him. He was able to schedule a few appointments over the phone or with the help of the office secretary, but when it was time to go to the scheduled meeting, he could not bring himself to follow through. He later called one or two customers to apologize for his failure to appear, claiming some unforeseen crisis; others he never contacted again, reporting them in his log as not having been home at the time of the proposed meeting. Weekly staff meetings with supervisors and other agents were difficult for Jason to attend because he had nothing but failed attempts to report. After three such meetings, Jason quit his job. He stayed at home, locked himself in his room, and refused to make any attempt to look for another job.

His parents were desperate. His father threatened to throw Jason out of the house, but his mother pleaded with her husband and got him to reconsider his threat. He gave Jason the opportunity to see a mental health professional to help him with his anxiety problem and his refusal or inability to interact with people. That was the beginning of Jason's long path of exploration, challenges, repeated failures and irrational justifications, recoveries, new attempts, and small successes that finally brought him to understanding and accepting reality and responsibility for his new life.

If we consider social anxiety disorder as a diagnostic entity by itself, relief as a result of any therapy process is likely to be short-lived. Anxiety reactions—as well as depressive or other emotional reactions—are part of the individual's basic overall responses to life events. In other words, individuals who experience the fear of future pain or discomfort and respond to those fears generally with withdrawal or avoidance will respond similarly not only to feared social interactions but also to any other feared situation. By focusing the treatment on the stated or identified complaint of social anxiety, relief of those symptoms might function as a smoke screen, leaving deeper levels of the phenomenon unexplored and able to continue their hidden existence until another eruption requires renewed attention.

Another Look at Psychological Hardiness

As discussed in chapter 3, the psychologically hardy mind operates on a belief system of commitment that persistence in goals will bring some results, that some control is possible in most situations, and that negative events can be turned around in some positive directions. By contrast, the lack of psychological hardiness leaves individuals with the conviction that the pain cannot be endured, whatever the goals in the situation might have been, that the individual is powerless in the situation, and that everything related to the situation will be negative with no possibility that the person can change it.

This generally defeatist attitude will prevail not only in situations that involve social interactions and the resulting anxiety but in every other stressful situation as well because the possibility of pain or discomfort will set the general mental-emotional process in action.

As soon as the possibility of a painful situation appears on the horizon, the defeatist belief system takes over, inducing the individual to avoid the situation at all costs. In turn, every act of avoidance makes the anxiety and the belief system grow stronger. Because the worst (death, humiliation, etc.) has not occurred, the individual thinks, "I must have done the correct thing by avoiding the situation." In other words, in the socially anxious individual's mind, the absence of the feared disaster is interpreted as evidence that avoidance was the correct action.

Sometimes individuals go so far as to distort information to feel justified in their avoidance behaviors. For instance, when Jason (discussed above) met with a psychologist, he hesitatingly admitted that he had told himself that setting up appointments with prospective insurance business customers was primarily for the business to make money, and it was the agents' responsibility to convince the customers to purchase insurance that they may not even need. Thus, describing to himself his job and his employer's intentions in a negative light made it easier for him to avoid calling customers or failing to appear at scheduled meetings with prospective customers. With this line of reasoning, he finally convinced himself that it was immoral to work in that line of business, and he could not possibly perform such immoral acts, thus working out a perfectly acceptable excuse to quit his job.

In the end, psychological hardiness is the determining factor of whether a person will decide to work on reducing the feared anxiety.

Considering fear as possessing the functional properties of a drive, as was suggested long ago by drive-reduction theorists, it can be understood that when a person is faced with a threatening situation or information about it, the person, motivated by the fear, will search for responses that reduce the threat.[13]

When a suggested protective action (persuasion to act) is successful in reducing the fear, the action is reinforced and can become part of the person's permanent response repertoire. But when the recommended action fails to reduce the level of fear, because it is perceived either to be ineffective or to be impossible to do, defensive reactions may be used to reduce the fear. In general, high levels of fear can be expected to evoke defensive reactions that can undermine rationalization and persuasion, and the emotional tension will not be sufficiently reduced. At that point, residual emotional tension may bring about defensive avoidance, causing a decrease in persuasion.[14]

Other models and theories that expanded from the drive-reduction model are the parallel-response model,[15] the protection-motivation theory,[16] and the extended-parallel-process model.[17]

According to the extended-parallel-process model, exposure to a fear-arousing situation or communication will initiate two appraisal processes—a threat appraisal and a coping appraisal. Individuals will estimate or appraise the threat reflected in the fear-arousing situation. The stronger they believe that they are vulnerable to a serious threat, the more motivated they will be to engage in a coping appraisal. In general, this response tendency toward a fear-inducing situation is not the likely one to expect within the population of socially anxious people who lack the motivation for coping with a threat.

In situations where the threat appraisal yields an estimate of the threat being irrelevant or insignificant, the extended-process model proposes that there is no motivation to proceed further. The model attempts to predict whether individuals who believe that they are vulnerable to a serious risk or danger will engage in danger control or in fear control. When individuals perceive the suggested action to be ineffective or their own inability to perform the action successfully, they will engage in fear control, eliciting such defense motivation and behaviors as denial, defensive avoidance, or reactance to alleviate their fear.[18]

The lack of psychological hardiness leaves individuals to believe that they cannot change the outcome of those fear-inducing situations because they do not have complete control and are unable to perform the necessary actions to successfully resolve the situation. Therefore, they neglect focusing on the second half of the model, the coping appraisal. During the threat appraisal, they tend to exaggerate the threat to the degree that defensive avoidance appears to be the only alternative.

Returning to Jason's story above, the psychologist appreciated Jason's admission of having described to himself his job as an immoral activity, which provided the excuse for quitting his job. Rather than arguing whether the job entailed an immoral basis, turning the conversation to the underlying fear had prompted Jason to formulate the excuse. Jason explained that his old speech defect might reappear in interactions with strangers in which Jason was expected to make a good impression and be persuasive.

Instead of inquiring about the most recent time such an event had occurred, the psychologist asked Jason to estimate how bad it would be if indeed it had happened. As might be expected, Jason's answer indicated that it would be "terrible."

"When you say terrible, how terrible do you mean? Can you give some kind of a rating like 50 percent, 75 percent, or 100 percent terrible?" the psychologist steered Jason's thinking into a more defined range. Jason thought for a moment and came back with "I would say about 85 percent at least."

Noticing Jason's hesitation to be specific and ascribing it to a combination of anxiety building up in Jason's mind and his tendency to be ambiguous regarding feared situations, the psychologist agreed, "That's pretty high; it must be uncomfortable. But at least it would not mean that you would die in a situation like that—that would be 100 percent."

Following a brief pause to give Jason time to absorb the answer, the psychologist asked, "Have you been in any situation with this 85 percent level of discomfort before?"

"No," Jason's answer came fast; then hesitatingly he continued, "There was one time when I was at my girlfriend Marla's house. Her parents had gone out for their anniversary celebration, a movie and dinner. Marla and I did not have many opportunities to be alone together. She said it would be safe to come over. We had been making out when we heard the garage door go up. I had managed to get into my pants but could not find my shoe; Marla's puppy had used it as a toy and run into the hall. Here I stood with one shoe in my hand and the other shoe missing when her parents came in. I could probably have made it out the side door, but looking for my shoe prevented me from getting out. I was so embarrassed standing there in front of Marla's parents with the shoe in my hand. I wished I could have died."

"That was a tough situation," the psychologist agreed. "How did you cope, what did you say to the parents?"

"I could not think of anything to say except the truth that the puppy had wanted to play with my shoes. Marla's mother left the room, saying she was going to get my other shoe from the puppy. Her husband was watching me. He did not invite me to sit down, so I remained standing until the mother came back with my shoe. I thanked her, stepped into the loafer, apologized, and left the house."

"Actually, you did quite well; you didn't even have to lie. Deciding to tell the truth—as much as you had to and could afford to—was a good coping strategy under the circumstances. Are you and Marla still dating?" the psychologist asked.

"No, we broke up some time ago when I graduated from college and didn't know what to do next. I miss her." Jason sounded sad.

With this interchange, the psychologist wanted to impress on Jason the fact that he had been able to cope in an embarrassing situation.

Recognizing the tendency of socially anxious clients to quickly exaggerate the threat appraisal to the degree of eliminating their focus on the coping appraisal, the clinician attempts to persuade the client to give a detailed rating of the perceived threat. By lowering the ratings of the threat from the initial panic-induced rating of 100 percent to a less exaggerated degree, the clinician is able to guide the client gently into the path of a coping appraisal. At least, the seed of possible coping can be planted in the client's mind. Socially anxious individuals are usually as capable of coping in other areas of their lives as most other people.

Solutions to Obesity—Mental or Medical?

The question of whether to approach medical or mental-health solutions to the problem of social anxiety takes on a different light in cases in which obesity is a reason for avoiding social interactions. Individuals in this category tend to believe that if their obesity problem was solved, they will not have to worry about interactions with others. So both a mental (adhering to a weight-loss diet) and a medically based approach, such as bariatric surgery, hold promise for a solution. But as many individuals who have entered either one of those paths have found out, it offers at best an incomplete solution. Why? It does not erase in the minds of the socially anxious persons the idea that there was something wrong, something missing in their personality structure, something more fundamental than diets or bariatric surgeries might resolve. The defeatist attitude has developed into a habit of facing or avoiding the world.

Bariatric Surgery Missing the Vulnerability Core

Having graduated from the process of bariatric surgery, followed by significant weight loss and a newly established exercise program, 34-year-old Heather felt ready for a new life. Most of her childhood, adolescence, and young adulthood had been overshadowed by obesity. She had graduated from college and found employment in a health-care facility. Aside from a few uneventful dates, the romantic part of life had not developed. However, with her new body, her future might hold new promises.

Heather's first decision was to embark on graduate school in the evenings after work. An advanced degree would not only assure her financial independence; she also felt ready to learn and to meet new challenges— she believed. Although she looked as slim and trim as many of her female classmates, Heather experienced a high level of anxiety in some of her classes. This was unexpected; Heather thought the anxiety had left her along with the excess weight. The classes she felt most anxious about were the ones that focused on discussion rather than strict lectures by the professor.

"What is so anxiety evoking about those classes with discussions?"

"What if somebody disagrees with what I am saying, telling me that I am wrong? What if someone laughs at my reasoning or my statements?" Heather responded to her psychologist's question.

"Well, did you answer your question? What would happen if someone does not agree with you?" the psychologist probed.

"That would be awful" was Heather's quick reply.

"How awful—you would be dead or crippled for life? The world would come to an end? You don't need to answer that now, but think about it. And something else, it seems that you insist on a 100 percent agreement with your opinion."

"I did not demand 100 percent agreement with my opinions. What made you say that?" Heather sounded defensive, something the psychologist tried to avoid but had to risk to help Heather understand her own behavior.

"Heather, you said, 'What if someone disagrees with what I am saying?' That means if just one person out of the particular group has a different opinion, it would be intolerable. Let's say you are in a group of 30 members or classmates, and one of them disagrees, it's awful, or whatever. That means you want all 30 members to agree with you, and that would be 100 percent of them. That's more than a professional speaker would or could demand."

Heather seemed stunned. "I never thought about it that way" was her reply.

"I have found myself disagreeing with the opinion of others. Of course, that did not always mean that my opinion was the correct one. For me, at times there was something to be learned from others' thoughts." The psychologist tried to direct the focus away from Heather's beliefs to neutralize the topic and give Heather a chance to reconsider her view on the topic.

"Come to think of it, I don't always agree with what others say," Heather said in a low tone of voice, "and I don't think people feel insulted. How come I take it so seriously?"

"Perhaps it is still left over from the years of being sensitive about what other people think of you. It had been a habit for so long, and although the surgery changed your outward appearance, your habitual thinking and feeling may still lag behind," the psychologist tried to explain. "Think about it for a bit. It is a complicated concept and it might take some time to get desensitized to your old way of responding emotionally."

As explained earlier, anxiety reactions, just like other emotional reactions, are basic elements in individuals' overall framework of responding to events in their lives. Faced with fear-evoking events, individuals habitually respond in ways they did in the past—even if the current anxiety-producing events are different from those in the past.

CHAPTER SEVEN

We Act as If Our Beliefs Are True

"I failed again!" Nancy announced at the beginning of her therapy session. She felt incompetent, disappointed, and rejected but also angry as she recollected the previous week's disturbing events to her therapist.

"What is it you think you failed at?" the therapist asked after Nancy had settled herself in her chair.

"It's my book club," Nancy answered. "Arlene, the founder of the club, is also our leader, and she makes most of the decisions about what we should read. She has a doctoral degree in world literature or something like that, so we all go with her leadership. As a newcomer to the club, I tried to get a bit closer to her, thinking she might be a good influence on my kids."

"How is she responding to your outreach attempts?" the therapist asked, thinking that this might be a sensitive issue for Nancy.

"She doesn't seem to be overly eager to be friends with me" was Nancy's response. "That's why I offered to take her place leading the discussion of this month's book. She apologized that she could not prepare for it or even be present because she had a conference to attend."

"So you offered to help out with leading the discussion about the book . . . ," the therapist encouraged Nancy to continue with her story.

"Yes, it was not an easy book to read; it seemed to carry several hidden messages. But I wanted to do it as a favor to the leader, and I hoped it would be an opportunity to impress her," Nancy explained.

"How did it work out?" the therapist asked.

"Well, I had difficulty fully understanding some of the parts, but I thought the rest of the group would help me with the discussion, especially since

Arlene might not even be there. But she did make it to the meeting, and she let me lead the group. Of course, I was nervous with her being there. Two or three of the other members disagreed with me on some points. That made me even more nervous. At the end Arlene thanked me for taking over for her, but she also added that apparently I missed some of the messages of the book and proceeded to explain those points. I was crushed." Nancy ended her report.

The therapist thought for a minute before questioning Nancy about the importance of Arlene's approval, remembering that Nancy believed Arlene might be a good influence on Nancy's children, but was there perhaps more to it? Nancy had indicated that Arlene did not receive her with open arms when she joined the book club.

"It's a challenge," Nancy answered the therapist's question.

"What exactly is the challenge in this case?" the therapist inquired.

"Something that is difficult to reach is worth working for. It makes you stronger." Nancy's answer came quickly, almost like it had been rehearsed or used often.

"How does that work when the challenge is too difficult or impossible to reach?" the therapist wanted to know, suspecting that this insistence on the difficulty might be part of Nancy's problem.

"My father always said that doing something that you know how to do is all right, but it does not advance your knowledge. The real learning is to confront a challenge, something that you and others think is impossible to do and then work on it," Nancy related from her childhood.

"Did your father always resolve the challenges he approached?" was a natural question to ask, thought the therapist.

"No, it didn't always work out, but my father never gave up. He believed that a person's strength develops by confronting challenges. He was very serious about it and taught me to do the same thing," Nancy answered, smiling as she remembered her relationship with her father.

"So what happened when some challenging projects did not work out?" the therapist wondered.

"My mother would call someone who could do it. I remember one time when my father tried to fix a water leak in our kitchen. He tried to turn the knob on the pipe to turn off the water before investigating how to fix the leak. But the knob broke off; it was old and the water could not be turned off. It just streamed into the kitchen. My father had to call the water company to have them turn off the water pipes outside the house. My mother tried to call a plumber to work on the problem, but it was late Friday evening and nobody would come before Monday morning."

"How did you make it through the weekend without water? I remember you have two siblings, so that would be five people without water," the therapist wondered.

"We tried to stay in the house the first night, but on Saturday morning my mother said we had two choices: check into a motel or drive to her parents' house some 50 miles away. My father voted for a motel, so we could be near home early Monday morning when the plumber was supposed to come. My mother said Dad didn't want to face her father when his latest 'challenge' failed; that's why he voted for the motel," Nancy ended her story.

Confronting and Conquering Challenges

Just as the belief in Santa Claus, discussed in chapter 2, can result in distortions in a child's mind about a person's value, other cultural ideas can lead to misconceptions in the minds of adult individuals. A phenomenon that often leads to social anxiety is people's obsession with gaining acceptance or recognition from those who do not seem interested in them and who remain distant in interactions with them, just as it happened in Nancy's story above. Why are the strivers for acceptance so invested in achieving the support and goodwill of those who prefer to be with other people rather than the ones who court them so ardently? It takes a lot of effort to invest energy into an almost certain disappointment.

Besides requiring a lot of effort, the endeavor entails much stress from the very beginning. Prior to any interaction, the approval-seeking person is filled with anxiety over how to behave, what to say, and how to express wishes and thoughts. By the time of the actual meeting, the individual is worn out. In addition, during the face-to-face interaction, the tension experienced by the approval seeker is at such a high level that he or she is almost unaware of some of the signals emitted by the other person as well as of some of his or her own words and actions.

Often, after the meeting, this is followed by a recapitulating step-by-step exploration of what the individual said and did and what would have been better to do. The criticism of one's own behavior goes on and on, leading to even higher levels of anxiety. And even though it would be easier and often also better to discontinue the efforts, the individual is driven to try again, to try harder and harder without necessarily reaching the desired goal. Those actions seem to indicate that the individual puts a higher value on the person who rejects him or her than on those who accept and enjoy the individual's company.

Just as the rare coin fetches a higher price on the market than the ordinary penny, the rare approval or acceptance from one person is worth more than the smiling approval from a generous person with a greater supply of approval. Following this line of logic through to the bitter end, we would soon extinguish niceness and easy acceptance from those around us. What a sad world it would become.

What is the reason (or excuse) people use when they first decide to pursue the low likelihood of success and then to continue the pursuit in the face of a high likelihood of failure? "It's a challenge," they might say. A challenge of what and for what? might be an appropriate question. According to *Webster's Ninth Collegiate Dictionary*, the word "challenge" carries the meanings of "to 'demand as due or deserved,' 'to order to halt and prove identity,' 'to confront or deny boldly: Dare,' 'to call out to duel or combat,' 'to invite into competition,' 'to arouse or stimulate esp. by presenting with difficulties.'"[1]

However, in common usage, the word "challenge" reflects the belief that the word itself contains the meaning of something honorable or almost sacred. People talk about accepting a challenge or being challenged to live up to a high standard. The word has been instilled with a strong positive valence, reflecting respect onto anything that is being faced or handled as a challenge. This positive valence automatically bestows the stamp of approval, of being filled with noble content, on any issue under discussion. Therefore, it lends an aura of acceptance or importance to any topic that claims to present a challenge.

The individual seeking acceptance from someone not interested in an interaction with the individual will persist in the efforts as long as it can be perceived as being a challenge. Even the steadily increasing level of anxiety often will not persuade the individual to give up the "challenge"—just as some people will continue striving toward goals, no matter how unlikely the probability of success appears to be—as long as it can be believed to be a challenge.

Beliefs—Based on Faith, Evidence, or Gut Feelings?

Beliefs are strong motivators; they determine our actions as well as our nonactions. At times, beliefs might be based on experiences that are incomplete, obscure in meaning, or just misinformed; nevertheless, people steadfastly hold on to their beliefs. People's belief systems are triggered by environmental influences and their thoughts about those influences. In their responses, "people act as if their perceptions are accurate and their beliefs are true. Beliefs are major components of attitudes about situations and values that include goals, morals, and ethics."[2]

"Strongly held beliefs are often more powerful than reality, because they can impact perception to the degree where, in the believer's mind, the conviction becomes reality."[3] Beliefs are held sacred. And yet, beliefs change; not all beliefs remain constant through a person's life. Emotional states can influence the accuracy and direction of beliefs. Specific ways in which emotional states function to influence beliefs have been suggested. For instance, emotions provide immediate, attention-gripping information about an individual's experiences. This information is experienced by the individual as being relevant to current perceptual and mental content, which in turn may eventually serve as the object of newly formed beliefs or as evidence that confirms or disconfirms already-held beliefs. Furthermore, because affect is directly experienced, it is self-evident and therefore believable.

This is to say that belief-consistent and belief-inconsistent affect may function as confirmatory or disconfirmatory evidence of already-established beliefs. Although moods lacking an object and having an unconstrained informational value may lend themselves as evidence to any associated belief, emotions function as evidence for beliefs that are directly related to the object of emotions.[4] Thus, it seems that incidental affective states have a tendency to distort people's perceptions and beliefs about objects in an assimilative fashion, especially if the target situation is ambiguous.[5]

Consulting again *Webster's Collegiate Dictionary* for a definition of the word "belief," we find the following entry:

1.   a state or habit of mind in which trust or confidence is placed in some person or thing
2.   something believed; a tenet or body of tenets held by a group
3.   conviction of the truth of some statement or the reality of some being or phenomenon, esp. when based on examination of evidence

In addition, we learn that the words "faith," "credence," and "credit" are synonyms and that "belief" and "faith" are often used interchangeably.[6] People like Nancy and her father, as described above, seem to have a tendency to substitute "faith" for "belief" at times.

On the other hand, most psychological definitions of beliefs focus on two main features, the content of a belief (i.e., a mental representation of a particular object) and people's convictions (i.e., to hold a belief, one must be convinced that the object of the belief exists). In other words, beliefs are about objects that can be mentally represented, such as people, places, things, and events, whereas the content of a belief is achieved through experience. Because one can potentially mentally represent any experience, beliefs can be about any part of any experience, whether the experience is based on reading an account of something or on contemplating future events. Secondly, to hold a belief in something, one must be convinced above the level of chance that the object of the belief exists (or does not exist).[7]

Thinking that the existence of the belief's object is merely possible (i.e., not being convinced one way or the other) does not count as holding a belief, but instead as having an idea of a possibility.[8]

The term *conviction* is used here to refer to what some call *subjective probability*[9] and what others label as *units of confidence* or *certainty*.[10]

There has been some debate about whether belief conviction is dichotomous (one does believe or one does not believe) or continuous (one believes with some level of probability), and it seems reasonable that belief conviction can be measured dimensionally, and dimensional measures of belief conviction have utility.[11]

Others suggest that conviction is both a defining feature and a dimension because a certain level of conviction is needed to have a belief. In other words, although it can widely vary, without conviction about the existence of the belief object, one does not have a belief.[12]

As mentioned earlier, beliefs change, and belief conviction does not remain constant over time. It has been found that belief conviction varies continuously over time and context, and continuous measures of belief conviction are systematically related to factors ranging from emotional arousal[13] to anterior cingulate activity.[14]

People, no matter what age, cultural background, sex, or any other factor, have the potential to form and hold an infinite number of beliefs. Some may be of little importance, but others are of great importance. Some beliefs are adaptive and provide comfort; others are maladaptive and distressing to the holder of the belief. The fact that people hold so many distinct beliefs, including those that are maladaptive, bizarre, and distressing, raises the question why anyone would want to hold on to the maladaptive and distressing ones.[15]

One might want to think that people believe that which is supported by evidence, and it is clear that many beliefs have a great deal of supporting evidence. However, there are many beliefs that lack tangible supporting evidence.[16] This would suggest asking oneself, "Are my beliefs grounded in evidence and reality, or are they situations of conviction without evidence and based on faith?"

Another notion might be that people hold beliefs that make sense of their experience, and those beliefs that do so successfully are held with high levels of conviction. But just as many beliefs that people hold apparently do not make good sense out of experience. Yet another response might be that people hold beliefs that help them make sense of their emotional experiences and help regulate affect in valued directions.[17]

Some research within goal-orientation theory has shown that individuals' beliefs about their abilities determine the types of goals they set for themselves. For instance, Leah, a talented young woman, believed that her ability to paint was fixed (referred to as "entity view"). As she explained, "If I were really talented and meant to be a painter, the quality of my paintings would fall into the category of 'artist'—but I am just a 'Sunday painter.'" The belief in her "fixed" ability prevented her from engaging in further development of her talents. If, on the other hand, Leah had believed that her abilities were changeable (referred to as "incremental views"), she might have enrolled in art classes to see whether she could improve her skills and talents.

In a way, Leah's belief that her talents were limited and that therefore the level of her artwork remained the same made sense to her, and, by the same token, the constant or stationary level of her performance reinforced her "entity views." Entity views lead to self-validation goals in which the focus is on proving one's ability, whereas incremental views lead to learning goals with the intention of improving one's ability.[18]

Another example of subscribing to an entity view is seen in the story of Alex, told in chapter 2. From his school years on, Alex held on to the notion of a "certain level of intelligence" as the basis for his functioning in his professional career. Considering the level of intelligence as an entity, there seemed to be little call for further preparation or learning about the production processes in his department at work.

Another example of the strength of people's (often unfounded) beliefs is related to decision making. Generally, people tend to select a solution that elicits the most pleasant feelings in them, even if another alternative might appear more sensible or logical. Being drawn by the desire to feel good, a person may justify a given choice with the person's explanation that while a particular choice would appear reasonable, the person's strong positive feelings regarding another choice would indicate that this would actually be a better option. The person's decision is based on the correctness of his or her gut feelings.[19]

Emotional State and Risk Perception

It has been observed that individuals' emotional states have an effect on their risk perception; people perceive risks as higher when they are in a negative emotional state than when their mood state is positive.[20] Similarly, risks appear higher when under incidental states of fear than under incidental states of anger.[21] In other words, in a dangerous-appearing situation, the individual's fear makes any risks inherent in the situation seem much greater, inducing the person to retreat or avoid the situation. On the other hand, when in an emotional state of anger, the person is more inclined to retaliate than to withdraw, making the risk appear smaller than it actually might be. Thus, in a process of misattribution, people may misinterpret these incidental emotional states as integral affective responses to the target situation.[22]

When exploring the relationship, or "value function," between objective and subjective values of various possible outcomes without emphasis on the individual's mood, it was observed that the value function for losses is steeper than for gains. The findings indicated that a certain increase in possible loss carries a greater impact on a decision than an objectively equal increase in possible gain. The risk of losses far outweighs the risk of gains.[23]

The observation that people perceive the degree of risks as stronger when they are in a negative mood than when they are in a positive mood is reminiscent of the hypothesis that bad is stronger than good. In other words, negatively valenced events will have a greater impact on individuals than positively valenced events of similar types.[24]

Although good may prevail over bad, it will do so only through a superior force of numbers. A superior number of good events can overcome the psychological effects of a single bad event. In situations of equal measures of good and bad, however, the good ones are outweighed by the psychological effects of the bad ones. This finding was considered to be a general principle of psychological phenomena, perhaps reflecting the innate predispositions of the human psyche.

Other observations regarding the impact of everyday events demonstrated that bad events had longer-lasting effects than good events. Having a good day did not produce noticeable effects on people's well-being the following day, but having a bad day carried over and influenced the mood of the next day.[25]

Applying the hypothesis of bad being stronger than good to the area of people's beliefs would imply that bad or frightening beliefs will promote stronger and longer-lasting impacts on people's minds than good or encouraging beliefs. Unfortunately, those strong beliefs—whether they are accurate in their basis or not—can act as hurdles to progress as they strengthen resistance to change. This is an important consideration when working with individuals' thoughts, attempting to change some of the self-defeating thoughts into more self-enhancing or, at least, logical or rational ones. On occasion clients may give lip service to attempts to change by admitting hesitatingly, "I know those thoughts are not rational or logical," but inwardly still hanging on to their long-standing beliefs. The powerful effects of one's beliefs on one's behavior are illustrated by the following story.

It Sounds So Logical

When Sonja, a young German woman, and her German husband came to the United States, they settled in New Jersey and bought a home in a neighborhood where another German family lived. Naturally, the two families became acquainted, and Sonja asked Martha, their new German neighbor, to converse in English with her, so that she could progress faster in learning English and being able to communicate within her new environment. Martha's response, "Oh, no, my English is so good; I am afraid of losing my native language. You and I will communicate in German," took Sonja by surprise, but she did not have a choice in the matter.

To help Sonja become more familiar with her new environment, Martha introduced her to all the neighbors, and they welcomed Sonja freely. In those days in the late 1950s, the neighborhood women met for coffee several times a week. Through Martha, Sonja became a part of the group, but her facility with the English language still needed a lot of improvement. Surprisingly, Sonja seemed to have greater difficulty understanding Martha's English than that of the other women. But that did not make sense to her because she knew that Martha was introduced to English while in high school in Germany, just as Sonja was. Therefore, it should be easier for her to comprehend Martha's English statements because the pronunciation they were being taught in German high schools was English, not American.

Remembering that Martha had informed her of her competence in the English language, Sonja reasoned to herself that if she could not understand another German person's English, she would have even more trouble understanding her American neighbors' English. This belief became so strong that whenever one of her neighbors talked to her directly, Sonja could not understand her as she felt her anxiety rise. Overhearing others talk, she could comprehend some of what they said, but as soon as the conversation was directed at her, the overwhelming anxiety turned her mind into a blank, which kept her from comprehending what they said.

One day, looking out the window, Sonja saw some of her neighbors approaching her house. She panicked when she saw that Martha was not with them. The doorbell rang a few times, but Sonja did not open the door even though she was aware that the neighbors knew she was at home. The state of fear Sonja was engulfed in made her exaggerate the risk of opening the door and facing her neighbors without Martha's assistance—very much as explained above in the observations regarding the effects of one's emotional mood on one's beliefs. Following that incident, Sonja refused to participate in the neighborhood coffee visits. She felt like a prisoner in her own home.

Fortunately, she learned about some community schools in New Jersey that had opened their doors to adult learners in evening classes. Among those were classes for adult immigrants who wanted to improve their knowledge of the English language. The courses usually ran from September through the end of the year and again from January through May. Sonja signed up for the learning experience. The class membership included two young women from Japan, one woman from France, one from Brazil, two young men from Italy, one woman from Austria, and two from Germany. The students were fortunate to have a dedicated teacher, who conducted two class meetings per week. One meeting was devoted to the English language and its grammar, spelling, and sentence structure. The focus of the second class was on citizenship, community affairs, relevant laws, and similar topics.[26]

Sonja was progressing well in the class and decided to take the next-level class. While in the second-level class, she reasoned to herself that she must have learned enough to be able to converse with her neighbors. As before when Sonja developed the strong anxiety, her reasoning now again turned into a belief.

One afternoon Sonja observed some of her neighbors sitting outside her next-door neighbor's house. She mustered all her courage and marched over to the neighbor's house. Facing the women, Sonja apologized for not having opened the door when they had tried to visit with her some time ago. Then she explained to them that she had experienced difficulties understanding Martha's speech, which made her think that it was hopeless for her to think that she could understand what her American neighbors talked about.

Listening to Sonja's explanation, the women burst into laughter. Sonja's immediate thought was "I am worse off than I thought; I must not have made sense talking to them." After a brief pause, the women explained that they, too, had difficulty understanding Martha, but they did not say anything because they did not want to hurt her feelings. They tried to half understand and half guess what Martha was talking about.

For Sonja this was a valuable lesson about the impact of beliefs on one's behavior. The first belief that if she could not understand a German person's English, comprehending American people's English was impossible, although sounding logical on the surface, was not so logical in reality, and it made her develop increasing anxiety that paralyzed her whenever she thought about having to communicate with her neighbors.

Sonja's second attempt at logic made her believe that if she studied and participated actively in class, her overall knowledge of the language should improve to the level of being able to communicate reasonably successfully with her neighbors. Thus, acting on the second belief, which was based on evidence that she had progressed in improving her language skills, finally repaired the damage incurred by holding on to and acting on her first belief.

It is this second type of belief construction that Sonja applied in her future endeavors, such as if she could communicate adequately with her neighbors, she might have a good chance at obtaining a job. Being able to hold employment as a bookkeeper and secretary strengthened her belief and increased the probability that she might be accepted at a college to further her language skills and training in other areas. Completion of a college degree served as evidential basis for the belief that the probability for achieving a PhD degree was high enough to attempt it. Because she followed this reasoning process, Sonja's beliefs became reality.

But it was not easy sailing; there were many hurdles and setbacks to overcome. In her first job, she worked for an insurance agency that shared office space with the local motor vehicle bureau, where people stood in line, talking while waiting their turn to be helped. This made it difficult to understand customers over the telephone. At the time, it was important to be able to detect prospective customers' racial backgrounds from the sound of their voices and their manner of speech because regular insurance companies were strict in their criteria about accepting customers. Those that did not qualify had to be offered "assigned risk" policies.

In addition, the other female employee, a woman in her fifties, took an instant dislike to Sonja, mainly because of her German background. Behind Sonja's back, she talked about Sonja as the "Nazi"—which was ironic in a way, considering the company's discriminatory business practices. It did not help that the owner of the business, a former navy officer, had many friends and acquaintances who called frequently and that Sonja had some difficulty understanding their names over the telephone. After two months Sonja was let go from her job. It was a great disappointment, and the temptation to hide from the world was great. The combination of the language difficulties, the coworker's unfriendliness toward the "Nazi," and the shame over being fired from her job was hard to accept, and for a while Sonja doubted the soundness of her decision to leave her native country.

Again, she withdrew for a while from social contact, except for continuing to attend evening classes with different subjects, all to improve her language skills. Because she was running out of courses to take and the only one left was a class in millinery—at a time when hats were not in fashion for women—Sonja applied for another job. This was a part-time bookkeeping position with a local newspaper firm, to be followed by another part-time job, and Sonja finally took the GED examination and a little later the SAT. The college atmosphere presented another anxiety-inducing environment for this woman from a foreign country, who was older than the average college students at the time.

The Elevator Training

Through all those events, Sonja remained aware of her still-unresolved underlying shyness. She decided it was time for a change, but how could she accomplish that? She thought about various uncomfortable moments in the presence of strangers. The situation that stood out immediately in her mind was riding in an elevator with one unfamiliar person sharing the ride. Avoiding facing the stranger, people usually focus on the walls or the door of the elevator, while sharing the heavy silence with the temporary companion. This was going to be her training ground, Sonja decided. Her goal was to become involved in a conversation with whoever shared the elevator ride with her. And to make sure that there would be a conversation, Sonja had to be the one to start it.

Sonja's plan of action was to start those conversations by saying something complimentary about the stranger sharing the elevator with her. If she encountered a mother with a child, Sonja focused on the child and said something nice about the child. A woman without a child might receive a compliment on her clothing or her hair. Encountering a man she did not know made the situation slightly more difficult. If he wore an interesting tie, Sonja would focus on that object, stating that the tie reflected his good taste. More often than not, the man would respond with "My wife bought that tie for me." Sonja's answer came fast; with a smile at the man, she repeated, "Yes, you do have good taste—you chose your wife."

Those little compliments quickly broke the ice, leading to a brief, friendly chat. Sonja put one condition on herself: she was not allowed to lie; the object she decided to focus on had to elicit a positive reaction in her. At the end of the elevator ride, the participants smiled and nodded to each other, wishing the other a good day. Their smiles could still be seen as they took a few steps toward their destination. For a brief moment the interaction provided a warm, friendly bond between two strangers.

Sonja found this practice rewarding and extended it to other situations in which strangers come together for a short time, turning these meetings into friendly encounters. The encounters allowed Sonja to assume control over the interaction, but even more significant was the fact that forcing herself to find and focus on something pleasant in the stranger's appearance reduced her fear and anxiety of interacting with him or her. The search for the pleasant aspect in the stranger created a mental shift from anxious anticipation to friendly expectation.

Beliefs and Trust

Closely linked to our beliefs is the issue of trust; as mentioned earlier, belief and trust are often used interchangeably. Trust (more often than knowledge) is the foundation of our beliefs; we believe in what we trust, and we trust our beliefs. Not surprisingly, one of the most heavily studied constructs in social and economic sciences is the issue of trust.[27]

Today, one type of trust seems to be particularly relevant: the trust between strangers. For instance, purchasing products online requires people to trust in unknown others. Although it may seem irrational to trust strangers, with those purchases people do trust unknown others. Some researchers explain that trust between strangers represents a behavioral tendency that once developed remains stable across the lifetime as people's beliefs in this type of trust grows.[28]

The ability to rely trustingly on others can be regarded as strength, a kind of self-reliance, different from the cultural stereotype of needing no one. It is the strength of knowing when and on whom to rely and "to permit oneself to be relied upon."[29]

But trust has also been described as "the willingness of a party to be vulnerable to the actions of another party based on the expectation that the other will perform a particular action important to the trustor, irrespective of the ability to monitor or control that other party."[30] This definition implies *uncertainty* and *risk*, given the truster's absence of control, and it is based on an *expectation* (not knowledge) that the partner in this interaction, the trustee, will act in the truster's interest. This scenario requires accepting a personal *vulnerability* in terms of potential betrayal. In deciding to trust, the trusters have to rely on their expectations about the trustee's trustworthiness.

From a rational perspective, trusters should only trust when it is sufficiently likely that the trusted person will react in a benevolent fashion;

otherwise, trusting would be self-destructive on the trusters' part.[31] Even with the most optimistic expectations about the trustees' trustworthiness, trusters can never be certain that their trust will be honored by the trustees. Therefore, trusting is necessarily closely linked to vulnerability, a fact that is not wasted on the socially anxious person.

For many socially anxious people, self-disclosure constitutes a risky trust issue. Sharing personally sensitive information with trusted others seems to bind them in a special relationship as the truster is rendered vulnerable to the trustee, the confidant.[32] In general, people are careful in protecting sensitive information that might be used against them, either by purposefully deceiving others or by omitting the information.

Considering the explanations above, trust behavior indicates a risky choice of depending on another person versus maintaining control over a personal resource, thus relating trust behavior to risk-taking versus risk-avoiding actions.[33] People with a risk aversion have a tendency to regard a prospect indicating positive probabilistic outcomes as being lower in value or as being equal to the expected value in a situation of risk neutrality, while risk-seeking people would evaluate the prospect as higher.[34] In other words, risk aversion describes an individual's preference for choosing a sure (positive) outcome over a potentially higher but risky outcome.

Translating this to the decision to trust, a risk-averse individual would require a larger subjective probability that the other is trustworthy (and therefore likely to honor trust) before actually trusting. On the other hand, a risk-seeking individual would be willing to trust even with the expectation of a smaller probability that the other is trustworthy (and thus unlikely to honor trust). Therefore, dispositional risk aversion can be seen as a determinant of trust behavior.

Effects of Prior Trust Experiences

Considering the notion that trust refers to a basic social behavior, one could expect that in general, people can look back on a substantial number of experiences related to trust behavior. Such prior trust experiences should influence people's current trust behavior in similar circumstances by influencing their expectations about others' trustworthiness.[35] For example, people who had been betrayed in an online purchase generalized their reduced trust to all sellers, while buyers whose trust had been rewarded in online transactions maintained their general trust in the sellers.[36] Thus, trusting can be seen as a "learned behavior" because it is based on past experiences with the trustworthiness of others.[37]

Applying these explanations to the lives of socially anxious people, one could expect that most of these individuals would fall into the risk-aversive category. Furthermore, considering trust involving situations in terms of "bad being stronger than good" as discussed earlier, one bad experience in having trusted another person would far outweigh future positive trust experiences, rendering the socially anxious person devoid of current or future trust after just one or two prior negative trust situations.

The case of Trina, introduced in chapter 3, is a fitting example. Trina's disappointment at a very young age after having confided in her mother regarding her wishes was a tremendous blow to her trust. Mothers and their concern for their children are generally held in high esteem. "If you can't even trust your mother to remember your wishes, who is there to trust? Nobody!" she assured herself. Those few childhood experiences of disappointed trust formed her staunch belief that to avoid future vulnerability and disappointments she could never trust in anybody again. And that is exactly how she lived; if trust makes me vulnerable to the risk of disappointment, no more trust in anybody.

Actually, "disappointment" is an understatement, because Trina believed that if people (including her mother) knew what she wanted, they would on purpose deprive her of her desire's fulfillment. Those paranoid tendencies resulted in her emotional isolation—she was not emotionally close to anyone. This scenario is reminiscent of Betty's refusal to let anybody into her life. In her case, the reason for her voluntary isolation was that she could not trust herself. Emotional distance kept her in control of herself, she believed.

The Special-Person Misconception

Perhaps one of the oldest and hardest-to-kill beliefs is that of having to be a special person in one's sphere of life, to be accepted, admired, and even envied by others in one's reference group. This is what Victor Raimy called the "special person misconception"—a cluster of misconceptions with a psychological core of exaggerated self-importance. Those who suffer from this misconception are doomed to compulsively draw from others confirmation of their specialness. If that specialness is "threatened, vigorous efforts are made to defend it; if it is shattered, serious psychological problems occur. Reducing anyone's self-esteem is usually a hazard to his mental health; reducing the exaggerated self-esteem of the special person is often disastrous."[38]

In general, several beliefs make up the cluster of misconceptions, and individual beliefs may vary from person to person, but they usually include striving for perfection (as discussed in chapter 3), along with statements similar to these: "I must do everything in special ways to stand out," "If people don't recognize my specialness, I have failed and must try harder," "I am working harder and suffering more frustrations than others, but it is important to be special," "I can't relax or trust others because they might try to outperform me," and others. However, it is almost impossible to detect those underlying beliefs in initial interactions or even within therapeutic contact, because individuals holding those beliefs do not freely verbalize them to others. After all, there are some cultural guidelines about modesty. Sometimes individuals might realize that other people harbor similar demands about themselves, and that may indicate a need for silence to keep the competition from knowing their own secret ambitions.

In the cluster of one's misconceptions, the attitude about specialness may be found right next to inferiority feelings, particularly in special individuals who are unsuccessful, and may reflect a picture of depression and anxiety. The lack of trust in others adds to the special individual's anxiety and frustration; unless openly admired and indulged, the individual cannot relax. Lack of admiration breeds the suspicion that the individual's specialness is not recognized by the other, either because the other harbors ill feeling toward the person or because more energy expenditure by the special person is needed to establish his or her position.

Unfortunately, some special persons can be quite critical of others, displaying little empathy, which often combines with poor social skills brought about by their need to distance themselves from the critical reactions of others to maintain their own high self-esteem. It has been hypothesized that indiscriminate and noncontingent positive reinforcements, which ignore the appropriateness of the reinforcement, in early childhood, may produce the faulty beliefs or misconception. But this type of affliction can also be found in individuals who as children were strongly encouraged by a parent to excel (see Annabel's story in chapter 9).[39]

The literature of psychotherapy and psychopathology has noted the problem of exaggerated self-importance of the "special person" for a long time, as Alfred Adler (neurotic striving for personal superiority), Sigmund Freud (narcissism), Karen Horney (idealized self-image), Ludwig Binswanger (will to power, to dominate), and others have written and talked about the concept and its link to depression, social anxiety, and obsessive-compulsive trends. However, the underlying cluster of misconception does not yield easily to psychotherapy, and the psychotherapist faced with the secondary symptoms of anxiety and depression, which result when the special person is unsuccessful in his or her strivings, will need to attend to those complaints "before the more difficult task of treating the special-person cluster becomes feasible."[40]

Denise, a busy professional woman, is familiar with some of the symptoms that trouble people with special-person syndrome. On her way to a professional meeting she had to organize in a different town, she stops to pick up a colleague, who is also attending the meeting. In the backseat of the car is Nicole, Denise's attractive 18-year-old daughter. Denise introduces Nicole, explaining that Nicole had wanted to accompany her mother to this interesting town and that they thought it might be a good learning opportunity for Nicole to observe her mother in action in her profession. It is quite obvious that Denise is very proud of Nicole. While driving to their destination, Denise talks about Nicole's intelligence and many talents. Apparently, she has inherited her father's musical and her mother's artistic talents, practicing them both to a greater accomplishment than her parents did.

As Denise's colleague turns her head to look at Nicole while expressing some appropriate encouragements, she notices Nicole looking tense as she bites her fingernails. The colleague turns back to face Denise, who continues to praise her daughter's accomplishments but then adds, "The poor kid can't even enjoy her talents because she always wants to do better until she does it perfectly. Socially, she is very sensitive and has a lot of anxiety when she meets people, especially new people, because she wants to make the best impression on them."

Nicole agrees, "I want them to like me and take me seriously, which means I have to be special." As Denise introduces her daughter to the other attendees of the meeting, Nicole is polite but hardly ever smiles and never asks any questions of the other participants. Denise's colleague observes Nicole and tries to give her special attention to make her feel more comfortable. Nicole's facial expression is tense like earlier in the car; she smiles very little and appears preoccupied. When she thinks nobody is watching her, Nicole bites her fingernails again in an attempt to calm herself down. "Poor Nicole, she is so pretty and talented; how sad that she is too anxious to enjoy all the gifts and resources she has," thinks Denise's colleague when they part at the end of the evening.

Thus, it seems that the special-person misconception is passed down from generation to generation.

Beliefs—Inherited and Passed On

Across most cultures, many beliefs are passed on from generation to generation without being questioned. As the Christmas myth comes alive every year, certain beliefs seem to dominate our thinking (see discussion in chapter 2). Other mythical beliefs, such as the images of masculinity and femininity confronting us almost daily, are not restricted to particular seasons but can influence our lives at any time.

In general, the concept of masculinity is infused with images and demands of power. The focus of the male gender identity is on the ideology of masculinity with the essential characteristics of fearlessness, toughness, and denial of vulnerability. Female gender identity, on the other hand, seems to revolve around the notions of submissiveness, emotionality, indecisiveness, and seductiveness. Taken together, the descriptions of both gender identities might tend to reflect the male-female "reason-emotion dichotomy"—nurturing behavior and expression of intimacy are associated with female behaviors and could be called *extravagant expressiveness*, whereas *manly emotion* can best be described as a "subtle expression of intense emotion under control."[41]

What happens to males and females whose actual behaviors do not conform to the stereotypical images people believe in? Many men in heterosexual relationships believe that it is their responsibility to provide well for their families and that they should be the primary provider. However, economic constraints may present a situation in which the "good provider" role may conflict with the men's more meaningful career aspirations. Should they let their wives carry some of the financial responsibilities in order to follow the path of their desire? How would their male and female friends respect them if they let some of the financial responsibility slip off their shoulders in order to follow their dreams?

The struggle between what one wants to do and what one believes one ought to do is something some men carry silently within themselves, not allowing themselves the freedom to express sadness or disappointment.[42]

Jeremy, the younger of two brothers, was named after his mother's father and grew up in the shadow of his older brother, Marvin. Everybody loved Marvin, a lively, outgoing boy, who loved to explore how things worked. Jeremy admired his brother, just as everyone else seemed to do, and Marvin was always protective of his "little brother." Jeremy was a quiet, gentle, and somewhat shy boy, although he did not shy away from conflicts but tried to handle them in what he thought was a just manner. In fact, Jeremy seemed to be fanatic about justice, and everyone expected him to become a lawyer.

Early in his young life, Marvin decided to become a chemical engineer to follow after his father, who had started a small chemical company. While still in college, Marvin married Martina, his high school sweetheart, and soon they became the proud parents of Elliot, their little son.

In his second year of college, Jeremy was still undecided about his future. Officially, he had stated that he was considering applying to law school; inwardly, he was not so sure about it. For one thing, he did not consider himself to be a convincing speaker, able to discuss in public his opinions and ideas. Jeremy never disclosed to his family or friends how petrified he was in his speech class. Fortunately, nobody paid much attention to his low grade in that class.

Taking a general psychology class as one of his elective credits, Jeremy met and fell in love with Cheryl, whose future goal was to become a human-resources representative for a hospital or a big company. They dated for a while and things looked good, except for the uncertainty Jeremy still felt about his professional future. Jeremy had never been close to his friends; his shyness kept him from letting them know his real hopes, wishes, and fears. The only one he disclosed some of his doubts to was Marvin; Jeremy could trust him to keep Jeremy's concerns a secret until he was willing to unveil them.

For some time, Jeremy had felt the urge to be in a profession in which he could help people, have direct contact with them, and be part of a healing aspect in his involvement with people. The nursing profession was the place to apply his energy and compassion. He discussed his plans with Marvin, who after initial surprise encouraged him to follow his calling. That was the brothers' last conversation. Marvin soon left for a business trip to the West Coast, from which he never returned. Marvin was killed in a fatal crash in the rental car he had been driving at the time.

Following his disclosure to his brother, Jeremy told Cheryl about his plans to apply for admission to nursing schools. Cheryl laughed; she thought Jeremy was joking. After Jeremy convinced her that he was serious, she replied, "You won't make enough money to support a family the way you should as a man." That was the end of their relationship.

As could be expected, Jeremy's father had a difficult time accepting the loss of his oldest son, the one who was expected to carry on the business the father had started. He turned to Jeremy, impressing upon him what he thought Jeremy's responsibilities were now. Jeremy's answer that he planned to enroll in nursing school came as a shock to his father. He refused to accept his son's decision and told him to think it over and give him his answer in a week. The next morning, Jeremy received a phone call from his mother. He could hear her crying. When he asked his mother what was troubling her, she told him that his father had asked her the night before what she had done to Jeremy as a child that had turned him into a wimp.

What was Jeremy to do? He lost his girlfriend; his father strongly disapproved of him; his mother put a guilt trip on him; and—above all—he had just lost his brother and best friend. Remembering Marvin's encouragement regarding Jeremy's career choice, Jeremy decided to remain firm in his decision. He believed in it as a path for his future; he had to do something he believed in. Jeremy's father was furious when he heard that Jeremy had not changed his mind, and in a way he seemed to disinherit him when he told Jeremy that he would not be able to stay in his room when he returned home for semester breaks. Both Jeremy's and Marvin's rooms with their bathroom would be occupied by Marvin's widow and her infant son. Apparently, Jeremy's father wanted to make sure that Marvin's son would be the next heir to the family business as well as to the father's affection.

Jeremy was crushed; it appeared that with his brother's death he had also lost his parents and his home. Some of his former friends called him "Florence" (after Florence Nightingale), and another started the rumor that Jeremy might be gay to explain Cheryl's withdrawal from the relationship. Jeremy had never been very active socially because he had often felt out of place; now he had become even more isolated, and he was fearful about the reception he might receive in nursing school. Would he be the only male student in the class? How would the female students treat him; would they regard him as an outcast from the male world?

Another question to consider was the possibility that his anxiety in interactions with others might impair his effectiveness when working as a nurse, just as he had feared when he decided some time ago not to follow his interest in law.

It seems that with Marvin's death Jeremy lost his only support, and the beliefs in cultural stereotypes held by his parents, friends, and girlfriend significantly increased Jeremy's social anxiety, which had its beginning in his boyhood shyness.

The Impact of "Dangerous Belief Domains"

It is of interest that some researchers have identified "dangerous belief domains"—beliefs that have a tendency to lead to conflict between people in groups. The five domains include beliefs about superiority, vulnerability, injustice, distrust, and helplessness.[43] At least four of the five belief domains—superiority (the striving for it), vulnerability, distrust (expectations of being rejected by others), and helplessness—are at the base of inter- and intrapersonal conflicts that socially anxious people experience frequently. In addition, if we consider socially anxious individuals' notion that they should not have to be victimized by fears and anxiety—despite their fear-producing thoughts—the injustice- or unfairness-related domain is relevant to their suffering, too.

Researchers have suggested that perceptions of unfairness and subsequent responses to the unfairness are influenced by a sense of helplessness.[44] In turn, the felt helplessness may lead to deficits in cognitive, emotional, and motivational functioning.[45] Constructive responses to the perceived unfairness may be inhibited or made difficult by those deficits, whereas less helpless individuals are able to mobilize more constructive responses. Thus, perceiving unfairness may bring about cognitive, emotional, and motivational changes that result in psychological stress responses.

Cognitive consequences of perceiving unfairness may occur because the situations of perceived unfairness take on the sense of threatening rather than challenging, which is in general more stressful[46] and may lead to decreased problem-solving abilities and narrowing of attention.[47]

Perceived unfairness may also affect the more general motivational categories of approach and avoidance.[48] Under some circumstances, perceiving unfairness may motivate individuals to approach sympathetic others, attempting to make emotional connections,[49] whereas in other instances perceiving unfairness may cause people to distance themselves from others because of distrust and fear.[50]

An example of distancing oneself because of perceived unfairness can be seen in the story of Norman in chapter 3, who isolated himself from people because of the history of his family, which he believed was the cause for people's (assumed) judgment of him. Similarly, Lionel, to be encountered in chapter 8, had moments of perceived unfairness when his life did not furnish him with the financial resources that his family of origin possessed. And when Clarence, introduced in chapter 5, believed that women's lives contained fewer responsibilities than men's lives, he attempted to resolve or cope with the perceived unfairness by turning to cross-dressing to reduce the stress by imagining himself to be a woman. The attempt— as might be expected—increased his stress and anxiety. Just as he had felt uncomfortable and anxious in the company of men, the women in his life were not supportive of his preferences; they might have had their own perceived unfairness to cope with as the situation developed.

CHAPTER EIGHT

Process of Change: Recognizing the Illogical Logic of Social Anxiety

There is nothing more certain than change. Whatever aspect of life we look at, not much remains the same. Change involves processes rather than isolated momentary actions. Changing vocabulary, changing meaning—changing beliefs? The process of change contains many elements. Pitfalls occur when hurrying through the process, leaving some aspects unresolved or incompletely resolved. If after exploration of the originally feared situations with changed thoughts and changed vocabulary, a proposed change in action is not forthcoming, chances are that the person's belief system has not changed sufficiently.

Whether our thoughts are rational or irrational has been the main focus of cognitive-behavioral therapists. Although it would be difficult to find fault with the logic of this approach, at times it might not reach the deepest meaningful level of clients' thought processes. Clinicians representing a compassion-focused approach may instead inquire whether individuals' thoughts are useful to them or supportive of their efforts. The reasoning for emphasizing this aspect of thinking is that people have a right to be irrational, and in many instances human beings, although aware of it, are irrational in their thoughts and actions. Asking ourselves whether our thinking is helping or sabotaging our efforts to reduce our social anxiety in certain situations would appear less criticizing than to have to admit to being irrational. This gentler approach is considered by some to have a soothing and balancing effect on people's minds that can in turn direct them toward encouragement and emotional support.[1]

One conception of rationality that is basic to standard economic theory focuses on the consistency between a person's decisions and actions and between the person's behavioral compassion-focused approaches. As stated by economist Amartya Sen, "Rationality . . . demands cogent relations between aims and objectives actually entertained by the person and the choices that the person makes."[2]

Cognitive processes like thoughts, judgments, and decisions as well as behavioral processes are all influenced by emotions. Two types of emotional phenomena affecting mental and physical processes have been distinguished, the *incidental* emotional state and the state in which the source is unrelated to the object of the decision. These emotional states include current emotions that are not caused by the target object, preexisting mood states, and such lasting emotional dispositions as chronic anxiety. Integral emotional responses are those feelings experienced in connection with the object of judgments or decisions. In particular, integral affective responses are emotions that are elicited by features of the target object, whether they are real, perceived, or just imagined.[3]

It has been observed that when integral emotional responses are used as proxies for value, the responses are not scaled accurately for either magnitude or probability. For instance, judgments and decisions based on integral emotional responses appear to be sensitive to the presence or absence of affect-producing stimuli but relatively insensitive to variations in the stimuli's magnitude.[4] Likewise, evaluations and decisions based on integral emotional responses tend to reflect an insensitivity to probability, except for the presence or absence of uncertainty.[5] In summary, "affective decisions under uncertainty rely on discrete images of the options that do not incorporate probabilities."[6]

As emotional states influence people's reasoning processes, their logical rationality is also affected. Most intense emotional states tend to impair working memory capacity and consequently reduce sound reasoning ability. It has been found that people with anxiety tend to have lower ability to recall information and organize it in memory. It also takes longer to verify the validity of logical inferences while a high anxiety level persuades these individuals to select an option without considering every alternative. "Intense emotional states, such as anxiety, therefore appear to produce deficits in people's reasoning abilities."[7] Therapists working with socially anxious individuals need to make sure that their clients understand and accept the various influences of their emotional states on their rationality. Without that understanding and acceptance, their efforts in therapy will not reach beyond the surface layer.

Yet another way of checking our thinking and functioning can be found in the suggestion that human beings rely on two main modes of operation—the being mode and the doing mode. The being mode includes resources for learning, healing, and well-being. Those resources are not available to us while functioning in the doing mode, which is goal oriented and concerned with performing and striving.[8] The being mode is the sphere of mindful awareness without judging, which creates a distance from worrying and competing.[9]

Anxiety in Response to Change and Uncertainty

Changes in life are unavoidable and are usually accompanied by conditions of uncertainty. Due to their negative expectations about changes, many people experience discomfort in the face of uncertainty. On a purely logical level, however, people's hesitancy about change and uncertainty does not seem to make sense because uncertainty does not necessarily guarantee a dark or threatening outcome of the changing situation. There may be promising opportunities as well as less desirable options to choose from.[10]

At this point we need to remind ourselves that being fearful of change is very closely related to being afraid of interacting with people new or unknown, as the unknown (people or situations) is generally considered to be a change from the known. The possibility of change introduces an element of instability and uncertainty, something the socially anxious person tries to avoid. It is difficult enough for the anxious individual to participate in certain uncomfortable but known situations. On those occasions in which the outcome cannot be predicted because of unknown variables involved, the anxiety may not find a lid to contain it. The anxiety was high enough in situations experienced before, but it rises much higher when unknown variables are likely to enter a given situation.

Another illogical jump in logic on a surface level can be seen when individuals witness someone else in distress or in dangerous circumstances. "It could have been me" might be a seemingly logical thought, especially if the unfortunate person in distress is engaged in an activity normal or usual for many of us. Martin, the young man introduced in chapter 3, who could not eat in the presence of others, is an example of this jump in logic. Yes, many of us could find ourselves in such situations. However, not everyone would draw the conclusion that it would be terrible to go through such an experience without any chance to recover our dignity.

Some individuals in the "it could have been me" situation might resolve to be extra careful in situations similar to the observed one, whereas others might regard the scenario in a raised emotional upheaval as a life-or-death situation. Those with raised emotional levels tend to pathologize normal behavior instead of normalizing pathological behavior. In their thought processes, the brain's frontal lobes are temporarily out of order, leaving the old midbrain to determine what actions to take.

The Smoke Screen of "Why?"

A frequently encountered question from anxious individuals is "Why can't I do this or that like everybody else can?" A question like that constitutes something of an incision point. A question like that should not pass unchallenged because doing so would affirm its content in the anxious individual's mind and thereby unwittingly strengthen the underlying belief that the person is unable to do what would be necessary to resolve the difficulty. Asking why is just like putting up a smoke screen to hide the true concern. The underlying issue here is that the individual is holding on to the belief that he or she is unable to perform the task in question. Getting stuck on the "why" path turns into a detour that never returns to the originally considered goal. The question of "Why can't I?" needs to be changed to "How can I do this?" before serious work can begin. The "why" approach characterizes a stationary position; the person asking why is not moving toward anything. However, the "how" approach tends to invite movement toward a solution.

Cognitive Openness

Cognitive openness refers to the willingness to pay attention to new information, even when it seems to contradict our previous knowledge. Its importance is connected not only to learning but also to adapting to new situations and to psychological well-being in general. Some research has focused on a particular part of cognitive openness, that of openness about oneself. It was found that after experiencing an initial rejection from a potential pen pal, children who tended to hold self-validation goals were less likely to share information about themselves than children who focused on learning goals.[11]

Furthermore, people with self-validation-related goals were less likely to express (and thus try to resolve) their concerns in romantic conflicts and in daily social conflicts.[12] And individuals persisting in following their self-validation-related goals with their actions exhibited a lack of psychological openness about themselves, which creates a distance between them and those around them because the disclosure resistance elicits a discomfort in those they interact with. Thus, the lack of psychological openness becomes a psychological vulnerability in interaction with others.

Goals and Beliefs as Links to Anxiety

An investigation about how goals and beliefs are linked to depression may also apply to the development of avoidance behaviors, encountered in anxiety states and phobias.[13] Citing evidence that beliefs (cognitive vulnerabilities) and goals (to prove self-worth) contribute to depression, the authors proposed that cognitive vulnerabilities (attributing negative events to stable and global causes while making negative inferences) are closely linked to goals of self-worth, whereas the opposite beliefs are closely connected to learning goals. When confronted with stressors, people concerned with self-worth goals become anxious with their main focus of searching for ways to refuse acknowledgment of possible proof of worthlessness. And while they are engulfed in anxiety, they tend to adopt defensive strategies that turn out to be handicapping moves rather than calming and enhancing actions.

Maladaptive emotion regulation strategies have been observed in people with goals of defending their self-worth. For instance, as part of a study, a subgroup of adults concerned with self-validation goals (seeking to prove their ability) responded to failure with strong negative emotion and ruminations. Another subgroup of adults who wanted to perform better than others responded with denial.[14] Similarly, it was observed that a subgroup of individuals with insecure attachment engaged in more overt expressions of negative emotions.[15]

Interesting observations were made on subgroups of self-validating defensive individuals, who generally perform well and appear to be fine except when they are under high levels of stress. Apparently, the appearance of well-being is due to a suppression of negative emotion, a coping style that has been shown to backfire under stress.[16] Evidence of these individuals' "hidden vulnerabilities"[17] prompted researchers to conclude that "although avoidant people often display adequate levels of psychological adjustment and well-being in daily life, they exhibit relatively poor coping and high levels of distress in severely and persistently stressful situations."[18] Similar observations—the appearance of performing well except when stressors continue—were reported for a subgroup of participants with self-validation goals.[19]

Additional research showed that those people who cope with stress through suppression are likely to use shallow processing during problem solving. It has also been suggested that shallow processing may be the result of defensively blocking out any information that might indicate failure or other threats to self-esteem.[20] This seems to agree with the implication that individuals with self-validation goals lack cognitive openness under stress, as discussed in the previous section.

Closely linked to self-validation goals is the notion of contingencies of self-worth.[21] Contingencies constitute the domains in which people base their self-esteem.[22] Whether or not individuals engage in defensive behavior in a domain, such as physical attractiveness or intellectual achievement or other areas of achievement, depends on whether their worth is contingent on that domain.

Deciding Which Self-Worth Goals to Pursue

Denise was torn between her artistic ambitions and her physical fitness aspirations. Both interests involved expenditure of time and financial costs for training and monitoring, and both also represented self-worth goals because Sarah wanted to be special among her friends, either as an artist or a physical fitness expert. Fearing that her artistic endeavors would require more time while presenting in her opinion a lower guarantee of success, she opted for the physical fitness category of her aspirations, reasoning to herself and others that the physical exercises would be beneficial for the back problems she had been experiencing lately, and it would also offer the possibility of becoming a certified personal trainer. She signed up and paid for a particular course of physical training with a personal trainer in her area and embarked on several organized walks for worthy causes—to give her training the extra workout of distance walking.

The first walk was a success; Sarah crossed the finish line with the majority of the walkers. It felt great, as she posted on Facebook, "My first walk and I finished not at the end but with many who had more training and experience than I!" The congratulations from her friends and praise from her personal trainer felt great. They seemed to confirm that Sarah had made the right decision for reaching her (self-worth) goals.

Unfortunately, her success was short-lived. A few weeks after the walk, Sarah's back problems increased, and her pain kept her from progressing as well in her training as she had hoped. For an additional fee, her personal trainer offered to modify the exercises so that the stress on her back would be reduced. Sarah could not afford the additional cost; in fact, she had been shocked when she first found out how much money personal trainers were able to charge for their services. At the time she saw herself in that enviable position at the end of her training process. Instead now she was stuck with nowhere to go. Would her experiences have been more rewarding if Sarah had chosen to focus on her artistic endeavors instead of on the physical fitness training? It is difficult to say. However, because her goals in that area were also tied to self-worth, she might not have fared much better.

Cognitive Vulnerabilities Slowing Down the Process

Cognitive theories of depression suggest that people's vulnerability stems from a tendency to interpret stressful life events as having negative implications for their future and for their self-worth.[23] Additionally, the hopelessness theory of depression focuses on several cognitive vulnerabilities, such as attributions of negative events to stable and global causes and the tendency to infer negative consequences and negative self-characteristics from those events.[24] Both of these theoretical explanations are equally applicable to anxiety states.

Similar cognitive vulnerabilities, called *dysfunctional attitudes*, were identified by others.[25] These attitudes included themes of worthlessness, inadequacy, failure, and loss. "If I make a mistake, that means I am incompetent" would be an example of a dysfunctional attitude. Characteristics such as low self-esteem, self-blame, low effort, lack of persistence, poor performance, and appraising adversity as a threat rather than a challenge are all parts of helplessness.[26] Having failed at a task, people with fixed and global beliefs usually display several of those helplessness characteristics.[27]

Acknowledging that cognitive vulnerabilities (beliefs) are related to self-worth goals, some authors used the term *vulnerable self-beliefs* to indicate that certain beliefs are cognitive vulnerabilities focused on the self.[28] Cognitive vulnerabilities relate to beliefs about the world as well as the self, whereas vulnerable self-beliefs pertain to positive as well as negative events. Other research has shown that vulnerable self-beliefs are linked with goals to self-improve self-worth.[29]

Evaluating and proving one's talents in intellectual, social, athletic, or work-related abilities involves skills that are part of performance goals. As discussed in chapter 1, people who subscribe to performance goals strive to seek positive evaluations or avoid negative judgments of their competence. They want to avoid appearing incompetent in whatever skills they possess, and therefore, they avoid situations that would require the exhibition of those skills unless success is guaranteed.

Another kind of cognitive vulnerability can be seen in certain attachment styles. Based on Bowlby's theory, research studies within the "Strange Situation" paradigm focused on the behaviors of infants who were separated temporarily from their mothers. At the time three infant attachment styles were defined—secure, anxious-ambivalent, and avoidant.[30] Both the anxious-ambivalent and the avoidant styles are relevant to the lives of socially anxious people. For instance, as described in chapter 7, individuals who seek self-acceptance through recognition from others exhibit a preoccupied attachment style as they continuously (anxiously-ambivalently) attempt to get closer in their relationships with others, perhaps consider-ing it to be a "challenge." Nancy's story in chapter 7 serves as an example reflecting this attachment style. On the other hand, the fearful attachment style, mentioned in chapter 1, can be observed in people who have con-structed negative internal models of self and others.[31] They don't feel the urgency to bond intimately with others. In addition to avoiding intimacy, individuals with a fearful attachment style also tend to avoid conflict. "Because they have a negative view of others as well as of themselves, they might expect malevolence or punishment from their partners, and they fear rejection."[32]

In addition to the originally defined three attachment styles, a fourth childhood attachment style, a style that lacks consistent behavior patterns, has been observed.[33] This disorganized attachment style reflects chaotic and conflicted behaviors, such as simultaneous approach and avoidance behaviors—approaching the caregiver and freezing in midstride.[34]

Anxiety-Specific Beliefs and Goals

Listening to people who are socially anxious reveals a wide repertoire of situations the individuals feel uncomfortable or embarrassed in. In the past, various models of embarrassment were identified, such as the loss-of-self-esteem model,[35] the social-evaluation model,[36] the personal-standards model,[37] the dramaturgic model,[38] the transgression-of-others'-expectations model,[39] and the center-of-attention model, as mentioned in the relevant literature.[40]

When speaking of embarrassment, one is usually thinking of a fear of speaking in public, but so far we have also encountered individuals who are afraid to eat while being observed by others, as in the case of Martin in chapter 3, or—as in the story of Andrew, in chapters 2 and 4—just having to move about while being seen. Still others are afraid of being judged by others for the decisions they have made in the past or even for what their parents did or did not do. And even if the anxiety-producing situation involves verbal interactions, there are differences within this group of suf-ferers. While some individuals are afraid that their "mind will go blank," others are able to talk without difficulty in certain situations while stead-fastly avoiding to participate in other situations.

For instance, in chapter 3, the story of Jonathan, a young comedian, was briefly mentioned. Although Jonathan was plagued by anxiety when inter-acting with customers in his father's furniture store and with people in general, he was relatively free from anxiety when on the stage performing on a part-time basis as a comedian in a local nightclub. Actually, his act on the stage was a façade he could hide behind, very similar to the approach of Ralph, the magician and his colleague on the stage.

Middle-aged Donald, a married father of two small children, breaks down interactions with others into two broad categories within his life: one category includes situations in which he can verbally interact with others without experiencing significant anxiety, and the other category includes situations that he tends to avoid; if avoidance is not an option, he experiences paralyzing anxiety. Much like Jonathan and Ralph above, Donald spends part of his free time onstage as a musician. His day job is that of a schoolteacher. No anxiety problems plague him in his job or when approached by people in the audience.

What accounts for the difference? Or what might be similarities in the situations? Careful exploration of Donald's thoughts and beliefs as they relate to the different situations provides clues that help interpret Donald's reactions. In the job environment where Donald was hired years ago and is paid for his work, his presence there has been approved; he is accepted. His presence on the stage as part of the band has also been approved of, and any audience member who might address him came there to see or hear Donald. Again, his presence has already been given the stamp of approval. This fact is reflected in Donald's thoughts: "They came here to see and hear me. I don't have to prove myself to them." Similarly, in social situations in which other individuals approach Donald, his anxiety is contained even if he does not know the person well. Again, the approaching person carries and reflects approval of Donald.

As people in the performing arts can often be quite comfortable onstage, like Jonathan, Ralph, and others, but suffer from social anxiety in private situations, people in other professions can as well. Doctors can, too, as explained by one doctor: "Doctors are not immune to anxiety, but in stressful situations we can adopt our roles as doctors, which gives us a sort of script to follow."[41] Similarly, Donald's presence at school and his performance as a musician were protectively "covered" by his role in the particular situation.

What might be Donald's thoughts in situations in which he is expected to attend to or approach people he is unfamiliar with? Here are some samples: "I don't know anything of substance to say" or "I need to be able to say something solid and meaningful, or they will think I am stupid." Those thoughts reflect Donald's self-valuation goals. Because self-valuation goals usually lead to avoidance, Donald's responses to those thoughts are of an avoidant nature. Following the avoidance events and often prior to similar upcoming situations, Donald repeatedly ruminates and criticizes himself. "Loosen up and mingle," he tells himself. But then his thoughts turn to "I should be able to discuss important issues and I should be able to feel comfortable interacting with these people, just like everybody else does." It is noteworthy here that Donald does not settle for reduced discomfort, which could be further reduced at future opportunities. Donald's beliefs can be summarized as "with people who approach me, I don't have to prove myself; they have already approved of me." His goal seems to be a total lack of discomfort, possibly indicating an entity type of thinking approach rather than an incremental style approach. If Donald were to decide to work with a therapist on resolving his social anxiety, those aspects of his cognitive system would be significant indicators for the treatment process.

Donald also feels discomfort when exposed to people he is expected to be involved with in "small talk," which in his opinion constitutes a waste of time. Here his discomfort seems to be a mixture of anger and anxiety. Why should he be bothered with this demand on his time as well as have to familiarize himself with some of the rituals embedded in small talk?

Illogical Self-Protective Self-Handicapping

In order to discount responsibility for failure and defend self-worth, people sometimes focus on obstacles inherent in certain tasks. This has the added advantage of augmenting the credit for success (if success is the outcome) because of the obstacles they had to overcome. Self-protective (defensive) forms of self-handicapping, such as withdrawal of effort, wallowing in negative emotion, and rumination, are particularly favored by people who have self-worth goals and who experience threats to their self-worth.[42]

A quintessential form of self-protective (defensive) self-handicapping can be observed in the excuse-generating system of rumination. When ruminating, individuals come up with a multitude of reasons why they fail and how their failures lead to negative consequences. The causes listed by ruminators, such as lack of energy, inability to concentrate, feeling ill, or being unlucky, are not intended to overcome failure. They serve as evidence to justify avoiding taking action or responsibility.[43]

Self-handicapping behaviors like ruminations, failures, self-blame, and self-derogation are costly in terms of self-worth, while ironically they are attempts to avert new assaults to self-worth. As an example, ruminatory self-blame may feel less noxious than others' blame because it is diluted by the tendency to think of many blameworthy forces that reduce chances for success, and ruminatory self-blame is controlled by the self.

Replacing self-worth goals with approach or learning goals and vulnerable self-beliefs with malleable beliefs would constitute a beneficial change in the individual's cognitive system.[44] The existence of learning goals is thought to move people to appraise stressors as challenges and opportunities for growth rather than as threats to self-worth.[45] Beliefs underlying learning goals focus on the self as being malleable[46] and on the notion that self-worth is not dependent on one's abilities.[47]

The logic behind individuals' attempts to hide any shortcomings or personal failures in order to maintain their sense of self-worth may appear reasonable, except that all the hiding efforts will not make the deficiencies disappear in the individual's mind, where they do the most damage. Anyone who believes that they can hide what hurts them most have a rude awakening in store; instead, the fear burns the unmet self-worth goals into the individual's mind, where they remain indefinitely. Thus, something the person wishes did not exist stays alive for what seems like an eternity. Ever-expanding self-worth goals fill the individual's brain, leaving little room for new learning. Consequently, the fearful brain has no space for explorations of paths to new learning that can help create new opportunities and new realities. The fearful brain is like a cage with its walls pushing inward under outside pressure, becoming smaller and tighter all the time.

Self-Worth Goals' Link to Competition

Another painful aspect involving self-worth goals that is often not openly pronounced is the element of competition involved. In setting up goals and deciding whether they have been met or failed, individuals usually look at others who may have set similar goals for themselves. Have these others met their goals or perhaps even surpassed them? This can constitute a threat to the condition of one's own self-worth goals.

Robert, a man in his late forties, had joined a group of people in his community who were interested in participating in marathon runs. But more recently, he had withdrawn from joining the meetings, although he was still involved in the races. When asked why he had discontinued going to their social meetings, he replied that the other runners in this particular group were cliquish and did not like newcomers. He decided he wanted nothing to do with them.

Upon further questioning, Robert related the story of his first experience with the group. He said he had joined a group of three men standing around talking about their participation in different marathons. One of the men was telling the group that he had started running almost 10 years ago and had participated in several marathons in different parts of the country but that he had not made it to the Disney World Marathon yet. Anxiously trying to fit in with the group, Robert spoke up: "I only started running five years ago, and I made it to the Disney World race last year. That was an awesome experience!"

One of the other men replied, "I made it to Disney World a couple of times. It is a memorable event." With that he turned to the other two men, nodding and proceeding to walk away with them. Robert just stood there speechless, feeling, as he said, like he had egg on his face. He felt rejected by the three men and decided not to be a part of that group anymore. He admitted feeling anxious now before the races because he dreaded running into any of the group members. What Robert failed to recognize was that he had taken somewhat of a competitive position when he told the men that he had only been training and running for five years and had already made it to the Disney World race. Apparently, the three men had not appreciated his competitive stance and had just left the scene to avoid further verbal competition.

As suggested earlier, leaving self-worth goals behind and adopting approach or learning goals instead would seem to lead to individuals' healthier conditions overall.[48] Becoming invested in self-worth goals means that individuals need to have some basic foundation to place their self-worth on and to make estimates of how to set goals for their self-worth, always assuming that the goals have to be higher than the present set of worth. Then the next issue raising its head is how to measure the level of self-worth as well as the level of those goals. It does not take long to fall back on comparisons with others to establish a certain threshold of acceptable worth, and this opens the door to competition, which in turn is the most fertile breeding ground for social anxiety.

People with self-validation goals tend to view stressors, such as anxiety about failure to perform successfully, as threats to their self-worth, and in turn they react defensively by trying to prevent their own and others' negative judgments regarding their worth.[49] Focusing instead on approach and learning goals, which are associated with high persistence compared with self-validation goals, would help the individual to ease away from the anxiety by directing attention to what could be gained knowledge of.[50] This shift in attention would serve to at least reduce the level of anxiety, and with continuing practice, the individual would feel more competent and in control during social interactions. However, the process is not without difficulty for the socially anxious person.

Retreating into the Shadow

Eric had been a promising student. His curiosity led him to search for answers along different paths than he was exposed to in his childhood. His parents were divorced, and in an unusual settlement, the court had awarded full custody of Eric's older brother Edwin to the father, while the mother had full custody of Eric. With that type of arrangement, there was not much contact between the brothers and their respective noncustodial parents.

During his junior high school year, Eric had participated in a junior-students-in-science fair that the school had been sponsoring on a biannual basis. Interested in physics, Eric had come upon a challenge that aroused his curiosity, and he entered the fair while working toward a solution. When it came time to select the finalists for the competition, Eric was taken aside by the science teacher, who informed him that just a few years back, another student had worked on a very similar problem and had come close to a solution. At the time, the student had withdrawn, asking for an extension to work out the final steps because the family was moving out of state.

That student had been Eric's older brother Edwin. The teacher explained to Eric that because of the closeness of the subject matter and the fact that the two boys were brothers, Eric and his project had to be disqualified from the competition because it might be seen as a collaboration of the two brothers instead of Eric's achievement.

As might be expected, Eric was crushed. Not only had his father chosen his older brother as the son to live with him, but the brother also had proven himself to be a budding scientist. All Eric could amount to in his opinion was a cheap imitation of his older brother. Eric did not talk to his mother about his disappointment. By this time, she had married again and was pregnant with his stepfather's child.

Eric's further career in school was unremarkable; he did not get into any trouble, but he also did not excel in anything. He kept his interests a secret because he feared that any disclosure of his endeavors would be met with another public acknowledgment that his ideas were only repetitions of what others had already contemplated and solved. With that fear, his relationships to other students remained on a superficial level.

Eric's grades were good enough to be accepted at a local college, so he could remain living with his family to keep expenses down. And he managed to find a part-time job in a nearby restaurant. Otherwise, the years of his college experience were not much different from his high school years. Eric kept his goals and ambitions secret and did not participate in any competition. The speech class constituted an ordeal for him because he felt physically and emotionally uncomfortable with the teacher's and his classmates' attention on him. Nevertheless, he stumbled through the exercises, earning acceptable grades. For the remainder of his classes, he blended in almost seamlessly with his environment. Eric's story also seems to reflect a lack of psychological hardiness, as discussed in chapter 3. His commitment to persistence in working toward goals that would bring meaningful results was lacking, as was his sense of being able to influence what was happening and the belief that negative events can be changed or modified to yield some positive outcomes.

After graduation from college, Eric's greatest hurdle was to face job interviews. Just thinking about them put him in a state of panic. No matter how he described himself and his goals and talents, he was sure to appear as a less accomplished imitation of the applicants that were interviewed before him. He felt unable to make a good impression. Instead of what he could say to the interviewer, Eric's thoughts focused on what the interviewer would see and think of him.

As most socially anxious individuals do, Eric focused attention mostly on himself, his goals being found worthwhile, and his fears of making mistakes and being judged and rejected. Accepting judgment and rejection as facts of life for him, he saw himself unable to extend his attention to the people he would be interacting with. If these interviewing people were as judgmental and negative as he believed, why would he want to work for them? Why not look for a friendly future boss or supervisor? Because in Eric's mind they were all going to dislike him, even though statistically that would not seem realistic.

Absorbed in his own fears, Eric did not realize that the persons interviewing him would face risks too. Unless the company was small enough for the owner to be interviewing prospective employees, department heads and supervisors interviewing applicants put their reputation on the line when they recommended one or the other applicant for a position. If the applicant of their choice did not work out well in the work setting, the supervisor would face consequences. Therefore, it was as important for a job applicant to make the interviewers comfortable with him or her as it was for the interviewer to make the right choice.

Unfortunately, this fact is often overlooked by the socially anxious job applicant because of his or her narrowed focus, the focus on their own discomfort and their self-worth goals rather than on a learning goal about those they interact with. As focus on self-worth goals is also often associated with an insecure attachment style, Eric's story can be understood within attachment theory. The loss of his father and older brother due to his parents' divorce and his mother's subsequent remarriage may have resulted in Eric's insecure attachment. Attachment insecurity has been found to be associated with avoidance motivation, including performance-avoidance goals,[51] characteristics found during Eric's school performance following the disappointment he endured during his science-project competition.

Persistence Inviting Failure

A generally accepted notion in psychology is the principle that behavior eventually ceases if it is not followed by reward, at least occasionally. But while many individuals' behaviors follow this principle, in some cases, especially those of socially anxious individuals, people's self-changing actions persist despite this notion.

Some researchers have looked at the cycle of failure, interpretation, and renewed effort in what they called people's "false hope syndrome," when individuals undertake a difficult self-change task, such as ridding themselves of undesirable but intrinsically rewarding behaviors.[52]

Dieting and attempts at weight loss represent perhaps the most prominent self-change resolutions. Many overweight people believe that the corrective action of dieting will not only enable them to lose weight but bestow increased attractiveness, health, and popularity on them. The promise of those additional desired benefits often leads to failure because of individuals' unrealistic expectations regarding the speed, amount, ease, and desired side effects of the self-change process. "Expectations often exceed what is feasible and lead people to reject more modest, achievable goals. The best is the enemy of the good."[53] The initial overconfidence frequently contributes to failure to maintain abstinence from excessive food, alcohol, and tobacco.

In addition, individuals who attempt to reduce participation in one activity (such as overeating) while trying to control another behavior are less likely to succeed in either one due to their unrealistic expectations of being able to make both changes.[54] Many socially anxious people are overweight, which may actually in many cases be the reason for the anxiety; trying to control the anxiety while dieting involves unrealistic expectations of self-change, and they are often doomed to failure.

One way self-changers look at their failures is to focus on deficiencies within themselves that will prevent the successful change from occurring. Those with unrealistically high expectations regarding their mental control abilities may become excessively self-critical and may panic following behavioral slips.[55]

The way self-changers interpret (or misinterpret) their failures determines whether they will try again or whether they will refrain from future attempts to reach their goals. Some people do not accept defeat easily and conjure up seemingly logical explanations for the current failure, which include the notion of being an almost success, which in turn spurs them on to regard the situation as a challenge to succeed with the next attempt.

On the other hand, those attributing failure of their self-change process to external factors making success impossible, to an exaggerated difficulty of the undertaking, or to their own shortcomings tend to be more likely to refrain from repeated attempts.[56]

This type of rationalizing can often be observed in participants in a time-limited program, such as an exercise or particular training program, who are less successful than they had expected to be. Their responses may indicate that succeeding in the program brought fewer benefits than they had originally predicted, adding that failure actually had fewer negative consequences than they had thought, thus making both success and failure seem less important.

A Fleeting Moment of Recognition

"Lionel—what a name for a flunky," he introduced himself.

"Why did you volunteer to tell your story?" the interviewer asked.

"Because if I heard myself saying it out loud, it might be enough of a challenge for me to want to change my life," and looking up at the interviewer, he continued, "I have been afraid of saying those things out loud. It was bad enough to have thoughts about it."

"What are those things you are referring to?" inquired the interviewer.

"My life," Lionel responded, relating his story. Lionel's two brothers had moved away as young men, but Lionel remained in the town he was born and grew up in. Where could he go that would make a difference? Nowhere, he thought. However, it did make a difference because here, in his hometown, people might remember the social status of his family.

His grandparents and great-grandparents were well-to-do. One of the daughters, Lionel's mother, was a meek, unassuming young girl, who fell in love with a man who was something of a fortune hunter, her fortune. They married, got a house to live in from the family estate, and had three sons before the father left the family because he couldn't lay his hands on his wife's inheritance as soon as he wanted. The three boys were mainly raised by their grandparents with some loving attention from their mother, who was not a good disciplinarian. While the older boys were developing a sense of responsibility under their grandfather's influence, Lionel, the youngest, was left to spend more time with his mother, who indulged his every whim.

Unlike his older brothers, Lionel did not recognize the need to train for a profession. In fact, much of his free time during his teenage years was spent in a marijuana haze. When his mother died and the money flow suddenly stopped, Lionel was forced to look for a job. With his mother's death, the door to the family fortune closed, the grandparents moved into an upscale, gated retirement community, and the money was secured in trusts to which Lionel had no access, except for a specified amount to purchase an automobile to replace the old secondhand car he was driving or to be paid out over time for a four-year tuition-only college education. His older brothers had moved away, working on their careers.

To pay for his living expenses, Lionel was forced to find a job quickly—any job. He did finish high school, but four years seemed like a long time, and he still had to work to be able to pay rent and feed himself. Lionel chose the new automobile, a brand-new Buick that looked big and powerful. However, Lionel had no training for any occupation after that choice. Unskilled labor or apprenticeship positions were the only paths open to him. Being in need of immediate resources, he chose unskilled labor. A brief early marriage did not improve Lionel's life as his new wife soon complained about the limits of Lionel's earning power. There was not much change after the divorce; Lionel settled into cheap, small apartments as he changed from one low-paying job to the next. But he became increasingly reluctant to interact with people from the past as well as people he met in his current environment.

Meeting people who had known his family of origin was especially painful because Lionel knew that they would see his current position in life as a big failure from his beginnings. Similarly, with new acquaintances, he felt intimidated as soon as they asked any questions about his past. In due course Lionel felt judged harshly by everyone around him for not being as wealthy as his family of origin had been. With that notion he experienced strong feelings of anxiety and anger toward interactions with others, and he, by acting in self-defense or self-protection as he saw it, reduced his contact with others to the point of becoming socially isolated.

Long ago when he chose the new car over the college tuition, Lionel was thinking of the four years being a long time to be short on money. He looked at the time span as an entity, not considering the possibility of trying college one semester at a time.

For Lionel, money was directly related to self-esteem because he suspected that people blamed him for his lack of riches. Shaped by our culture, self-esteem is a crucial human motivation, something that everyone wants to maintain.[57] Within the relationship between self-esteem and money, the three exchange principles of augmentation, substitution, and competition seem to be operating factors.[58] The financial costs of seeking or maintaining self-esteem have been explored by exchange theory. One of the main components of self-esteem is competence. The ability to earn money serves to prove people's level of competence—the greater the amount of money earned, the greater the level of competence, based on the augmentation effect.

The substitution effect indicates that money and self-esteem partially compensate for one another. But the degree to which money and self-esteem are interchangeable is determined by the symbolic meaning of money, individual differences, and the situational need for money.

The competition effect points to factors that determine people's choices between money and self-esteem. Making a choice between money and self-esteem also emphasizes the element of competition because earning more money than the next person means competing for it with the next person.

Now at age 58, what are Lionel's chances of being able to change beliefs that have been entrenched in his mind for almost half a century? How could his thought processes, which seem to endorse the entity view rather than the incremental view, change to the point of entertaining the possibility of taking small steps in considering the opinions of others without immediately becoming defensive? How could he bridge the distance between his own concerns and fears to consider the thoughts and concerns of others around him? How could he allow himself to lower his defenses and listen to suggestions from others? If he put a lid on his suspicions of others, could he learn to open up to them without the fear that they would betray his trust?

Or would it seem impossible to make all those changes during the remaining years of his life—and would it be worth the effort and time needed to accomplish that? As one might have guessed, Lionel opted out of this opportunity for a friendlier life and decided to remain socially on the periphery of life. He may not have realized that with increasing age, a friendless life becomes even more painful to live than at younger ages. But because his self-esteem depended on the possession of money, he might have considered the likelihood of earning a substantial amount of money too small to even try at this time in his life. Thus, the moment of opportunity when he talked to the interviewer passed without effecting a change in Lionel's lifestyle.

One might say that in terms of Ego Development Theory, Lionel had not entered higher stages that show the individual's increasing capacity to think about the self and others in a differentiated and integral manner, to be aware of the emotional and developmental causes of psychosocial conflicts, and to decrease levels of defensiveness while being able to transcend narrow self-interests.[59]

After the long and winding process of confronting and challenging old ideas, considering changes and trying to convince oneself that new paths might lead to better endings or destinations, how is one to make sure to remain on the new path to one's life? Good intentions are plentiful, but to keep the efforts meaningful, some successes along the way are needed to reinforce the good intentions. It may be worth looking at other areas of life to see what has been shown to be successful.

Building Psychological Momentum

One of the most frequently discussed phenomena among sports fans and stock traders is the notion of psychological momentum (PM), the idea that success leads to perceptions of momentum with an increased sense of confidence in people. Important to note is that not just athletes and stock brokers but the public at large are convinced about the performance-enhancing effects of PM.[60] Simply stated, the theory of PM means that people's previous performance significantly affects their subsequent performance.[61]

In general, PM is based on and demonstrated in two altered perceptions: (a) oneself as a performer (without any social or competitive comparison), and (b) oneself as a performer relative to an opponent (i.e., perceived superiority over the opponent). Combinations of these two perceptions yield the third perceptual component of PM, the perceived likelihood of winning or being successful in achieving a future goal.

However, the PM evolves only when these perceptions have been created by a recent or sudden success. Thus the basic model is success builds PM, in turn leading to more success. Although PM has been observed in both short- and long-term time frames, longer PMs (longer series of success) seem to lead to greater likelihood of success.

In general, the length of the chain of individual successes strengthens the PM; however, it can easily be disrupted by external events and agents, rendering it short-lived and temporary in nature. It is the initial success that is critical for the formation of PM; without it, PM does not develop. But the longer the length of the chain of successful events, the stronger will be the PM. In summary, the theory proposes that success breeds success because the effect of the initial success is psychological in nature rather than instrumental or technical. In turn, this leads individuals to attribute the success to their skills and effort, believing in their own abilities.[62] The buildup of PM can be applied within exposure treatment, often used as part of Cognitive-Behavioral Therapy, expecting that exposure to the anxiety-producing situation will decrease the actual level of anxiety by habituation.[63]

Applying those thoughts to the situations of our socially anxious individuals, we realize how important it is for them to be successful in their attempts to interact with others in a satisfying manner to build up their PM. And it is equally as important to follow up immediately with another try of reaching out to others before the PM fades into obscurity.

Pamela, a 20-year-old college student, experienced frequent anxiety attacks when interacting with other students and even more so when she could not avoid face-to-face encounters with any of the faculty members. Recently she had sought help for her anxiety problem from a psychologist who also was an adjunct faculty member at the same college. In her sessions with the psychologist, Pamela traced the beginnings of her difficulty back to her early school years. Although she was a good student, Pamela's mind "went blank" when asked questions in class by the teacher.

The first time this had occurred was in her English class when the teacher asked where Pamela had lived before entering the public school because her pronunciation of a particular word was different from the way it was pronounced in this part of the country. Some of the other children started to giggle as Pamela tried to answer the question. However, she was so embarrassed that she did not know what to say. Unfortunately, the teacher interpreted Pamela's lack of response as stubbornness and in a stern voice instructed her that here in this area and in this school, children were expected to answer when asked a question by an adult.

At the end of the class period, Pamela thought about approaching the teacher and explaining her silence, but her classmates seemed to watch her as she rose from her chair. Her seat was relatively close to the exit, and the distance to the front of the room where the teacher stood seemed much greater to her. Taking that walk under the watchful eyes of her classmates raised her anxiety level; all she could think of was to escape. With her head bent down, she quietly headed for the door.

This early experience set the tone for her school career; Pamela was an excellent student as long as she did not have to verbalize her ideas or otherwise participate in verbal discussions with others. Now she was attending college, and her psychologist was aware that Pamela tried to take as many online classes as she was allowed. While online studies in themselves constituted a convenient way for some students to obtain the credits while holding jobs during regular class hours, for Pamela it would serve to reinforce her social anxiety problem.

One day the psychologist observed Pamela in the hall to the classrooms listening to another faculty member. As the psychologist passed them, the teacher asked the psychologist to stop for a moment. The teacher wanted to inform the psychologist about the excellent essay Pamela had written for the class assignment. Of course, the teacher was not aware of Pamela's relationship with the psychologist; the teacher just wanted to express to another faculty member her pride in Pamela's insightful and logical style of writing. Pamela was downcast, trying to shrink into herself and avoiding the attention while her teacher praised her work. But she had to raise her eyes to face the psychologist, who made some encouraging remarks, smiling and nodding toward Pamela.

Perhaps her psychologist's presence helped Pamela to maintain composure as her teacher continued to mention particular details from Pamela's essay. At some point the teacher suggested that the essay had parts that might be of interest to the students in the psychologist's class. The psychologist, recognizing this turn of events as a good opportunity to work on increasing her client's self-esteem, obtained Pamela's agreement that she would be available to share some parts of her essay with the students in the psychologist's class later that week.

Pamela was pleased to be praised for her good work, although she probably would have preferred to learn about it in a note from her professor rather than have to face two faculty members. As would be expected, the aspect of talking to her psychologist's students frightened her, but she could not afford to reject the idea and embarrass her teacher as well as her psychologist. Besides, she trusted her psychologist enough to feel some support.

After Pamela and the psychologist had a preparatory session, the actual class discussion with Pamela went quite well, being thoughtfully conducted by the psychologist. Some of the students expressed the wish to hear more about the topic of Pamela's essay. The psychologist's smile and agreement with the students' wish ensured Pamela's performance in the psychologist's class. In the meantime, during their sessions the psychologist used Pamela's successful interactions to create and raise the PM to strengthen Pamela's self-confidence.

It was fortunate that the series of encouraging events had been started by Pamela's teacher and the psychologist was able to continue the trend. Had the psychologist been the first one to praise Pamela in the presence of others, it might have been less effective and convincing because Pamela might have believed it was just the psychologist's attempt to make Pamela feel better.

As summarized by some researchers, PM starts and builds up in situations where initial success significantly increases an individual's subjective probability of success by enhancing either (a) the person's perception of him- or herself as a performer in and of itself or (b) the individual's perception of him- or herself as being a superior performer over the opponent.

Contemplating Change

After reviewing above some of the hurdles along the path to possible change, there are additional considerations to attend to when contemplating changes in parts of one's lifestyle. For instance, many people are convinced that their personality is determined at birth, whereas others assume the ultimate control to design and mold their own personality. Re-creating the self and making conscious decisions to forge a new persona instead of accepting the roles that one's society and culture has enforced on the person can be a lifetime process. Decisions regarding which characteristics to include in one's new identity, trying them on, and modifying them require great effort as well as much patience.[64]

When deciding to reconstruct parts of their personal identity, as a rule, individuals don't just make up a wish list without some consideration of their abilities to accommodate their desires. Expectations about the likelihood of achieving desired traits and competencies in dealing effectively with obstacles that may stand in the way of those desired entities determine the degree and duration of efforts expended toward the goals.[65]

The person's estimate of how effectively a certain change will lead to a given outcome is the person's outcome expectancy. There is also an efficacy expectancy, which is the degree of the person's conviction that the behaviors necessary to yield the outcome can be successfully performed by the person. Both expectancies are thought to work together in influencing people's decisions about what behaviors to initiate. The expectancies are generally defined in terms of likelihood rather than in an "either-or" framework.[66] Reconstructing one's life can be an exciting undertaking when done by choice; for socially anxious people contemplating change—perhaps with the help of a mental health clinician—their experiences of change likely feel less exciting and more cumbersome.

CHAPTER NINE

Reconstructing One's Life

From the "decade of anxiety" in the 1980s, when the American Psychiatric Association officially recognized social anxiety disorder as a psychiatric disorder, to the year 2013, when 5.6 percent of American people were filling benzodiazepine prescriptions and 6,973 of them died of an overdose,[1] can we say we have found a solution to the problem? What once was considered to be a solution for social problems—a healthy dose of self-esteem—did not seem to deliver on the promises.[2] Now anxiety disorders in children and adolescents are called the "emerging epidemic" by those who want to teach professionals how to recognize and treat this epidemic.[3]

While having self-esteem would not hurt, dealing with the pain of social anxiety is much more complicated than handing someone a bag of self-esteem. For those who embark on changing their painful lifestyle, every individual's path will be different from every other one. Some will travel along the path alone, while others might engage the help of a psychiatrist, psychologist, or other mental-health clinician.

Learning from a Famous Example

Perhaps following the example of Albert Ellis, PhD, the founder of first Rational Emotive Therapy (RET) and then Rational Emotive Behavior Therapy (REBT), might be a good starting point for contemplating change.

In a recent interview with his widow, Debbie Joffe Ellis, it was stated that during his teenage and young adult years, Albert Ellis had been intensely shy. He was too afraid to speak to girls, and even though in college he was voted president of his political group, he felt very anxious when he had to speak in public. But he did not give up and instead forced himself to speak more often, deliberately pushing himself to do what felt uncomfortable, all with the understanding that eventually he would feel less threatened. He reminded himself that the worst that could happen would not amount to a tragedy, and he most likely would not die from it either.

As he was able to overcome his fear of speaking in public, Albert Ellis discovered that he was actually good at it, and he began to enjoy it. Applying his "just do it" approach, he assigned himself the task of talking to 100 girls in the month of August of that year and managed to make one date. But she did not show up! He still was able to overcome his fear of talking with females.

When the girl he fell in love with did not return his feelings, he became depressed. But he had an epiphany during a lonely midnight walk: it was not the girl's rejection that caused his depression; rather his demand that she *should* love him caused his bad feelings. His belief that he could *never* be happy without her caused his depression. Strongly disputing his own "shoulds" and "musts," Ellis created healthy rather than debilitating emotional responses to disappointing events in his life.

This practice of "in vivo desensitization" and applying encouraging, positive, and realistic self-talk became a core part of REBT. In the early years of RET/REBT, Albert Ellis was condemned by many of his peers and colleagues, who called him and his theory superficial and simplistic. But his persistence in talking, teaching, and writing about it led to changes in the world of psychology and counseling with the recognition of REBT. His qualities of persistence, tolerance for frustration, and not needing the approval of others contributed to reaching his goals. Those attitudes are basic elements within REBT.[4]

And those are the attitudes he taught me in individual supervision sessions, as well as reminding me to develop my own style within the REBT format and to repeat important issues because the anxious client may not hear or remember them when mentioned only once. I still follow his advice.

Progressing with Professional Help

When the anticipated process of change involves the socially anxious individual and a mental-health clinician, the situation becomes a work setting where "if those ideas or conceptions of a client which are relevant to his psychological problems can be changed in the direction of greater accuracy where his reality is concerned, his maladjustments are likely to be eliminated."[5] The therapist's task in such a setting is to present evidence when challenging the client's misconceptions, and the client's task is that of *cognitive review*, the process occurring within the client that brings about changes in misconceptions.[6] The fact that those misconceptions have been endowed with the strength and power of beliefs by the client makes the challenging and the cognitive review processes more difficult than might be expected at first glance.

Two for the Price of One?

When two socially anxious people meet and form a union, such as marriage, their difficulties don't just double but may increase exponentially. The arena where hurt feelings can cause the deepest pain is intimate relationships. Individuals are most vulnerable when the hurt comes from the words or actions of those they love. The fear of that hurt leads individuals to hide their vulnerability by refusing to disclose their emotional state to the other. As they remain outwardly emotionally closed or distant, they deprive the other person of the opportunity to really know them, and, similarly, the other person may be equally afraid of being emotionally hurt and may engage in similar hiding maneuvers. Socially anxious people's attention is focused on the turmoil within themselves, leaving them unable to concentrate on the interests and feelings of the other. Their self-consciousness destroys the intimacy, keeping them mentally and emotionally isolated within the relationship they once desired.[7]

While some socially anxious individuals resort to online dating services in their attempts to find a romantic partner, others are drawn by the similarity to another social anxiety sufferer, in the hope that they will find understanding and empathy for their own difficulties in the personality characteristics of this other socially anxious person. However, as discussed above, being plagued by similar fears and threats does not necessarily breed empathy for the other's pain, as Annabel and Mark discovered.

Annabel and Mark were seen together in their first session with the presenting problem that their marriage had lost its glow. Although they liked each other, they were not passionate about each other. Annabel did most of the talking while Mark sat quietly in his chair, occasionally nodding his head. When the psychologist addressed him directly, Mark responded with "Annabel is doing a good job describing our situation. I love her as much as I ever did, but I think she is bored with me."

The psychologist looked at Annabel as if to invite her response before asking Mark for more details about the "boredom." This also provided the psychologist with the insight that the two spouses had discussed this issue in the past when Annabel quickly responded, "It's true; it seems that Mark has no ambition for himself or for us, and I find that disappointing—it feels like we are 100 years old." If they had not discussed this issue before, Annabel might have been surprised by her husband's statement, and her response would not have been as quick.

"If you were to redesign your marriage now, how would you want it to be? What things would the two of you be doing to keep you from feeling like you are 100 years old?" The psychologist's question was meant for Annabel, but Mark decided to answer.

"I think she is referring to my dead-end job. I am not in a position to advance where I work. A couple years ago I went back to get my master's degree, hoping that would help. But it hasn't really made a difference."

"Because you are not looking for jobs anywhere else. And what about your idea of buying old houses and fixing them up for resale? That was a great idea, but it did not go anywhere." Annabel seemed to have a list of things Mark could or should have done but apparently did not act on.

"Perhaps there are some circumstances in your present job that you don't want to give up?" The psychologist tried to get the conversation back to Mark.

"No, there is nothing special. It's just that I feel safe because I know all about this place. I don't like change," Mark responded, looking down at the floor as if studying his shoes.

Exploring other areas of their marriage, the psychologist found out that the couple had two children, who seemed to be well adjusted overall. There was some financial stress, probably because of Mark's low-paying job. Annabel did not like her own job because of her work schedule, which in the past had allowed her to be at home with her children during part of the day. Now that the children were spending more time at school, Annabel wished for a regular daytime job. But she did not quit her job for fear that Mark's salary would not be enough to hold them over until she found another job to her liking.

Mark had an interest in metal sculpting and spent much of his free time on his hobby, hoping to develop that into a money-making activity in the future. Their sex life was functioning on a regular, about once-a-week basis, but it was obvious that Annabel was not excited about it.

At the end of the session, the psychologist scheduled individual sessions for each one of the spouses to obtain more in-depth information about their individual feelings.

Annabel in her individual session admitted that she had thought about leaving the marriage for quite some time. She liked Mark as a person; he was kind and gentle, but she did not feel any passion for him. How would Annabel develop her life if she left the marriage? was the psychologist's question.

"I always wanted to go back to school for an advanced degree, but it never seemed the right time. When Mark went back to graduate school, I was envious. But I thought it was more important that he do that, so as a man he would make more money. And when I thought about the years it would take for me to finish the next educational level, I was not sure that I could take that time away from being with my children."

"What did you want to focus on in your studies? Did you start taking courses and then drop out?" the psychologist inquired.

"No, it did not seem right to even start when I was not sure that I could finish it. I thought about literature and poetry. I used to write poems and my friends thought they were pretty good," Annabel elaborated on her interests.

Wanting to know more about Annabel's love for poetry, the psychologist asked, "Are you still writing poems or stories?"

"No," Annabel responded in a low voice. "I have not done any writing for quite a while; it just doesn't turn out well." She paused for a moment before continuing. "A couple years ago a friend of mine asked me to write a poem for her wedding. She and her future husband had planned to recite a poem for each other in the 'exchanging vows' section of the ceremony. She told me what ideas and emotions she wanted to express and thought I might be able to frame all that in a poem."

"What a great idea. Did you do it?" the psychologist asked.

"I tried, but the more I thought about it, the less I was able to get anything great sounding together. My friend was disappointed and said it could be something simple, just to express her feelings in a form of a poem. I did not want her to say something that sounded stupid. They wanted to print it in their little brochure for the guests, so everybody would have been able to read and criticize my words. I ended up not going to the wedding because she had already told some of her friends that I would write a poem for her. I feel uncomfortable in social situations anyway."

"Your friend's wish could have meant that she really thought your writing was very good and that it would be an honor for her to verbalize it on this important occasion," the psychologist suggested. "What is it about social situations that makes you feel uncomfortable?"

"I feel people expect me to say something profound, especially since I had talked about writing poetry. Now when I participate in a conversation my words sound so superficial. After any social event, I go over what I said, trying to come up with clever and meaningful things I should have said. I ruminate about it for hours."

"Do you think your friends criticize you as harshly as you criticize yourself?" the psychologist probed.

"I know my friend who got married was disappointed. I have been ashamed ever since for letting her down; but I could not let myself down," Annabel responded thoughtfully.

"By not letting yourself down, do you mean that giving your friend a poem that was not perfect in your mind would have amounted to letting yourself down?" the psychologist inquired.

"Definitely, as much as I had wanted to do it, not being able to do it right could only mean ridicule for me from those who saw it."

"If anybody saw your poem in the brochure, wouldn't that have meant that your friend liked it and had considered it to be good enough to recite at her wedding?" the psychologist thought out loud.

"I never showed it to her" was Annabel's brief answer. It was obvious that she did not want to continue with that topic of conversation.

Having made a mental note about the likelihood that Annabel tended to an entity view of thinking when she mentioned the years that it would have taken for her to complete studies to the next level and her apparent self-valuation goal approach, the psychologist thought that returning to the school issue might not be as pressing and therefore turned the conversation to the presenting problem of the marriage.

"You mentioned earlier that although you like your husband, you are not passionate about him. Have you thought what Mark might be able to do that would bring back your feelings for him?"

"Mark doesn't seem to have any goals for himself or for us other than just all living together. He doesn't talk much to people because he feels guilty about the past. It is depressing to watch him. At first I assumed that he would get over it, but I was wrong. I am getting tired of it." Annabel's voice reflected a mixture of depression and anger.

"What does he feel guilty about, do you know?" the psychologist asked, expecting it to be important information.

"Oh, it's all about his childhood when his father left the family. Mark does not want to talk about it." After a brief pause Annabel added, apparently impatient with herself, "Why can't I make up my mind whether to leave Mark or stay with him? I go back and forth. There is some safety in being with him but it gets me down to live without any goals, except for raising the children, but nothing exciting for us. Why can't I decide?"

"It seems you have painted yourself into a corner, not knowing which way to turn," the psychologist agreed with Annabel. "When you ask yourself 'Why can't I . . . ?' that sounds like you have accepted the fact that you can't decide, and all you want to know now is why you can't. That's a dead-end street."

"What do you mean . . . ?" Annabel sounded doubtful.

"As long as you accept that you can't do something, it does not really matter why; it would not change the situation. If you asked yourself 'How can I change this, or how can I make a decision?' that question might lead you to a beginning of making a decision," the psychologist explained, considering the importance of carefully strengthening Annabel's psychological hardiness by entertaining the possibility that she might be able to change or do something about a given situation.

Annabel thought for a moment; then to the psychologist's pleasant surprise, she followed the line of thinking when she slowly reflected, "In other words, if I say, 'I can't' and convince myself of that, I will not do anything; but if I ask how I could do it or start doing it, I might come up with an idea—is that how you meant it?"

"That's exactly how it works. You understood the process correctly. That's great!" After a brief pause the psychologist continued, "Now there might be another trouble point if you were to insist that you will make the absolutely best decision, the perfect decision. That could keep you from starting to work on a decision."

The psychologist's excitement seemed to please and encourage Annabel, as the big smile on her face indicated. But she also a little hesitatingly admitted that she had been concerned about the perfect decision. The psychologist's praise made it easier for her to accept the warning. All in all, it was a good ending to their first individual session.

Avoiding Facing the Risk

Mark, in his individual session, admitted feeling guilty about his past decisions. As he related his story to the psychologist, he seemed to be fighting back some tears. His father had left the family when he lost his job, leaving Mark, his mother, and his two younger sisters stranded for money and support. When they found out about the abandonment, Mark's sister Diana, who was about 18 months younger than Mark, suggested trying to get jobs in the neighborhood that they could perform while still attending high school. Their mother would look for some house-cleaning jobs, but above all Diana stressed the point that they should stay together and support each other. Mark felt he had to agree. But after his high school graduation, Mark enlisted in the army. Diana was outraged, and Mark tried to calm her down by saying that he would send money home from what he got paid in the army.

During his tour of duty, Mark was mostly stationed in Europe, and he was able to enroll in college courses offered by extension programs for members of the armed forces provided by stateside American universities. He did send some money home, but he never came home for visits because he did not want to lose out on the classwork for his education. Even when he could have left, he remained on the military base. Before his discharge from the army, Mark had been able with the help of some faculty members to be accepted to the university's main campus to continue with his studies, and that is where he established himself as a student and community member.

Shortly before his discharge, Diana had written that their father had returned home with a little boy in tow. Although Mark's parents had never divorced, the father had moved in with another woman and had fathered a child, the little boy. When the woman died unexpectedly, Mark's father went back to his previous home and family, taking his new son along. Apparently, Mark's mother did not have the strength to refuse him shelter, and the father with his new son settled into their home again. Diana was livid because she was expected to help raise the little boy and take care of the family. Danielle, Mark's youngest sister, was planning to get married soon after her graduation from high school.

Following his discharge from the army, Mark made one visit to his hometown and family. It was a rather unpleasant visit. Danielle acted as if she did not know him. His parents expected him to stay, get a job, and help the family. His worst encounter was with Diana. As soon as she saw him, she confronted him in a sharp voice, "You might have received an honorable discharge from the army, but you are a traitor to your family. I don't ever want to see you again." With that she walked out the door to her beat-up old car and started the ignition. She was leaving home.

Mark never forgot his sister's words, and his shame made it impossible for him to talk about his family. He did not make friends and did not socialize because, as he said, "sooner or later people ask you about your family, and I could not face that."

In contrast to embarrassment, the reason for much of the discomfort experienced by socially anxious individuals, shame and guilt are usually associated with interactions with loved ones rather than acquaintances. And those feelings seem to have longer-lasting effects because shame and guilt may carry moral implications rather than embarrassment following an individual's awkward behavior.[8]

Had Mark ever considered approaching Diana and discussing his feelings with her? No, he had not. This silent retreat had been characteristic of his general response to problems. As Mark admitted to the psychologist, he was aware of Annabel's dissatisfaction with their marriage, but as long as she was still there, he could make believe that things were all right. He did not even want to talk about their difficulties because that would mean acknowledging them and having to make decisions about changes. Changes were frightening to Mark because he did not know how to cope with them.

Mark added that on occasion he had agreed with Annabel that something needed to be changed in their marriage, but if she did not continue to pursue the subject, he was just as happy to not bring it up, hoping it would die down.

Many socially anxious people, as long as their worst fears don't come true, tend to tell themselves they have done the right thing by avoiding acting on the conflict or threat. And true to his chosen path of avoidance, Mark refused to participate in further therapy sessions, individual or conjoint.

Single-Sided Relationship Therapy?

Although conjoint sessions are the primary vehicle for marital therapy, there may be situations when conjoint sessions are impossible because one partner is unable or unwilling to attend, or it may be ill advised because one partner may appoint him- or herself as cotherapist, blaming the other or waiting for the other to implement changes. A single-sided relationship therapy model can function as a helpful alternative in situations like those.[9]

Annabel continued with individual sessions on a greatly reduced frequency of meetings because of her limited financial resources. But she surprised the psychologist when she disclosed her tentative plans of action. She did not want to start with a separation from Mark; instead she wanted to work on her own social anxiety and competitive goal expectations first. As she explained, that would give Mark more time to reconsider his reluctance to work on change, and it might put her in a more stable condition if she later decided not to stay in the marriage.

"This is my attempt to change 'why' into 'how,'" she explained with a smile.

The psychologist agreed that was a wise course of action for Annabel to follow. "You are off to a good start." The psychologist continued, "When you made the decision to start working on your fears, that was the first step of 'How can I?'"

"How am I going to take the next step?" Annabel asked, carefully pronouncing the word "how."

"We could take the next step by exploring what is going on in your mind when you start feeling anxious in a social interaction," the psychologist suggested. "What are you thinking then?"

"My thoughts? . . . That's embarrassing to tell . . ." While Annabel's voice trailed in hesitation, the psychologist interrupted, "It is not easy; but you know, Annabel, I believe you have the courage to tell me the thoughts that are important for the process of change to take place. I have confidence in you."

"That is more than I can say for myself," Annabel smiled weakly. "When I meet with people, other than family or very close friends, I am worried what they think of me. I want to make a good impression, and I want to be somebody special, not just a mother and wife with a part-time job to make ends meet."

"And your writing stories and poetry might have been that special talent?" The psychologist tried to turn the conversation to a narrower focus before asking Annabel for specific thoughts she might have had on the topic.

"Since I had been talking about poetry in the past, I was afraid that people would see me as bragging because nothing came of it. I was afraid people would ask me how many poems I had written. Then I would have to admit that I was a fake. I hadn't done anything worthwhile," Annabel answered.

The psychologist chose not to challenge Annabel on not having done anything worthwhile by pointing out her role as mother, housekeeper, and employee; most likely, she had encountered those affirmations from a few well-meaning friends, and this was not at the core of her self-criticism.

"At our previous meeting, you mentioned that you had considered going back to school, but then you thought about the years it would take to get to the next level, and you felt discouraged." The psychologist brought up the issue of people's mental views—such as entity versus incremental thinking—for exploration. "Sometimes when we consider our goals within the framework of big chunks of time, money, or energy that would be required, we might become overwhelmed by it and give up on it. But if we think about it in little steps or increments, it might not be so gigantic."

Annabel thought about the psychologist's statement for a moment before replying, "But if I could not finish the degree, it would be a waste of time and money. And people would know that I don't have the intelligence or stamina to finish."

As the psychologist had observed in the previous session, Annabel was motivated more by self-enhancement goals than learning goals. "Yes, one could consider the money and time involved as a loss; on the other hand, by starting with the process, the person would be able to learn some things that would encourage the person to increase his or her skills and talents through continued practice. And if for some reason the person had to interrupt the educational process, there might be opportunities to continue at a later point and feel good about one's persistence."

Realizing that those mental views would require repeated attention throughout the therapy process, the therapist waited patiently for Annabel's response, allowing time for Annabel to absorb this aspect of learning possibilities.

"I don't know where to begin right now," Annabel said, shrugging her shoulders in uncertainty. But her words indicated a willingness to consider some options.

"There might be a beginning with joining a local writers' group that is affordable. Your public library might have information about such groups. You could slowly get back into your poetry and stories by joining other aspiring writers. And you would not have to worry about criticism from them because they are trying to define their own voice and style." Annabel's initial hesitation about disclosing her writing attempts to others was deflated by the psychologist's suggestion. She promised to look into that possibility.

A Vehicle for Building Psychological Momentum

After some searching, Annabel joined a local writers' group not too far from her home. As could be expected, her anxiety level was high at her first meeting with the group. Fortunately, she had taken along two of her poems from years ago, just in case they asked her about her writing, which they did. Annabel selected one of the two poems, explaining that she had written it some time ago but felt differently about it now and was considering reworking it to reflect more current inspirational terms. The group's responses were favorable; members not only praised Annabel's previous work but also offered some suggestions on how to modernize the poem's approach.

Even though Annabel would have liked instant total approval, she gratefully accepted suggestions for change rather than demanded a complete acceptance of her poem. Although not aware yet of the importance of this development, Annabel was able to shift her mental attitude from the all-or-nothing entity approach to incremental thinking, which emphasizes learning.

What a wonderful experience. Annabel could have sworn that her little car had developed wings when she drove back home from the meeting. Upon her arrival at home, Annabel sat down and rewrote several passages of her poem. She even started a new one. Truly, the psychological momentum had been brought about by the writers' group's favorable responses; now it was of the utmost importance to keep it going with additional positive responses. Continued attendance at those meetings provided a framework for keeping the psychological momentum activated.

Proceeding to a Deeper Level

Although joining a writers' group was definitely a successful first step, the psychologist had serious doubts that it would be sufficient to free Annabel from her anxiety. A change on a deeper level would be required for that solution to occur. It was time for Annabel to disclose and evaluate important events and influences from the past.

In her next session, Annabel related some of her childhood experiences. As an only child, she was aware that her father would have been happier with a son; however, Annabel's mother was not able to have more children. Annabel's mother was a pretty but somewhat timid woman, and the father would jokingly say that he married her for the outside of her head, not the inside, indicating that there was not much substance to his wife's brain.

Annabel tried to please her father; praise from him would be the greatest reward. But most often she fell just short of that mark. With her father's encouragement, she joined the school's gymnastics team. She was one of the better gymnasts, but never *the* best at the right age. Her father let it be known that she did not live up to his expectations. When at a certain age it became clear that she would not excel in gymnastics, Annabel quit. It was too emotionally painful to continue just for the sake of doing gymnastics.

Not long afterward, her parents divorced, and Annabel lived with her mother while her father remarried and started a new family. Annabel's physical attractiveness found many young male admirers, but unfortunately, she was drawn to men who were like younger versions of her father—criticizing, complaining, blaming, and destroying what little self-confidence she had left.

In college she focused on a career in medical technology for her financial independence. Her love for poetry and writing found expression in the few elective credits open to her in her curriculum. And here a repetition of her earlier strivings in gymnastics occurred. When she did not excel dramatically after a semester or two, she gave up on it. As in the past, when achievement of her goals at a certain stage seemed doubtful, she would quit her efforts, considering additional learning or practice to be useless.

She believed that she had to be established as a success at a certain point in time and to defend her position from then on. If she could not reach success by that time, she had to either hide the fact that she had ever tried or defend or justify why her goals could not be achieved.

"When you told me about your strivings to excel as a gymnast, it seemed like there was a lot of stress and pain involved, and it was probably worse when you realized that you would not be that special person receiving your father's praise and your friends' admiration," the psychologist gently tried to guide Annabel's thoughts back to that event. "Let's look at what it entails to be a special person as you see it. To be the very best at something takes a lot of training, patience, and self-sacrifice (you don't have much time or energy left for fun activities)—as you already know."

"But it's worth it to be special," Annabel broke in.

"Well, that would be for you to decide," the psychologist resumed the line of thought regarding the special-person misconception. "If you want to remain that special person, you would have to work harder and harder, all the time watching that nobody else excels you in that particular skill or activity. And how much do most people like others who perform better at tasks that they are proud of being able to do?"

Observing Annabel's face clouding over, the psychologist continued, "And even more distressing, if a person excels in some task domain to the point that he or she has achieved the special-person status, then if they want to keep that status, they have to work for the rest of their lives on that task. When demanding to keep the special-person status, the individual gives up control over what to do and for how long, even if some other activity would seem preferable at some time." The psychologist paused to give Annabel time for the impact of the meaning.

After several minutes passed, Annabel spoke again. "When I quit gymnastics and later on writing too, I thought I had no choice but giving up because I did not have what it takes to make it."

The summary of her life approach had been either to have proved her competence at a certain point or to defend her lack of accomplishment by justifying why success could not be achieved. At that point there was no reason to continue learning or improving, Annabel believed.

How did Annabel determine the point of stopping the pursuit of her goal? was the question the psychologist addressed in the next session. Annabel seemed surprised, indicating her opinion that the reason for the stopping point was obvious. Upon the psychologist's further questioning, Annabel addressed the situation when her gymnastics training ended. "Well, it became obvious that I could not make the rank while still in school, so what was the point in continuing? Besides, my father had left us, and there would not be any praise coming from him."

"And when you stopped writing, what prompted your decision then?" was the psychologist's next question.

"Although some of my writing was favorably acknowledged in class, it did not stand out as the best. Two semesters of trying should have been long enough to make me excel," Annabel stated reluctantly. "Perhaps my father's leaving kept me from progressing; I felt abandoned by him," Annabel continued.

"Who told you that two semesters of classes would be enough to become an accomplished writer? Did your teacher suggest that you quit?" The psychologist probed further.

"My teacher did not say anything like that," Annabel admitted, "it just seemed to make sense that I did not have what it takes to be great."

"So nobody told you that you would not become a great writer?" The psychologist wanted to be sure that this was all the information Annabel had based her decision on.

"If I had continued taking more classes, it would have been obvious that I wanted to be a writer, and every one of my friends would know that I failed if I did not have something great to show for my efforts," Annabel admitted hesitatingly. "Besides, when I could not even come up with a poem for my friend's wedding, that was enough of a failure to admit." She finished her statement.

"So you were the one to decide when you had given your attempts the right amount of time and effort, but how did you know that it was the correct time to stop? In our previous session we looked at how insisting on the permanence of the special-person status takes away the control over what activities one wants to engage in and for how long."

Annabel nodded, indicating that she remembered the previous discussion.

"It seems to me that sometimes we hear of cases where people's talents or expert skills take quite a while to develop."

After a moment's pause, the psychologist apparently remembered a relevant case. "You are too young to know of Grandma Moses, but this woman was in her late seventies; her husband had died and her children had become adults when she started to paint and became a member of a long tradition of American folk artists. She was very successful, and every American president from Truman through Kennedy paid homage to Anna Mary Robertson Moses. At the time of her death at the age of 101, she had produced more than 1,600 works of art."[10]

The psychologist used this opportunity to present evidence to challenge the client's misconception or misguided belief, hoping that she, in turn, would take on her task of cognitive review and reevaluate her assumptions, as described earlier.[11]

Did some people laugh at Grandma Moses when she started to paint at her advanced age? the psychologist pondered. Perhaps some did—but if so, not for long. Actually, it had been Anna Mary's sister who suggested she try to paint because the arthritis in her hands made it too difficult to continue with her needlework. And this was not the only example. Perhaps Annabel could think of others; the psychologist encouraged her.

The reason or meaning behind the particular activity contemplated by the individual was still a hurdle in Annabel's mind. Was it sufficient to engage in an activity just because one enjoyed it?

The activating force in Grandma Moses's case appeared to be a distraction from loss and loneliness, or perhaps even boredom. In many other cases—Annabel's most likely included—people's driving force seems to be the desire to be awarded special status, to be acknowledged and admired permanently by those around them, eliminating the necessity to repeatedly prove their capabilities (as discussed earlier).

An eternal condition of perfection does not exist in actuality. Even if one has a moment of near-perfect ability, there will always be another human being coming along, younger, stronger, more attractive, smarter, better trained, and of superior skills. In order to preserve that 'moment of perfection' in the memories of others and oneself, the individual has to retreat into hiding at the end of that moment. And that, indeed, is the tragedy in the lives of many of the socially anxious people we encounter.

The elusiveness of perfection does not seem to deter people from pursuing it. Attaining perfection promises peace of mind about one's assured elevated place in society. The statistical impossibility of it and its at best fleeting existence in anybody's life are facts the brain refuses to acknowledge when under the influence of a mixture of threat, fear, anxiety, and wishful thinking.

Indeed, Annabel encountered difficulties when focusing on the meaning of perfection and the striving toward perfection as a life goal. As she remembered from her childhood, her father had emphasized the importance of striving for perfection. As he told her, to strive for perfection is a noble goal, one that reflects honorably on the person. Anybody can set easy or simple goals that can be attained without great effort, but a high goal, such as perfection, bestows dignity and significance on the individual who strives toward it. Those messages from one's childhood are difficult to extinguish.

At the time Annabel did not realize that her father's statement placed more value on conceptualizing a goal than on actually working toward achieving it. And now she was still wrestling with recognizing and accepting its meaningless content.

The learning experience within Annabel's therapy process so far included recognizing and challenging several strong but misguided beliefs (misconceptions):

(1) As many socially anxious people believe, Annabel also thought she should be able to interact with others without experiencing anxiety—eventually leading to a sense of perceived unfairness. (2) Success or accomplishment has to occur at a certain time in one's life. (3) Accomplishments have to be perfect and remain perfect forever. In her opinion, her happiness and her acceptance by others depended on those demands.

Annabel's freeing from her "false assumptions" was considered to be the main part of the learning experience. Instead of trying to change emotions, behaviors, or symptoms, the therapy process, according to some therapists, should focus on changing goals, concepts, and notions because those are the only changes that can lead to permanent improvement.[12] And those changes had to occur before Annabel could plan and design her future life.

Her continued participation in the writers' group prompted Annabel to rework the poem she had read to the group and to work on others. Also, as she listened to the work of the other group members, she was able to notice changes and improvements as they went along. This was an important observation on her part because, as she admitted, she had not worried about her own writing as she focused on that of the others. The psychologist congratulated her on that important self-observation and emphasized the significance of it in the learning process. Annabel's discovery that her listening and comprehension skills improved when she was not distracted by anxiety over her own performance opened the door for new learning to occur.

With continuing participation in the writers' group, Annabel also regained some of her earlier satisfaction in expressing her thoughts and feelings in short stories and poems. This was a good sign of progress on Annabel's part. The psychologist expressed praise for Annabel's astute observation and seized the opportunity to guide Annabel onto a decision path, emphasizing that this was not going to be a one-time decision but rather a path of repeated mindful contemplations and decisions.

The psychologist outlined Annabel's options along the path. As she continued writing and improving her skills of expression, she was keeping the source of her current satisfaction alive, and in addition, the chances of her becoming an accomplished writer were part of her future. There was no guarantee that she would become famous, but the opportunity existed as long as she continued with her writing activities. If on the other hand, she insisted on only writing "perfect" stories or poems, her creativity might be crushed under that heavy demand. And if she had to hide her failure to be successful, she would have to give up the activities that right now gave her a good feeling. In addition, she would have zero opportunities to ever be acknowledged and admired for her creative work.

In other words, every time she quit, she would deprive herself of the good feelings that accompany creative endeavors; she would also make sure that the recognition or fame she desired would never come her way. That was guaranteed. But if she abandoned her unrealistic insistence on perfection, she not only could continue to enjoy her creative activities but could possibly still excel in her writings.

After outlining the two options, the psychologist added, "Thirty or fifty years from now, which option do you think you would want to have chosen?"

Annabel was stunned by the psychologist's explanation. She sat in silence for a while, apparently not knowing what to say. Finally, she looked at the psychologist with moist eyes, her voice quivering, as she slowly said, "You are saying that if I want perfection, demanding 100 percent, I will most likely end up with zero," and after a brief pause she continued, "but if I ask for 50 or 80 percent quality in my writing, I might get 30 or 40 percent with the possibility of increasing that percentage with time and more learning?" Her words were heavy as she spoke, giving the impression of a mental and physical struggle going on in her.

"That is well summarized on your part. The only thing you did not mention is the loss of the gratification you are now deriving from your creative endeavors that you would experience if you insisted on 100 percent."

Just before leaving this session, Annabel turned around to face the psychologist again. "And all this is not even dependent on the marriage; this is all about just me!"

The psychologist nodded yes.

Moment of Choice

How would Annabel respond? The psychologist had thought that the progress she had made so far allowed for the introduction of the next challenge, the decision that would mean starting and implementing the steps of change or giving up and continuing to live with paralyzing anxiety.

When Annabel returned for her next session after trying to weigh her options and arrive at a decision she could live with, she disclosed her thoughts to the psychologist.

"This is a difficult decision to consider. I am not sure that I am ready to make it yet, but if it's all right with you, I would like to continue with the process of change—at least for now. There might still be a time when I decide to quit."

The psychologist agreed. "That is totally all right, Annabel. It makes sense to carefully consider the different possibilities in such an important issue."

Pulling a piece of paper from a drawer, the psychologist faced Annabel with a smile. "I wanted to share this with you. Some time ago a former radio announcer developed a phobia of speaking. After about 11 years he entered treatment and was able to overcome his phobia. As he wrote about his experience and the treatment program, he ended with words spoken in 1899 by Theodore Roosevelt, words that have a special meaning for people afflicted with this kind of fear and anxiety.

> Far better it is to dare mighty things,
> to win glorious triumph
> even though checkered by failure,
> Than to rank with those poor spirits
> who neither enjoy much
> nor suffer much,
> Because they live in the great twilight
> that knows neither
> victory nor defeat.[13]

Annabel sat in silence, listening to the words. Finally, she said, "Wow—that is powerful! So those are my options: possible victory or certain defeat," and added after a brief pause, "Where do I start?" With her words Annabel demonstrated a cognitive openness, a willingness to listen to the words and opinions of others. Several of Annabel's cognitive vulnerabilities seemed to have resolved during the therapeutic process.

The psychologist was pleased to note that Annabel apparently remembered the discussion of the previous session well enough to attend to the psychologist's abstaining from pronouncing something like "guaranteed" or "100 percent" victory.

"The good part is, you have already started. When you joined the writers' group, you took the first steps onto the path to triumph; you are a courageous person," the psychologist attended to Annabel's question.

One of the next hurdles to tackle was the area of interactions with friends and acquaintances (not the writers' group members) when topics such as her writing or other goal-directed activities might be brought up.

"Another step on the road to change might be to consider how you want to act and feel if in an interaction with your friends the topic of your writing comes up," the psychologist led Annabel to that for Annabel uncomfortable topic. "Did you have any such encounter yet?"

"No" was Annabel's quick answer, "but I have thought about it a lot without coming up with an answer."

"Let's try to imagine such a situation and find out how you would want to handle it. Although you might want to be free of all anxiety, that might be a bit unrealistic to expect. Would you be willing to settle for some anxiety?"

When Annabel nodded her head, the psychologist continued, "What would be the most likely reason for the anxiety?"

"What are they thinking of me?" was Annabel's quick response.

"That in itself is just a question, and unless you ask the person, you will not know the answer. Are you sure that the question will raise the anxiety in you, or are you perhaps trying to guess the answer, and that brings up the anxiety?" the psychologist wanted Annabel to identify the actual trigger for the anxiety.

"Well, it's not that difficult to guess what they think, probably something like 'She'll never be a real writer; she doesn't have the talent' or 'How long is she going to try to be somebody special? She is a hopeless case.'"

"Your guesses are all negative thoughts, reflecting your thinking when we started our work," the psychologist pointed out. "But they are only guesses or causal inferences you are making about the unobservable mental activities of those other people. And in a way, you are doing what you suspect them to do, thinking negatively about the other."

Annabel's face turned pink as she asked, "You mean that I am anxious because I am afraid other people will be as judgmental as I apparently am?"

"That might be one of your fears," the psychologist agreed with Annabel, "and let's not forget, the other people may not really have those negative thoughts about you. We don't really know for sure. Is that reason enough to become fearful and distance yourself from those others?"

"If that is true, how can I change my fearful expectations?" Annabel seemed to be ready for the next step.

"If you find yourself in a conversation with a friend or acquaintance and the topic of your writing comes up, why don't you answer the way you would have wanted to with opening up about your interests. Please don't expect to be completely free of any anxiety, but instead just see if the world is coming to an end or if you faint dead away during the interaction," the psychologist suggested.

"That reminds me of my starting with the writers' group," Annabel remembered. "I was nervous at the beginning, but with time I was able to listen to the group members and actually hear what they said as my anxiety level went down."

"Yes, I remember when you mentioned it; it had been such an important step forward. I am glad you did not forget that experience because it is evidence that you will be able to reduce the level of anxiety. In fact, it would be a good thing to remind yourself repeatedly that you were able to make that happen."

"And from what we talked about earlier," Annabel offered as a suggestion, smiling a bit sheepishly at the psychologist as she spoke, "I could also remind myself that I have no evidence that the other people will not like me or will judge me harshly—as harshly as I am apparently judging myself."

"Annabel, you are an excellent student. I am proud of you!" was the psychologist's answer.

Over the next several months, Annabel made slow but good progress in her interactions with others. It still remained a difficult area in her overall change. Her father's influence of criticizing her through most of her childhood years was difficult to lay to rest. Surprisingly, Annabel's children helped her when they told her that she was more fun to be with now than earlier. That compliment meant a lot because she knew her children well enough to realize that they told the truth.

Annabel remained a member of the writers' group; eventually the group members became her most important support system. She continued to write and attend workshops from time to time, as she could afford it. It was a very emotional moment when she presented a framed poem to the friend who had asked her for a poem for her wedding. This poem was about the birth of the woman's first child. The woman thought the poem beautifully expressed her feelings about this event. She hugged and kissed Annabel while tears were rolling down her cheeks. Their friendship was restored.

It was a happy day when Annabel entered the psychologist's office, excitedly announcing that she had been invited to contribute a story for an anthology the local writers' center was planning to publish. It was a story she had already started, and one of the group members had told a representative of the writers' center about it. As if she could read the psychologist's mind, Annabel said, "This is not going to be a repetition of the wedding poem situation."

A Reminder: This Is Not a Fairy Tale

Annabel's progress became obvious to Mark as he observed the changes in her mood and her activity level as well as the children's positive attitude. Because he feared change, he feared what his life would become. As in the past, he did not express his fear or his thoughts about the marriage. But much like his father years ago, Mark left the home after informing Annabel that he had met a previous girlfriend quite by accident. She still seemed to love him. He felt accepted as he was—no need for change. So he decided to share his future life with her.

Of course, Annabel was shocked. Even though she knew that Mark was not happy, she did not expect him to consider his changes secretly and only tell her about them at the end. For a moment she felt tempted to offer that they go back to their old lifestyle if he would remain in the marriage. That moment passed when she realized the dishonesty as Mark had kept his thoughts and plans a secret from her. Anger rose up in her over the betrayal, and she experienced a moment of perceived unfairness that could lead to feeling sorry for herself and jeopardizing the progress she had made. That moment passed.

Considering Annabel's life changes within the framework of Binswanger's three worlds of human existence,[14] it would appear that the *Mitwelt* lost a seemingly important ingredient, her husband. However, her relationship with her children had moved to a more meaningful level, and she also had added several good friends to this sphere of her life. Both the *Umwelt* and *Eigenwelt* had experienced significant expansions. The world around her had enlarged, including many more people and adding experiences to it. Her personal self and its meaning now appear almost limitless.

Notes

Chapter 1

1. *Diagnostic and statistical manual of mental disorders, fifth edition* (*DSM-5*) (Washington, DC: American Psychiatric Association, 2013).

2. Pierre Janet, *The major symptoms of hysteria*, 2nd ed. (New York: Macmillan, 1920).

3. Joseph F. Rychlak, *Introduction to personality and psychotherapy* (Boston: Houghton Mifflin, 1973).

4. Karen Horney, *New ways in psychoanalysis* (New York: Norton, 1939), 74–75.

5. Eric Luis Uhlmann, "American psychological isolationism," *Review of General Psychology* 16, no. 4 (2012): 381–90.

6. Erving Goffman, *Stigma* (Englewood Cliffs, NJ: Prentice-Hall, 1963).

7. Arthur Lange and Patricia Jakubowski, *Responsive assertive behavior* (Champaign, IL: Research Press, 1976).

8. J. K. Meyer et al., "Six-month prevalence of psychiatric disorders in three communities: 1980 to 1982," *Archives of General Psychiatry* 41 (1984): 959–66.

9. R. A. Schurman, P. S. Kramer, and J. B. Mitchell, "The hidden mental health network treatment of mental illness by non-psychiatric physicians," *Archives of General Psychiatry* 42 (1985): 89–94.

10. W. Katon et al., "Panic disorder: Epidemiology and primary care," *Journal of Family Practice* 23 (1986): 233–39.

11. R. C. Scaer, *The body bears the burden: Trauma, dissociation, and disease* (New York: Haworth Press, 2001).

12. Aaron T. Beck, Gary Emery, and Ruth I. Greenberg, *Anxiety disorders and phobias: A cognitive perspective* (New York: Basic Books, 1985).

13. Thekla Morgenroth, Michelle K. Ryan, and Kim Peters, "The motivational theory of role modeling: How role models influence role aspirants' goals," *Review of General Psychology* 19, no. 4 (2015): 465–83.

14. Herbert Freudenberger and Gail North, *Situational anxiety* (New York: Carroll & Graf, 1982).

15. Matthew McKay and Patrick Fanning, *Self-esteem* (New York: St. Martin's Press, 1987).

16. McKay and Fanning, *Self-Esteem*, 3rd ed. (Oakland, CA: New Harbinger Publications, 2000).

17. Eric Hollander and Nicholas Bakalar, *Coping with social anxiety* (New York: Henry Holt, 2005).

18. K. Neff, "Self-compassion: An alternative conceptualization of a healthy attitude toward oneself," *Self and Identity* 2 (2003): 86–101.

19. Laura K. Barnard and John F. Curry, "Self-compassion: Conceptualization, correlates, & interventions," *Review of General Psychology* 15, no. 4 (2011): 289–303; A. Mills et al., "Paranoid beliefs and self-criticism in students," *Clinical Psychology & Psychotherapy* 14 (2007): 358–64; K. Neff, S. Rude, and K. Kirkpatrick, "An examination of self-compassion in relation to positive psychological functioning and personality traits," *Journal of Research in Personality* 41 (2007): 908–16; J. G. Williams, S. K. Stark, and E. E. Foster, "Start today or the very last day? The relationships among self-compassion, motivation, and procrastination." *American Journal of Psychological Research* 4 (2008): 37–44.

20. L. K. Barnard and J. F. Curry, "Self-compassion: Conceptualization, correlates, & interventions" (2011).

21. P. Gilbert and C. Irons, "Focused therapies and compassionate mind training for shame and self-attacking," in *Compassion: Conceptualizations, research and use in psychotherapy*, ed. P. Gilbert (New York: Routledge, 2005), 263–325.

22. K. Neff, "Self-compassion: An alternative conceptualization of a healthy attitude toward oneself," *Self and Identity* 2 (2003): 86–101.

23. C. Germer, *The mindful path to self-compassion: Freeing yourself from destructive thoughts and emotions* (New York: Guilford Press, 2009).

24. S. L. Shapiro et al., "Mindfulness-based stress reduction for health care professionals: Results from a randomized trial," *International Journal of Stress Management* 12 (2005): 164–76; S. L. Shapiro, K. W. Brown, and G. M. Biegel, "Teaching self-care to caregivers: Effects of mindfulness-based stress reduction on the mental health of therapists in training," *Training and Education in Professional Psychology* 1 (2007): 105–15.

25. J. Kabat-Zinn, "Mindfulness-based interventions in context: Past, present, and future." *Clinical Psychology Science and Practice* 10 (2003): 144–56.

26. M. H. Kernis, "Toward a conceptualization of optimal self-esteem," *Psychological Inquiry* 14 (2003): 1–26.

27. Roy F. Baumeister, L. Smart, and J. M. Boden, "Relation of threatened egotism to violence and aggression: The dark side of high self-esteem," *Psychological Review* 103 (1996): 5–33; M. H. Kernis, "Toward a conceptualization of optimal self-esteem" (2003); M. R. Leary et al., "Self-compassion and reactions to unpleasant self-relevant events: The implications of treating oneself kindly," *Journal of Personality and Social Psychology* 92 (2007): 887–904.

28. E. Deci and R. Ryan, "Human autonomy: The basis for true self-esteem," in *Efficacy, agency, and self-esteem*, ed. M. H. Kernis (New York: Plenum Press,

1995), 31–49; M. H. Kernis, "Toward a conceptualization of optimal self-esteem" (2003).

29. E. Deci and R. Ryan, "Human autonomy: The basis for true self-esteem" (1995); K. Neff, "Self-compassion: An alternative conceptualization of a healthy attitude toward oneself" (2003); M. Rosenberg, *Society and the adolescent self-image* (Princeton, NJ: Princeton University Press, 1965).

30. E. Deci and R. Ryan, "Human autonomy: The basis for true self-esteem" (1995), 32.

31. E. Deci and R. Ryan, "Human autonomy: The basis for true self-esteem" (1995); M. H. Kernis, "Toward a conceptualization of optimal self-esteem" (2003).

32. K. Neff, Y. Hsieh, and K. Dejitterat, "Self-compassion, achievement goals, and coping with academic failure," *Self and Identity* 4 (2005): 263–87.

33. K. Neff, "The development and validation of a scale to measure self-compassion" (2003); K. Neff, S. Rude, and K. Kirkpatrick, "An examination of self-compassion in relation to positive psychological functioning and personality traits" (2007).

34. P. Gilbert and C. Irons, "Focused therapies and compassionate mind training for shame and self-attacking" (2005); P. Gilbert and S. Procter, "Compassionate Mind Training for people with high shame and self-criticism: Overview and pilot study of a group therapy approach," *Clinical Psychology & Psychotherapy* 13 (2006): 353–79.

35. P. Gilbert and C. Irons, "A pilot exploration of the use of compassionate images in a group of self-critical people," *Memory* 12 (2004): 507–16.

36. D. Lee, "The perfect nurturer: A model to develop a compassionate mind within the context of cognitive therapy," in *Compassion: Conceptualizations, research and use in psychotherapy*, ed. P. Gilbert (New York: Routledge, 2005), 326–51.

37. P. Gilbert and C. Irons, "A pilot exploration of the use of compassionate images in a group of self-critical people" (2004).

38. L. K. Barnard and J. F. Curry, "Self-compassion: Conceptualization, correlates, & interventions" (2011).

39. E. Hollander and N. Bakalar, *Coping with social anxiety* (2005).

40. P. Muris et al., "The role of parental fearfulness and modeling in children's fear," *Behavior Research and Therapy* 34 (1996): 265–68.

41. E. Hollander and N. Bakalar, *Coping with social anxiety* (2005).

42. J. H. Flavell, "Cognitive development: Children's knowledge about the mind," *Annual Review of Psychology* 50 (1999): 21–45.

43. Jesse M. Bering, "Why hell is other people: Distinctively human psychological suffering," *Review of General Psychology* 12, no. 1 (2008): 1–8.

44. Richard S. Marken, "Looking at behavior through control theory glasses," *Review of General Psychology* 6, no. 3 (2002): 260–70.

45. Richard S. Marken, "The nature of behavior: Control as fact and theory," *Behavioral Science* 33 (1988): 196–206.

46. R. Gelman, F. Durgin, and L. Kaufman, "Distinguishing animates from inanimates," in *Causality and culture*, ed. D. Sperber, D. Premack, and A. Premack (Oxford, UK: Plenum, 1995), 150–84.

47. G. Gergeley, Z. Nadasdy, C. Gergeley, and B. Szilvia, "Taking the intentional stance at 12 months of age," *Cognition* 56 (1995): 165–93; D. Premack, "The infant's theory of self-propelled objects," *Cognition* 36 (1990): 1–16; R. S. Marken, "Looking at behavior through control theory glasses" (2002).

48. Brent Dean Robbins and Holly Parlavecchio, "The unwanted exposure of the self: A phenomenological study of embarrassment," *Humanistic Psychologist* 34, no. 4 (2006): 321–45.

49. P. Gilbert, J. Pehl, and S. Allan, "The phenomenology of shame and guilt: An empirical investigation," *British Journal of Medical Psychology* 67 (1994): 23–36; M. Lewis, *Shame: The exposed self* (New York: Free Press, 1992); M. Merleau-Ponty, "The child's relations with others," in *The primacy of perception*, ed. J. M. Edie (Evanston, IL: Northwestern University Press, 1964); B. D. Robbins and J. Goicoechea, "The psychogenesis of the self and the emergence of ethical relatedness: Klein in light of Merleau-Ponty," *Journal of Theoretical and Philosophical Psychology* 25, no. 2 (2005): 191–223; J. P. Tangney, "Self-conscious emotions: The self as a moral guide," in *Self and motivation: Emerging psychological perspectives*, ed. A. Tesser, D. A. Stapel, and J. V. Wood (Washington, DC: American Psychological Association, 2001), 97–117.

50. E. Hollander and N. Bakalar, *Coping with social psychology* (2005).

51. Signe A. Dayhoff, *Diagonally-parked in a parallel universe: Working through social anxiety* (Placitas, NM: Effectiveness-Plus Publications, 2000).

52. Steve Flowers, *The mindful path through shyness: How mindfulness and compassion can help free you from social anxiety, fear & avoidance* (Oakland, CA: New Harbinger Publications, 2009).

53. Gillian Butler, *Overcoming social anxiety and shyness: A self-help guide using Cognitive Behavioral techniques* (New York: Basic Books, 2008).

54. Lynne Henderson, *The compassionate mind guide to building social confidence: Using compassion-focused therapy to overcome shyness & social anxiety* (Oakland, CA: New Harbinger Publications, 2010).

55. Barbara Berckhan, *Einfach selbstsicher! Das Soforthilfe-Programm für mehr Gelassenheit und Souveränität* [Simply self-confident!] (Munich, Ger.: Gräfe und Unzer Verlag, 2007).

56. E. Hollander and N. Bakalar, *Coping with social psychology* (2005).

57. J. R. Marshall, *Social phobia from shyness to stage fright* (1994).

58. P. G. Zimbardo and S. Radl, *The shy child: Overcoming and preventing shyness from infancy to adulthood* (New York: Malor Books, 1999).

59. Murray B. Stein and John R. Walker, *Triumph over shyness: Conquering shyness and social anxiety* (New York: McGraw-Hill, 2002); Bernardo J. Carducci, *Shyness—a bold new approach* (New York: Quill, 1999).

60. B. J. Carducci, *Shyness—a bold new approach* (1999).

61. H. W. Marsh, "Age and sex effects in multiple dimensions of self-concept: Preadolescence to early adulthood," *Journal of Educational Psychology* 81 (1989): 417–30.

62. R. W. Robins et al., "Global self-esteem across the life span," *Psychology and Aging* 17 (2002): 423–34.

63. S. A. Baldwin and J. P. Hoffmann, "The dynamics of self-esteem: A growth-curve analysis," *Journal of Youth and Adolescence* 31 (2002): 101–13.

64. Chiungjung Huang, "Mean-level change in self-esteem from childhood through adulthood: Meta-analysis of longitudinal studies," *Review of General Psychology* 14, no. 3 (2010): 251–60.

65. Brittany Gentile, Jean M. Twenge, and W. Keith Campbell, "Birth cohort differences in self-esteem, 1988–2008: A cross-temporal meta-analysis," *Review of General Psychology* 14, no. 3 (2010): 261–68.

66. Michael W. Vasey and Mark R. Dadds, "An introduction to the developmental psychopathology of anxiety," in *The developmental psychopathology of anxiety*, ed. M. W. Vasey and M. R. Dadds (New York: Oxford University Press, 2001), 3–26.

67. D. Cicchetti and D. J. Cohen, "Perspectives on developmental psychopathology," in *Developmental psychopathology: Vol. I, Theory and methods*, ed. D. Cicchetti and D. J. Cohen (New York: Wiley, 1995), 3–20.

68. J. Kagan, "Temperament and the reaction to unfamiliarity," *Child Development* 68 (1997): 139–43.

69. D. Bell-Dolan, N. M. Reaven, and L. Peterson, "Depression and social functioning: A multidimensional study of the linkages," *Journal of Clinical Child Psychology* 22 (1993): 306–15.

70. N. A. Fox, S. D. Calkins, and M. A. Bell, "Neural plasticity and development in the first year of life: Evidence from cognitive and socio-emotional domains of research," *Development and Psychopathology* 6 (1994): 677–98.

71. Kenneth H. Rubin and Kim B. Burgess, "Social withdrawal and anxiety," in *The developmental psychopathology of anxiety*, ed. M. W. Vasey and M. R. Dadds (New York: Oxford University Press, 2001), 407–34.

72. K. H. Rubin and J. Asendorpf, eds., *Social withdrawal, inhibition, and shyness in childhood* (Hillsdale, NJ: Lawrence Erlbaum, 1993).

73. K. H. Rubin et al., "The transaction between parents' perception of their children's shyness and their parenting styles," *International Journal of Behavioral Development* 23 (1999): 937–58.

74. K. H Rubin and R. S. L. Mills, "Maternal beliefs about adaptive and maladaptive social behaviors in normal, aggressive, and withdrawn preschoolers," *Journal of Abnormal Child Psychology* 18 (1990): 419–35.

75. K. MacDonald and R. D. Parke, "Bridging the gap: Parent-child play interaction and peer interactive competence," *Child Development* 55 (1984): 1265–77.

76. Peter C. Whybrow, "Adaptive styles in the etiology of depression," in *Affective disorders*, ed. Frederic Flach (Markham, Canada: Penguin Books Canada, 1988), 4.

77. J. Bowlby, *Attachment and loss: Vol. II, Separation* (New York: Basic Books, 1973).

78. J. Bowlby, "Developmental psychiatry comes of age," *American Journal of Psychiatry* 145 (1988): 1–10.

79. Ross A. Thompson, "Childhood anxiety disorders from a perspective of emotion regulation and attachment," in *The developmental psychopathology of anxiety*, ed. M. W. Vasey and M. R. Dadds (New York: Oxford University Press, 2001), 160–82.

80. M. Ainsworth et al., *Patterns of attachment* (Hillsdale, NJ: Erlbaum, 1978); J. Bowlby, *Attachment and loss: Vol. I, Attachment*, 2nd ed. (New York: Basic Books, 1982); J. Bowlby, *Attachment and loss: Vol. II* (1973); J. Cassidy and P. R. Shaver, eds., *Handbook of attachment: Theory, research, and clinical applications* (New York: Guilford Press, 1999).

81. M. Mikulincer and P. R. Shaver, *Attachment in adulthood: Structure, dynamics, and change* (New York: Guilford Press, 2007).

82. J. G. Allen, L. Coyne, and J. Huntoon, "Complex posttraumatic stress disorder in women from a psychometric perspective," *Journal of Personality Assessment* 70 (1998): 277–98; K. A. Brennan and P. R. Shaver, "Attachment styles and personality disorders: Their connections to each other and to parental divorce, parental death, and perceptions of parental caregiving," *Journal of Personality* 66 (1998): 835–78.

83. B. E. Vaughn et al., "The quality of maternal secure base scripts predicts children's secure base behaviors at home in three socio-cultural groups," *International Journal of Behavioral Development* 31 (2007): 65–76.

84. J. Bowlby, *Attachment and loss: Vol. II* (1973); M. Main, N. Kaplan, and J. Cassidy, "Security in infancy, childhood, and adulthood: A move to the level of representation," *Monographs of the Society for Research in Child Development* 50 (1985): 66–104.

85. M. Ainsworth et al., *Patterns of attachment* (1978).

86. M. Mikulincer and P. R. Shaver, *Attachment in adulthood: Structure, dynamics, and change* (2007).

87. J. Bowlby, *Attachment and loss: Vol. II* (1973); M. Mikulincer and P. R. Shaver, *Attachment in adulthood: Structure, dynamics, and change* (New York: Guilford Press, 2007); L. E. Park, J. Crocker, and K. D. Mickelson, "Attachment styles and contingencies of self-worth," *Personality and Social Psychology Bulletin* 30 (2004): 1243–54.

88. C. S. Dweck, *Self-theories: Their role in motivation, personality, and development* (Philadelphia: Psychology Press, 1999).

89. Natalie Rusk and Fred Rothbaum, "From stress to learning: Attachment theory meets goal orientation theory," *Review of General Psychology* 14, no. 1 (2010): 31–43.

90. A. Kaplan and M. L. Maehr, "The contributions and prospects of goal orientation theory," *Educational Psychology Review* 19 (2007): 91–110.

91. A. J. Elliott, "A conceptual history of the achievement goal construct," in *Handbook of competence and motivation*, ed. A. J. Elliot and C. S. Dweck (New York:

Guilford, 2005), 52–72; A. J. Elliott, "The hierarchical model of approach-avoidance motivation," *Motivation and Emotion* 30 (2006): 111–16.

92. A. Kaplan and M. L. Maehr, "The contributions and prospects of goal orientation theory" (2007); C. M. Senko, A. M. Durik, and J. M. Harackiewicz, "Historical perspectives and new directions in achievement goal theory: Understanding the effects of mastery and performance-approach goals," in *Handbook of motivation science*, ed. J. Y. Shah and W. Gardner (New York: Guilford Press, 2008), 233–39.

93. C. Darnon et al., "Performance-approach and performance-avoidance goals: When uncertainty makes a difference," *Personality and Social Psychology Bulletin* 33 (2007): 813–27.

94. Victor Raimy, *Misunderstandings of the self* (San Francisco: Jossey-Bass, 1975).

95. M. Ainsworth et al., *Patterns of attachment* (Hillsdale, NJ: Erlbaum, 1978).

96. Jean Piaget, *The language and thought of the child* (London: Routledge & Kegan Paul, 1926).

97. W. Damon and M. Killen, "Peer interaction and the process of change in children's moral reasoning," *Merrill-Palmer Quarterly* 28 (1982): 347–78.

98. B. A. Barrios and S. I. O'Dell, "Fears and anxieties," in *Treatment of childhood disorders*, ed. E. J. Mash and R. A. Barkley (New York: Guilford, 1989).

99. M. Boivin, S. Hymel, and W. M. Bukowski, "The roles of social withdrawal, peer rejection, and victimization by peers in predicting loneliness and depressed mood in childhood," *Development and Psychopathology* 7 (1995): 765–85; S. Hymel, A. Bowker, and E. Woody, "Aggressive versus withdrawn unpopular children: Variations in peer and self-perceptions in multiple domains," *Child Development* 64 (1993): 879–96; S. C. Messer and D. C. Beidel, "Psychosocial correlates of childhood anxiety disorders," *Journal of the American Academy of Child and Adolescent Psychiatry* 33 (1994): 975–83.

100. K. H. Rubin and K. B. Burgess, "Social withdrawal and anxiety" (2001).

101. Carroll E. Izard, *Human emotions* (New York: Plenum Press, 1977).

102. E. Hollander and N. Bakalar, *Coping with social anxiety* (2005).

Chapter 2

1. Signe A. Dayhoff, *Diagonally-parked in a parallel universe: Working through social anxiety* (Placitas, NM: Effectiveness-Plus Publications, 2000).

2. Jerome Kagan, "Historical selection," *Review of General Psychology* 13, no. 1 (2009): 77–88.

3. Ibid., 82.

4. Vera Sonja Maass, *Women's group therapy: Creative challenges and options* (New York: Springer, 2006).

5. Christophe Gernigon, Robin R. Vallacher, Andrzej Novak, and David E. Conroy, "Rethinking approach and avoidance in achievement contexts: The perspective of dynamical systems," *Review of General Psychology* 19, no. 4 (2015): 443–57.

6. T. Hamamura and S. J. Heine, "Approach and avoidance motivation across cultures," in *Handbook of approach and avoidance motivation*, ed. A. J. Elliot (New York: Psychology Press, 2008), 557–70.

7. K. Murayama and A. J. Elliot, "The joint influence of personal achievement goals and classroom goal structures on achievement-relevant outcomes," *Journal of Educational Psychology* 101 (2009): 432–47.

8. D. D. Conroy, M. P. Kaye, and J. D. Coatsworth, "Coaching climates and the destructive effects of mastery-avoidance achievement goals on situational motivation," *Journal of Sport and Exercise Psychology* 28 (2006): 69–92.

9. P. Lockwood, "Could it happen to you? Predicting the impact of downward comparison on the self," *Journal of Personality and Social Psychology* 82 (2002): 343–58.

10. P. Lockwood et al., "To do or not to do: Using positive and negative role models to harness motivation," *Social Cognition* 22 (2004): 422–50.

11. C. S. Dweck, "Motivational processes affecting learning," *American Psychologist* 41 (1986): 1040–48; J. G. Nicholls, "Achievement motivation: Conceptions of ability, subjective experience, task choice, and performance," *Psychological Review* 91 (1984): 328–46.

12. Polly Wells, *Freaking out* (New York: Annick Press, 2013).

13. Emily Ford, with Michael Liebowitz and Linda Wasmer Andrews, *What you must think of me: A firsthand account of one teenager's experience with social anxiety disorder* (New York: Oxford University Press, 2007), 97.

14. Michael A. Tompkins, Katherine Martinez, and Michael Sloan, *My anxious mind: A teen's guide to managing anxiety and panic* (Washington, DC: Magination Press/American Psychological Association, 2010).

15. Chelsea Rae Swiggett, *Rae: My true story of fear, anxiety, and social phobia* (Deerfield Beach, FL: Health Communications, 2010), 39.

16. Laura K. Jones, "The evolving adolescent brain," *Counseling Today* 57, no. 7, Neurocounseling: Bridging brain and behavior (2015): 14–17.

17. Ibid.

18. Joseph Ciarrochi et al., "The development of compulsive internet use and mental health: A four-year study of adolescence," *Developmental Psychology* 52, no. 2 (2016): 272–83.

19. Brittany Gentile, Jean M. Twenge, and Keith W. Campbell, "Birth cohort differences in self-esteem, 1988–2008: A cross-temporal meta-analysis," *Review of General Psychology* 14, no. 3 (2010): 261–68.

20. M. Deutsch and H. B. Gerard, "A study of normative and informational social influences upon individual judgment," *Journal of Abnormal and Social Psychology* 51 (1955): 629–36.

21. Roy F. Baumeister et al., "Does high self-esteem cause better performance, interpersonal success, happiness, or healthier lifestyles?" *Psychological Science in the Public Interest* 4 (2003): 3.

22. S. Lyubomirsky, C. Tkach, and M. R. DiMatteo, "What are the differences between happiness and self-esteem?" *Social Indicators Research* 78 (2006): 363–404.

23. E. Diener and M. Diener, "Cross-cultural correlates of life satisfaction and self-esteem," *Journal of Personality and Social Psychology* 68 (1995): 653–63.

24. T. F. Heatherton and K. D. Vohs, "Interpersonal evaluations following threats to self: Role of self-esteem," *Journal of Personality and Social Psychology* 78 (2000): 725–36.

25. D. B. McFarlin, R. F. Baumeister, and J. Blascovich, "On knowing when to quit: Task failure, self-esteem, advice, and nonproductive persistence," *Journal of Personality* 52 (1984): 138–55.

26. J. P. Hewitt, *The myth of self-esteem: Finding happiness and solving problems in America* (New York: St. Martin's Press, 1998), 3.

27. J. M. Twenge and W. K. Campbell, "Birth cohort differences in the Monitoring the Future dataset and elsewhere: Further evidence for Generation Me," *Perspectives in Psychological Science* 5 (2010): 81–88.

28. J. M. Twenge et al., "Egos inflating over time: A cross-temporal meta-analysis of the narcissistic personality inventory," *Journal of Personality* 76 (2008): 875–902; J. M. Twenge and J. D. Foster, "Birth cohort increases in narcissistic personality traits among American college students, 1982–2000," *Social Psychological and Personality Science* 1 (2010): 99–106.

29. J. K. Bosson et al., "Untangling the links between narcissism and self-esteem: A theoretical and empirical review," *Social and Personality Psychology Compass* 2 (2008): 1415–39.

30. Brittany Gentile, Jean M. Twenge, and Keith W. Campbell, "Birth cohort differences in self-esteem, 1988–2008: A cross-temporal meta-analysis" (2010).

31. College Board, "College-bound seniors 2008," October 17, 2008, http://professionals.collegeboard.com/data-reports-research/sat/eb-seniors-2008.

32. J. M. Twenge and W. K. Campbell, "Birth cohort differences in the Monitoring the Future dataset and elsewhere: Further evidence for Generation Me" (2010).

33. C. J. Sykes, *Dumbing down our kids: Why American children feel good about themselves but can't read, write, or add* (New York: St. Martin's Press Griffin, 1995).

34. J. M. Twenge, *Generation me: Why today's young Americans are more confident, assertive, entitled—and more miserable than ever before* (New York: Free Press, 2006).

35. California State Department of Education, *Toward a state of esteem: The final report of the California Task Force to Promote Self-Esteem and Personal and Social Responsibility* (Sacramento, CA: Author; ERIC Document Reproduction, 1990).

36. W. Robins, H. M. Hendin, and K. H. Trzesniewski, "Measuring global self-esteem: Construct validation of a single-item measure and the Rosenberg Self-Esteem Scale," *Personality and Social Psychology Bulletin* 27 (2001): 151–61.

37. J. M. Twenge, *Generation me: Why today's young Americans are more confident, assertive, entitled—and more miserable than ever before* (2006).

38. Brittany Gentile, Jean M. Twenge, and Keith W. Campbell, "Birth cohort differences in self-esteem, 1988–2008: A cross-temporal meta-analysis" (2010), 267.

39. A. Caspi, G. H. Elder, and D. J. Bem, "Moving away from the world: Life-course patterns of shy children," *Developmental Psychology* 24 (1988): 824–31;

40. K. H. Rubin, "The Waterloo Longitudinal Project: Correlates and conse-quences of social withdrawal from childhood to adolescence," in *Social withdrawal and shyness in childhood*, ed. K. H. Rubin and J. Asendorpf, 291–314 (Hillsdale, NJ: Lawrence Erlbaum, 1993).

41. S. Hymel, A. Bowker, and E. Woody, "Aggressive versus withdrawn unpop-ular children: Variations in peer and self-perceptions in multiple domains," *Child Development* 64 (1993): 879–96; K. H. Rubin, H. S. Hymel, and R. S. L. Mills, "Sociability and social withdrawal in childhood: Stability and outcomes," *Journal of Personality* 57 (1989): 237–55.

42. K. H. Rubin et al., "The Waterloo Longitudinal Project: Predicting adoles-cent internalizing and externalizing problems from early and mid-childhood," *Development and Psychopathology* 7 (1995): 751–64.

43. C. R. Blease, "Too many 'friends,' too few 'likes'? Evolutionary psychology and 'Facebook depression,'" *Review of General Psychology* 19, no. 1 (2015): 1–13.

44. Erving Goffman, *The presentation of self in every day life* (London: Penguin, 1990).

45. M. H. Selfhout et al., "Different types of Internet use, depression, and social anxiety: The role of perceived friendship quality," *Journal of Adolescence* 32 (2009): 819–33; E. Kross et al., "Facebook use predicts declines in subjective well-being in young adults," *PLoS ONE* 8 (2013).

46. Larry Rosen, "The power of 'Like' on Facebook," *National Psychologist* 24, no. 2 (2015): 20.

47. N. Hampton et al., "Why most Facebook users get more than they give," Pew Internet and American Life Project, February 3, 2012, http://www.pewinternet .org/~/media/Files/Reports/2012/PIP_Facebook%20users_2.3.12.pdf.

48. Willie J., *Dancing on the dumpster* (Jesus Hands, 2014).

49. Albert Ellis, "Rational-emotive psychotherapy," in *Counseling and psycho-therapy*, by D. Arbuckle (New York: McGraw-Hill, 1967), 84.

Chapter 3

1. W. R. Crozier, "Blushing and the exposed self: Darwin revisited," *Journal for the Theory of Social Behavior* 31 (2001): 61–72.

2. Barbara Markway and Gregory Markway, *Painfully shy: How to overcome social anxiety and reclaim your life* (New York: Thomas Dunne Books / St. Martin's Press, 2001).

3. Isabel Thielman and Benjamin E. Hilbig, "Trust: An integrative review from a person-situation perspective," *Review of General Psychology* 19, no. 3 (2015): 249–77.

4. MeowLan Evelyn Chan, "Why did you hurt me? Victim's interpersonal betrayal attribution and trust implications," *Review of General Psychology* 13, no. 3 (2009): 262–74.

5. J. J. Koehler and A. D. Gershoff, "Betrayal aversion: When agents of pro-tection become agents of harm," *Organizational Behavior and Human Decision*

Processes 90 (2003): 244–61; I. Bohnet and R. Zeckhauser, "Trust, risk, and betrayal," *Journal of Economic Behavior & Organization* 55 (2004): 467–84.

6. MeowLan Evelyn Chan, " 'Why did you hurt me?' Victim's interpersonal betrayal attribution and trust implications" (2009); A. R. Elangovan, W. Auer-Rizzi, and E. Szabo, "Why don't I trust you now? An attributional approach to erosion of trust," *Journal of Managerial Psychology* 22 (2007): 4–24.

7. Lynne Henderson, *The compassionate mind guide to building social confidence: Using compassion-focused therapy to overcome shyness & social anxiety* (Oakland, CA: New Harbinger Publications, 2010).

8. Signe A. Dayhoff, *Diagonally-parked in a parallel universe: Working through social anxiety* (Placitas, NM: Effectiveness-Plus Publications, 2000).

9. Ludwig Binswanger, *Grundformen und Erkenntnis menschlichen Daseins* [Foundations and understanding of the human existence] (Munich, Ger.: Ernst Reinhardt Verlag, 1962).

10. Murray B. Stein and John R. Walker, *Triumph over shyness: Conquering shyness and social anxiety* (New York: McGraw-Hill, 2002).

11. Ibid.

12. Vera Sonja Maass, *Coping with control and manipulation: Making the difference between being a target and becoming a victim* (Santa Barbara, CA: ABC-CLIO/Praeger, 2010).

13. Roy F. Baumeister and M. R. Leary, "The need to belong: Desire for interpersonal attachment as a fundamental human motivation," *Psychological Bulletin* 117 (1995): 497–529.

14. Justin H. Park and Florian van Leeuwen, "The asymmetric behavioral homeostasis hypothesis: Unidirectional flexibility of fundamental motivational processes," *Review of General Psychology* 18, no. 2 (2014): 89–100.

15. M. R. Leary, "Sociometer theory and the pursuit of relational value: Getting to the root of self-esteem," *European Review of Social Psychology* 16 (2005): 75–111.

16. K. D. Williams, "Ostracism," *Annual Review of Psychology* 58 (2007): 425–52.

17. J. K. Maner et al., "Does social exclusion motivate interpersonal reconnection? Resolving the 'porcupine problem,' " *Journal of Personality and Social Psychology* 92 (2007): 42–55.

18. J. M. Twenge et al., "Social exclusion decreases prosocial behavior," *Journal of Personality and Social Psychology* 92 (2007): 56–66.

19. N. I. Eisenberger, M. D. Lieberman, and K. D. Williams, "Does rejection hurt? An fMRI study of social exclusion," *Science* 302 (2003): 290–92; G. MacDonald and M. R. Leary, "Why does social exclusion hurt? The relationship between social and physical pain," *Psychological Bulletin* 131 (2005): 202–23.

20. Roni Caryn Rabin, "More overdose deaths from anxiety drugs," *New York Times* (Mind), February 25, 2016, http://well.blogs.nytimes.com/2016/02/25/.

21. *Diagnostic and statistical manual of mental disorders, fifth edition* (DSM-5) (Washington, DC: American Psychiatric Association, 2013).

22. K. R. Blankstein, C. H. Lumley, and A. Crawford, "Perfectionism, hopelessness, and suicide ideation: Revisions to diathesis-stress and specific vulnerability

models," *Journal of Rational-Emotive & Cognitive Behavior Therapy* 25 (2007): 279–319.

23. Gordon L. Flett, Paul L. Hewitt, and Martin J. Heisel, "The destructiveness of perfectionism revisited: Implications for the assessment of suicide risk and the prevention of suicide," *Review of General Psychology* 18, no. 3 (2014): 156–72.

24. Helen Zook, "Perfectionism is a total confidence killer," *Cosmopolitan*, June 2016, p. 154.

25. Asher Pacht, "Reflections on perfection," *American Psychologist* 39 (1984): 386–90; B. Sorotzkin, "The quest for perfection: Avoiding guilt or avoiding shame?" *Psychotherapy* 22 (1985): 564–71.

26. P. L. Hewitt and G. L. Flett, "Perfectionism in the self and social contexts: Conceptualization, assessment, and association with psychopathology," *Journal of Personality and Social Psychology* 60 (1991): 456–70.

27. G. L. Flett et al., "Psychological distress and the frequency of perfectionistic thinking," *Journal of Personality and Social Psychology* 75 (1998): 1363–81.

28. D. M. Dunkley et al., "The relation between perfectionism and distress: Hassles, coping, and perceived social support as mediators and moderators," *Journal of Counseling Psychology* 47 (2000): 437–53; D. M. Dunkley, D. Zuroff, and K. Blankstein, "Self-critical perfectionism and daily affect: Dispositional and situational influences on stress and coping," *Journal of Personality and Social Psychology* 84 (2003): 234–52.

29. H. M. Roxborough et al., "Perfectionistic self-presentation, socially prescribed perfectionism, and suicide in youth: A test of the perfectionism social disconnection model," *Suicide and Life-Threatening Behavior* 42 (2012): 217–33.

30. P. M. DiBartolo, C. Y. Li, and R. O. Frost, "How do the dimensions of perfectionism relate to mental health?" *Cognitive Therapy and Research* 32 (2008): 401–17; K. Y. Kawamura and R. O. Frost, "Self-concealment as a mediator in the relationship between perfectionism and psychological distress," *Cognitive Therapy and Research* 28 (2004): 183–91.

31. G. L. Flett and P. L. Hewitt, "Disguised distress in children and adolescents 'flying under the radar': Why psychological problems are underestimated and how schools must respond," *Canadian Journal of School Psychology* 28 (2013): 12–27; P. L. Hewitt et al., "The interpersonal expression of perfectionism: Perfectionistic self-presentation and psychological distress," *Journal of Personality and Social Psychology* 84 (2003): 1303–25.

32. D. D. Burns, "The perfectionist's script for self-defeat," *Psychology Today* 3 (November 1980): 4–52.

33. S. J. Blatt and D. C. Zuroff, "Perfectionism in the therapeutic process," in *Perfectionism: Theory, research, and treatment*, ed. G. L. Flett and P. L. Hewitt (Washington, DC: American Psychological Association, 2002), 393–406.

34. C. A. Essau et al., "Prevention of anxiety symptoms in children: Results from a universal school-based trial," *Behavior Therapy* 43 (2012): 450–64.

35. R. Nobel, K. Manassis, and P. Wilansky-Traynor, "The role of perfectionism in relation to an intervention to reduce anxious and depressive symptoms in children," *Journal of Rational-Emotive & Cognitive-Behavior Therapy* 30 (2012): 77–90.

36. J. A. Shepperd, J. A. Ouellette, and J. K. Fernandez, "Abandoning unrealistic optimism: Performance estimates and the temporal proximity of self-related feedback," *Journal of Personality and Social Psychology* 70 (1996): 844–55.

37. L. J. Sanna and S. Meier, "Looking for clouds in a silver lining: Self-esteem, mental simulation, and temporal confidence changes," *Journal of Research in Personality* 34 (2000): 236–51; J. A. Shepperd, J. A. Ouellette, and J. K. Fernandez, "Abandoning unrealistic optimism: Performance estimates and the temporal proximity of self-related feedback" (1996).

38. J. D. Campbell and L. F. Lavallee, "Who am I? The role of self-concept confusion in understanding the behavior of people with low self-esteem," in *Self-esteem: The puzzle of low self-regard*, ed. R. F. Baumeister (New York: Plenum Press, 1993), 3–20.

39. R. Blaine and J. Crocker, "Self-esteem and self-serving biases in reactions to positive and negative events: An integrative review," in *Self-esteem: The puzzle of low self-regard*, ed. R. F. Baumeister (New York: Plenum Press, 1993), 55–85.

40. Patrick Carroll, Kate Sweeny, and James A. Shepperd, "Forsaking optimism," *Review of General Psychology* 10, no. 1 (2006): 56–73.

41. L. J. Sanna, "Mental simulations, affect, and subjective confidence: Time is everything," *Psychological Science* 10 (1999): 339–45; L. J. Sanna and S. Meier, "Looking for clouds in a silver lining: Self-esteem, mental simulation, and temporal confidence changes" (2000).

42. Bernard Guerin, "Individuals as social relationships: 18 ways that acting alone can be thought of as social behavior," *Review of General Psychology* 5, no. 4 (2001): 406–28.

43. D. B. Connor, D. K. Knight, and D. R. Cross, "Mothers' and fathers' scaffolding of their 2-year-olds during problem-solving and literacy interactions," *British Journal of Developmental Psychology* 15 (1997): 323–38; S. H. Landry et al., "Effects of maternal scaffolding during joint toy play with preterm and full-term infants," *Merrill-Palmer Quarterly* 4, no. 2 (1996): 177–99.

44. B. Guerin, "Individuals as social relationships: 18 ways that acting alone can be thought of as social behavior" (2001).

45. E. E. Sampson, *Celebrating the other: A dialogic account of human nature* (Boulder, CO: Westview Press, 1993).

46. I. E. Josephs and J. Valsiner, "How does autodialogue work? Miracles of meaning maintenance and circumvention strategies," *Social Psychology Quarterly* 61 (1998): 68–83; E. E. Sampson, *Celebrating the other: A dialogic account of human nature* (1993); B. Yngvesson and M. A. Mahoney, "'As one should, ought and wants to be': Belonging and authenticity in identity narratives," *Theory, Culture & Society* 17 (2000): 77–110.

Chapter 4

1. J. H. Fowler and N. A Christakis, "Dynamic spread of happiness in a large social network: Longitudinal analysis over 20 years in the Framingham Heart Study," *British Medical Journal* (2008), advance online publication.

2. J. Jetten et al., "The social cure," *Scientific American Mind* 20 (2009): 26–33.

3. R. A. Cummins, "The domains of life satisfaction: An attempt to order chaos," in *Citation classics from social indicators research*, ed. A. C. Michalos (Dordrecht, Neth.: Springer, 2005), 559–84.

4. J. Jetten et al., "The social cure" (2009), 29, 33.

5. J. K. Kiecolt-Glaser et al., "Emotions, morbidity, and mortality: New perspectives from psychoneuroimmunology," *Annual Review of Psychology* 53 (2002): 83–107.

6. Percy Black, "Thrust to wholeness: The nature of self-protection," *Review of General Psychology* 10, no. 3 (2006): 191–209; M. McPherson, L. Smith-Lovin, and M. E. Brashears, "Social isolation in America: Changes in core discussion networks over two decades," *American Sociological Review* 71 (2006): 353–75; R. D. Putnam, "Bowling alone: America's declining social capital," *Journal of Democracy* 6 (1995): 65–78.

7. R. D. Putnam, *Bowling alone: The collapse and revival of American community* (New York: Simon & Schuster, 2000).

8. C. S. Fisher, "The 2004 GSS finding of shrunken social networks: An artifact?" *American Sociological Review* 74 (2009): 657–69.

9. K. Wilber, *Integral psychology* (Boston: Shambhala, 2000).

10. R. D. Putnam, *Bowling alone: The collapse and revival of American community* (2000); Roger Walsh, "Lifestyle and Mental Health," *American Psychologist* 66, no. 7 (2011): 579–92.

11. James Verini, "Will success spoil MySpace?" *Vanity Fair*, March 2006, p. 243.

12. Ibid., p. 238.

13. Kim Mickenberg, "Headhunters for the heart: What do personal matchmakers have over your PC?" *Psychology Today*, May/June 2008, p. 32.

14. Laurie Meyers, "Fertile grounds for bullying," *Counseling Today* 58, no. 11 (May 2016): 26–35.

15. Ibid.

16. Janet Froeschle Hicks, "Empowering youth victimized by cyberbullying," *Counseling Today* 57, no. 9 (March 2015): 48–53.

17. Laurie Meyers, "Coming to terms with technology," *Counseling Today* 58, no. 1 (July 2015): 22–27.

18. Doug Shadel and David Dudley, "Are you real?" *AARP The Magazine* 58, no. 4C (2015), pp. 40–46, 65–66, 70.

19. L. Meyers, "Coming to terms with technology" (2015).

20. artoflove@evolvingwisdom.com (2016).

21. D. Shadel and D. Dudley, "Are you real?" (2015).

22. Sara Polanchek and Sidney Shaw, "Ten intimate relationship research findings every counselor should know," *Counseling Today* 58, no. 6 (December 2015): 36.

23. Laurie Meyers, "Confronting loneliness in an age of constant connection," *Counseling Today* 57, no. 7 (January 2015): 24–31.

24. "College students text a lot," *National Psychologist*, May/June 2015, p. 23.

25. L. Meyers, "Confronting loneliness in an age of constant connection" (2015).

Chapter 5

1. Roni Caryn Rabin, "More overdose deaths from anxiety drugs," *New York Times* (Mind), February 25, 2016, http://well.blogs.nytimes.com/2016/02/25/.

2. John R. Marshall, *Social phobia from shyness to stage fright* (New York: Basic Books, 1994).

3. S. M. Turner, D. C. Beidel, and K. T. Larkin, "Situational determinants of social anxiety in clinic and nonclinic samples: Physiological and cognitive correlates," *Journal of Consulting and Clinical Psychology* 54 (1986): 523–27.

4. Brian Mustanski, Rebecca Andrews, and Jae A. Puckett, "The effects of cumulative victimization on mental health among lesbian, gay, bisexual, and transgender adolescents and young adults," *American Journal of Public Health* 106, no. 3 (March 2016): 527–33.

5. L. Festinger, "A theory of social comparison processes," *Human Relations* 7 (1954): 117–40.

6. H. P. Buunk and F. X. Gibbons, "Toward an enlightenment in social comparison theory: Moving beyond classic and Renaissance approaches," in *Handbook of social comparison: Theory and research*, ed. J. Suls and L. Wheeler (New York: Kluwer Academic, 2000), 487–99.

7. J. V. Wood, "Theory and research concerning social comparisons of personal attributes," *Psychological Bulletin* 106 (1989): 231–48.

8. T. A. Wills, "Similarity and self-esteem in downward comparison," in *Social comparison: Contemporary theory and research*, ed. J. M. Suls and T. A. Wills (Hillsdale, NJ: Erlbaum, 1991), 51–78.

9. K. S. Beauregard and D. Dunning, "Turning up the contrast: Self-enhancement motives prompt egocentric contrast effects in social judgments," *Journal of Personality and Social Psychology* 74 (1998): 606–21.

10. B. Major, M. Testa, and W. H. Blysma, "Responses to upward and downward social comparisons: The impact of esteem-relevance perceived control," in *Social comparison: Contemporary theory and research*, ed. J. M. Suls and T. A. Wills (Hillsdale, NJ: Erlbaum, 1991), 237–60; R. H. Smith, "Assimilative and contrastive emotional reactions to upward and downward social comparisons," in *Handbook of social comparison: Theory and research*, ed. J. Suls and L. Wheeler (New York: Kluwer Academic, 2000), 48–67.

11. T. A. Wills, "Similarity and self-esteem in downward comparison" (1991).

12. S. E. Taylor and M. Lobel, "Social comparison activity under threat: Downward evaluation and upward contacts," *Psychological Review* 96 (1989): 569–75; H. Tennen, T. E. McKee, and G. Affleck, "Social comparison processes in health and illness," in *Handbook of social comparison: Theory and research*, ed. J. Suls and L. Wheeler (New York: Kluwer Academic, 2000), 443–83; J. V. Wood, "Theory and research concerning social comparisons of personal attributes" (1989).

13. R. Folger, "Reformulating the preconditions of resentment: A referent cognitions model," in *Social comparison, social justice, and relative deprivation: Theoretical,*

empirical, and policy perspectives, ed. J. C. Masters and W. P. Smith (Hillsdale, NJ: Erlbaum, 2000), 183–215.

14. R. H. Smith, "Assimilative and contrastive emotional reactions to upward and downward social comparisons" (2000).

15. P. Salovey, "Social comparison processes in envy and jealousy," in *Social comparison: Contemporary theory and research*, ed. J. M. Suls and T. A. Wills (Hillsdale, NJ: Erlbaum, 1991), 261–85.

16. P. Salovey and J. Rodin, "Some antecedents and consequences of social comparison jealousy," *Journal of Personality and Social Psychology* 47 (1984): 780–92.

Chapter 6

1. Signe A. Dayhoff, *Diagonally-parked in a parallel universe: Working through social anxiety* (Placitas, NM: Effectiveness-Plus Publications, 2000).

2. John R. Marshall, *Social phobia from shyness to stage fright* (New York: Basic Books, 1994).

3. Ibid.

4. Rachelle Blidner, "Scientists are studying if MDMA, ingredient in Ecstasy, can treat social anxiety in adults with autism," *New York Daily News*, March 26, 2015.

5. Roni Caryn Rabin, "More overdose deaths from anxiety drugs," *New York Times* (Mind), February 25, 2016.

6. David L. Charney, "Depression and agoraphobia—chicken or the egg?" in *Phobia: A comprehensive summary of modern treatments*, ed. Robert L. DuPont (New York: Brunner/Mazel, 1982), 126–39.

7. Ibid.

8. Charlotte Marker Zitrin, "Combined psychological and pharmaceutical approach to the treatment of phobias," in *Phobia: A comprehensive summary of modern treatments*, ed. Robert L. DuPont (New York: Brunner/Mazel, 1982), 57–76.

9. Murray B. Stein and John R. Walker, *Triumph over shyness: Conquering shyness and social anxiety* (New York: McGraw-Hill, 2002).

10. Rebecca Rialon Berry, "Advances in Cognitive-Behavioral Therapy for youth with anxiety disorders," *Current Psychiatry Reviews* 12, no. 1 (2016): 29–36.

11. M. B. Stein and J. R. Walker, *Triumph over shyness: Conquering shyness and social anxiety* (2002).

12. Roger Walsh, "Lifestyle and mental health," *American Psychologist* 66, no. 7 (2011): 579–92.

13. C. I. Hovland, I. L. Janis, and H. H. Kelley, *Communication and persuasion: Psychological studies of opinion change* (New Haven, CT: Yale University Press, 1953).

14. Natascha de Hoog, Wolfgang Stroebe, and John B. F. de Wit, "The impact of vulnerability to and severity of a health risk on processing and acceptance of fear-arousing communications: A meta-analysis," *Review of General Psychology* 11, no. 3 (2007): 258–85.

15. H. Leventhal, "Findings and theory in the study of fear communications," in *Advances in experimental social psychology*, vol. 5, ed. L. Berkowitz (San Diego: Academic Press, 1970), 119–86.

16. R. W. Rogers, "Cognitive and physiological processes in fear appeals and attitude change: A revised theory of protection motivation," in *Social psychophysiology: A sourcebook*, ed. J. T. Cacioppo and R. E. Petty (New York: Guilford Press, 1983), 153–76.

17. K. Witte, "Putting the fear back into fear appeals: The extended parallel process model," *Communication Monographs* 59 (1992): 329–49.

18. Ibid.

Chapter 7

1. *Webster's ninth collegiate dictionary* (Springfield, MA: Merriam-Webster, 1983), s.v. "challenge."

2. Vera S. Maass and Margery A. Neely, *Counseling single parents: A cognitive-behavioral approach* (New York: Springer, 2000), 18.

3. Vera S. Maass, *The Cinderella test: Would you really want the shoe to fit?* (Santa Barbara, CA: ABC-CLIO/Praeger, 2009), 91.

4. G. L. Clore and K. Gasper, "Feeling is believing: Some affective influences on belief," in *Emotions and belief: How feelings influence thoughts*, ed. N. H. Frijda, A. S. R. Manstead, and S. Bem (Cambridge, UK: Cambridge University Press, 2000), 10–44.

5. G. J. Gorn, M. T. Pham, and L. Y. Sin, "When arousal influences ad evaluation and valence does not (and vice versa)," *Journal of Consumer Psychology* 11 (2001): 43–55.

6. *Webster's ninth collegiate dictionary* (1983), s.v. "belief."

7. I. Ajzen and M. Fishbein, "A Bayesian analysis of attribution processes," *Psychological Bulletin* 82 (1975): 261–77; A. H. Eagly and S. Chaiken, *The psychology of attitudes* (Orlando: Harcourt Brace Jovanovich, 1993).

8. Matthew Tyler Boden and Howard Berenbaum, "The bidirectional relations between affect and belief," *Review of General Psychology* 14, no. 3 (2010): 227–39.

9. I. Ajzen and M. Fishbein, "A Bayesian analysis of attribution processes" (1975).

10. R. S. Wyer and D. Albarracin, "The origins and structure of beliefs and goals," in *Handbook of attitudes*, ed. D. Albarracin, B. T. Johnson, and M. P. Zanna (Hillsdale, NJ: Erlbaum, 2005), 273–322.

11. P. S. Appelbaum, P. C. Robbins, and R. Vesselinov, "Persistence and stability of delusions over time," *Comprehensive Psychiatry* 45 (2004): 317–24; M. Inzlicht et al., "Neural markers of religious conviction," *Psychological Science* 20 (2009): 385–92; H. M. Sharp et al., "Delusional phenomenology—Dimensions of change," *Behavior Research and Therapy* 34 (1996): 123–42; J. S. Strauss, "Hallucinations and delusions as points on continua function: Rating scale evidence," *Archives of General Psychiatry* 21 (1969): 581–86.

12. M. T. Boden and H. Berenbaum, "The bidirectional relations between affect and belief" (2010); D. T. Gilbert, "How mental systems believe," *American Psychologist* 46 (1991): 107–19.

13. H. M. Sharp et al., "Delusional phenomenology—Dimensions of change" (1996).

14. M. Inzlicht et al., "Neural markers of religious conviction" (2009).

15. M. T. Boden and H. Berenbaum, "The bidirectional relations between affect and belief" (2010).

16. D. W. Moore, "Three of four Americans believe in paranormal," June 16, 2005, http://home.sandiego.edu/~baber/logic/gallup.html.

17. M. T. Boden and J. Gross, "An emotion regulation perspective on belief change," in *Oxford handbook of cognitive psychology*, ed. D. Reisberg (Oxford, UK: Oxford University Press, 2013).

18. C. S. Dweck, *Self-theories: Their role in motivation, personality, and development* (Philadelphia: Psychology Press, 1999); A. Kaplan and M. L. Maehr, "The contributions and prospects of goal orientation theory," *Educational Psychology Review* 19 (2007): 91–110.

19. Vera Sonja Maass, *Lifestyle changes: A clinician's guide to common events, challenges, and options* (New York: Routledge / Taylor & Francis, 2008).

20. E. J. Johnson and A. Tversky, "Affect, generalization, and the perception of risk," *Journal of Personality and Social Psychology* 45 (1983): 20–31; W. F. Wright and G. H. Bower, "Mood effects on subjective-probability assessment," *Organizational Behavior and Human Decision Processes* 52 (1992): 276–91.

21. J. S. Lerner and D. Keltner, "Fear, anger, and risk," *Journal of Personality and Social Psychology* 81 (2001): 146–59.

22. N. Schwarz, "Feelings as information: Informational and motivational functions of affective states," in *The handbook of motivation and cognition: Foundations of social behavior*, vol. 2, ed. E. T. Higgins and R. M Sorrentino (New York: Guilford Press, 1990), 527–61.

23. D. Kahneman and A. Tversky, "The psychology of preferences," *Scientific American* 246 (1982): 160–73.

24. Roy F. Baumeister, Ellen Bratlavsky, and Catrin Finkenauer, "Bad is stronger than good," *Review of General Psychology* 5, no. 4 (2001): 323–70.

25. K. M. Sheldon, M. R. Ryan, and H. T. Reis, "What makes for a good day? Competence and autonomy in the day and in the person," *Personality and Social Psychology Bulletin* 22 (1996): 1270–79.

26. V. S. Maass, *Lifestyle changes: A clinician's guide to common events, challenges, and options* (2008).

27. Isabel Thielman and Benjamin E. Hilbig, "Trust: An integrative review from a person-situation perspective," *Review of General Psychology* 19, no. 3 (2015): 249–77.

28. M. Sutter and M. G. Kocher, "Trust and trustworthiness across different age groups," *Games and Economic Behavior* 59 (2007): 364–82.

29. Peter C. Whybrow, "Adaptive styles in the etiology of depression," in *Affective disorders*, ed. Frederic Flach (Markham, Canada: Penguin Books Canada, 1988), 1–18.

30. R. C. Mayer, J. H. Davis, and F. D. Schoorman, "An integrative model of organizational trust," *Academy of Management Review* 20 (1995): 709–34.

31. A. M. Evans and J. I. Krueger, "The psychology (and economics) of trust," *Social and Personality Psychology Compass* 3 (2009): 1003–17.

32. J. W. Pennebaker, *Opening up: The healing power of expressing emotions* (New York: Guilford Press, 1990); E. Zech, B. Rime, and F. Nils, "Social sharing of emotions, emotional recovery, and interpersonal aspects," in *The regulation of emotion*, ed. P. Phillippot and R. S. Feldman (Mahwah, NJ: Lawrence Erlbaum, 2004), 157–85.

33. I. Bohnet and R. Zeckhauser, "Trust, risk, and betrayal," *Journal of Economic Behavior & Organization* 55 (2004): 467–84; T. K. Das and B.-S. Teng, "The risk-based view of trust: A conceptual framework," *Journal of Business and Psychology* 19 (2004): 85–116; A. M. Evans and J. I. Krueger, "Elements of trust: Risk and perspective-taking," *Journal of Experimental Social Psychology* 47 (2011): 171–77; E. Ullmann-Margalit, "Trust, distrust, and in between," in *Distrust*, ed. R. Hardin (New York: Russell Sage Foundation, 2004), 60–82.

34. L. Glöckner and B. E. Hilbig, "Risk is relative: Risk aversion yields cooperation rather than defection in cooperation-friendly environments," *Psychonomic Bulletin & Review* 19 (2012): 546–53.

35. J. L. Glanville and P. Paxton, "How do we learn to trust? A confirmatory tetrad analysis of the sources of generalized trust," *Social Psychology Quarterly* 70 (2007): 230–42; J. Tullberg, "Trust—the importance of trustfulness versus trustworthiness," *Journal of Socio-Economics* 37 (2008): 2059–71; P. A. M. Van Lange, A. A. E. Vinkhuyzen, and D. Posthuma, "Genetic influences are virtually absent for trust," *PLoS ONE* 9 (2014); M. Yu, M. Saleem, and C. Gonzalez, "Developing trust: First impressions and experience," *Journal of Economic Psychology* 43 (2014): 16–29.

36. G. E. Bolton, E. Katok, and A. Ockenfels, "How effective are electronic reputation mechanisms? An experimental investigation," *Management Science* 50 (2004): 1587–1602.

37. A. R. Landrum, B. S. J. Eaves Jr., and P. Shafto, "Learning to trust and trusting to learn: A theoretical framework," *Trends in Cognitive Sciences* 19 (2015): 109–11.

38. Victor Raimy, *Misunderstandings of the self* (San Francisco: Jossey-Bass, 1975), 109.

39. Ibid.

40. Ibid., 115.

41. S. A. Shields, "The politics of emotion in every day life: 'Appropriate' emotion and claims of identity," *Review of General Psychology* 9 (2005): 9.

42. Vera Sonja Maass, "Images of masculinity as predictors of men's romantic and sexual relationships," in *Men in relationships*, ed. Victoria Hilkevitch Bedford and Barbara Formaniak Turner (New York: Springer, 2006), 51–78.

43. R. J. Eidelson and J. I. Eidelson, "Dangerous ideas: Five beliefs that propel groups toward conflict," *American Psychologist* 58 (2003): 182–92.

44. Benita Jackson, Laura D. Kuhzansky, and Rosalind J. Wright, "Linking perceived unfairness to physical health: The perceived unfairness model," *Review of General Psychology* 10, no. 1 (2006): 21–40.

45. R. C. Colligan et al., "CAVEing the MMPI for an optimism-pessimism scale: Seligman's contributional model and the assessment of explanatory style," *Journal of Clinical Psychology* 50 (1994): 71–95.

46. J. Tomaka and J. Blascovich, "Effect of justice beliefs on cognitive appraisal of and subjective physiological, and behavioral responses to potential stress," *Journal of Personality and Social Psychology* 67 (1994): 732–40.

47. P. A. Thoits, "Stressors and problem-solving: The individual as psychological activist," *Journal of Health and Social Behavior* 35 (June 1994): 143–59; B. L. Fredrickson, "Cultivating positive emotions to optimize health and well-being," *Prevention & Treatment* 3 (2000).

48. A. J. Elliot and K. M. Sheldon, "Avoidance personal goals and the personality-illness relationship," *Journal of Personality and Social Psychology* 75 (1998): 1282–99.

49. M. D. Foster and K. Matheson, "Perceiving and feeling personal discrimination: Motivation or inhibition for collective action?" *Group Processes and Intergroup Relations* 1 (1998): 165–74.

50. C. L. Hafer, "Do innocent victims threaten the belief in a just world? Evidence from a modified Stroop task," *Journal of Personality and Social Psychology* 79 (2000): 165–73.

Chapter 8

1. Lynne Henderson, *The compassionate mind guide to building social confidence: Using compassion-focused therapy to overcome shyness & social anxiety* (Oakland, CA: New Harbinger Publications, 2010).

2. A. K. Sen, "Rational behavior," in *The new Palgrave: Utility and probability*, ed. J. Eatwell (New York: Norton, 1990), 210.

3. J. B. Cohen, M. T. Pham, and E. B. Andrade, "The nature and role of affect in consumer judgment and decision making," in *Handbook of consumer psychology*, ed. C. P. Haugtvedt, P. M Herr, and F. R. Kardes (Mahwah, NJ: Erlbaum, 2007).

4. C. K. Hsee and Y. Rottenstreich, "Music, pandas, and muggers: On the affective psychology of value," *Journal of Experimental Psychology-General* 133 (2004): 23–30.

5. G. Loewenstein et al., "Risk as feelings," *Psychological Bulletin* 127 (2001): 267–86; Y. Rottenstreich and C. K. Hsee, "Money, kisses, and electric shocks: On the affective psychology of risk," *Psychological Science* 12 (2001): 185–90.

6. Michael Tuan Pham, "Emotion and rationality: A critical review and interpretation of empirical evidence," *Preview of General Psychology* 11, no. 2 (2007): 163.

7. Ibid., 157.

8. M. Williams et al., *The mindful way through depression: Freeing yourself from chronic unhappiness* (New York: Guilford Press, 2007).

9. Steve Flowers, *The mindful path through shyness: How mindfulness and compassion can help free you from social anxiety, fear & avoidance* (Oakland, CA: New Harbinger Publications, 2009).

10. Vera Sonja Maass, *Lifestyle changes: A clinician's guide to common events, challenges, and options* (New York: Routledge / Taylor & Francis, 2008).

11. C. Erdley et al., "The relations among children's social goals, implicit personality theories and response to social failure," *Developmental Psychology* 33 (1997): 263–72.

12. L. Kammrath and C. S. Dweck, "Voicing conflict: Preferred conflict strategies among incremental and entity theorists," *Personality and Social Psychology Bulletin* 32 (2006): 1497–1508.

13. Fred Rothbaum, Beth Morling, and Natalie Rusk, "How goals and beliefs lead people into and out of depression," *Preview of General Psychology* 13, no. 4 (2009): 302–14.

14. H. Grant and C. S. Dweck, "Clarifying achievement goals and their impact," *Journal of Personality and Social Psychology* 85 (2003): 541–53.

15. M. Mikulincer and P. R. Shaver, *Attachment in adulthood: Structure, dynamics, and change* (New York: Guilford Press, 2007).

16. R. M. Wenzlaff and D. M. Wegner, "Thought suppression," *Annual Review of Psychology* 51 (2000): 59–91.

17. M. Mikulincer, T. Dolev, and P. R. Shaver, "Attachment-related strategies during thought-suppression: Ironic rebounds and vulnerable self-representations," *Journal of Personality and Social Psychology* 87 (2004): 940.

18. Ibid., 952.

19. H. Grant and C. S. Dweck, "Clarifying achievement goals and their impact" (2003).

20. Ibid.; M. Mikulincer and P. R. Shaver, *Attachment in adulthood: Structure, dynamics, and change* (2007).

21. L. E. Park, J. Crocker, and K. D. Vohs, "Contingencies of self-worth and self-validation goals: Implications for close relationships," in *Self and relationships: Connecting intrapersonal and interpersonal processes*, ed. K. D. Vohs and E. J. Finkel (New York: Guilford Press, 2006), 84–103.

22. J. Crocker and C. T. Wolfe, "Contingencies of self-worth," *Psychological Review* 108 (2001): 593–623.

23. L. Y. Abramson, G. I. Metalsky, and L. B. Alloy, "Hopelessness depression: A theory-based subtype of depression," *Psychological Review* 96 (1989): 358–72; A. T. Beck, "Cognitive therapy: A 30-year retrospective," *American Psychologist* 46 (1991): 368–75; G. J. Haeffel et al., "Hopelessness theory and the approach system: Cognitive vulnerability predicts decreases in goal-directed behavior," *Cognitive Therapy and Research* 32 (2008): 281–90.

24. L. Y. Abramson et al., "Cognitive vulnerability-stress models of depression in a self-regulatory and psychological context," in *Handbook of depression*, ed. I. H. Gotlib and C. L. Hammen (New York: Guilford Press, 2002), 268–94; L. B. Alloy et al., "Prospective incidence of first onsets and recurrences of depression in individuals at high and low cognitive risk for depression," *Journal of Abnormal Psychology* 115 (2006): 145–56.

25. A. T. Beck, *Depression: Clinical, experimental, and theoretical aspects* (New York: Harper & Row, 1967); A. T. Beck, "Cognitive models of depression," *Journal of Cognitive Psychotherapy: An International Quarterly* 1 (1987): 5–37.

26. C. S. Dweck, *Self-theories: Their role in motivation, personality, and development* (Philadelphia: Psychology Press, 1999); A. Kaplan and M. L. Maehr, "The contributions and prospects of goal orientation theory," *Educational Psychology Review* 19 (2007): 91–110.

27. J. R. Z. Abela, R. P. Auerbach, and M. E. P. Seligman, "Dispositional pessimism across the lifespan," in *Risk factors in depression*, ed. K. S. Dobson and D. J. A. Dozois (Oxford, UK: Elsevier, 2008), 195–220; C. Peterson and N. Park, "Explanatory style and emotion regulation," in *Handbook of emotion regulation*, ed. J. J. Gross (New York: Guilford Press, 2007), 159–79.

28. F. Rothbaum, B. Morling, and N. Rusk, "How goals and beliefs lead people into and out of depression" (2009).

29. A. Kaplan and M. L. Maehr, "The contributions and prospects of goal orientation theory" (2007); H. A. McGregor and A. J. Elliot, "Achievement goals as predictors of achievement-relevant processes prior to task engagement," *Journal of Educational Psychology* 94 (2002): 381–95.

30. M. Ainsworth et al., *Patterns of attachment: A psychological study of the Strange Situation* (New York: Basic Books, 1978).

31. Hal S. Shorey and C. R. Snyder, "The role of adult attachment styles in psychopathology and psychotherapy outcomes," *Review of General Psychology* 10, no. 1 (2006): 1–20.

32. Vera Sonja Maass, *Coping with control and manipulation: making the difference between being a target and becoming a victim* (Santa Barbara, CA: ABC-CLIO/Praeger, 2010), 25.

33. E. A. Carlson, "A prospective longitudinal study of attachment disorganization/disorientation," *Child Development* 69 (1998): 1107–28; M. Main, "Introduction to the special section on attachment and psychopathology: 2. Overview of the field of attachment," *Journal of Consulting and Clinical Psychology* 64 (1996): 237–43.

34. M. Main and J. Solomon, "Procedures for identifying infants as disorganized/disoriented during the Ainsworth Strange Situation," in *Attachment in the preschool years*, ed. M. T. Greenberg, D. Cicchetti, and E. M. Cummings (Chicago: University of Chicago Press, 1990), 121–60.

35. A. Modigliani, "Embarrassment, facework, and eye contact: Testing a theory of embarrassment," *Journal of Personality and Social Psychology* 17 (1971): 15–24.

36. A. S. R. Manstead and G. R. Semin, "Social transgression, social perspectives, and social emotionality," *Motivation and Emotion* 5 (1981): 249–61.

37. M. K. Babcock, "Embarrassment: A window on the self," *Journal for the Theory of Social Behavior* 18 (1988): 459–83.

38. M. Silver, J. Sabini, and W. G. Parrott, "Embarrassment: A dramaturgic account," *Journal for the Theory of Social Behavior* 17 (1987): 47–61.

39. K. Sugawara, A study on embarrassment in new role situation: Using the data from university students at their probation in nursery school for the first time [in Japanese] *Communication & Society (Bulletin of Edogawa University)* 2 (1992): 31–39.

40. Brent Dean Robbins and Holly Parlavecchio, "The unwanted exposure of the self: A phenomenological study of embarrassment," *Humanistic Psychologist* 34, no. 4 (2006): 321–45; J. Sabini et al., "Who is embarrassed by what?" *Cognition and Emotion* 14 (2000): 213–40.

41. Eric Hollander and Nicholas Bakalar, *Coping with social anxiety* (New York: Henry Holt, 2005), 137.

42. R. L. Higgins, C. R. Snyder, and S. Berglas, *Self-handicapping: The paradox that isn't* (New York: Plenum Press, 1990); F. Rhodewalt and K. D. Vohs, "Defensive strategies, motivation, and the self: A self-regulatory process view," in *Handbook of competence and motivation*, ed. A. Elliot and C. Dweck (New York: Guilford Press, 2005), 548–65.

43. S. Nolen-Hoeksema, B. E. Wisco, and S. Lyubomirsky, "Rethinking rumination," *Perspectives on Psychological Science* 3 (2008): 400–424.

44. F. Rothbaum, B. Morling, and N. Rusk, "How goals and beliefs lead people into and out of depression" (2009).

45. C. S. Dweck and E. L. Leggett, "A social-cognitive approach to motivation and personality," *Psychological Review* 95 (1988): 256–73.

46. C. S. Dweck, *Self-theories: Their role in motivation, personality, and development* (1999).

47. Y. Niiya, J. Crocker, and E. M. Bartmess, "From vulnerability to resilience: Learning orientations buffer contingent self-esteem from failure," *Psychological Science* 15 (2004): 801–5.

48. F. Rothbaum, B. Morling, and N. Rusk, "How goals and beliefs lead people into and out of depression" (2009).

49. B. M. Dykman, "Integrating cognitive and motivational factors in depression: Initial tests of a goal-orientation approach," *Journal of Personality and Social Psychology* 74 (1998): 139–58.

50. L. Blackwell, K. Trzesniewski, and C. S. Dweck, "Implicit theories of intelligence predict achievement across an adolescent transition: A longitudinal study and an intervention," *Child Development* 78 (2007): 246–63.

51. A. J. Elliot and H. T. Reis, "Attachment and exploration in adulthood," *Journal of Personality and Social Psychology* 54 (2003): 5–12.

52. J. Polivy and C. P. Herman, "The effects of resolving to diet on restrained and unrestrained eaters: The 'false hope syndrome,'" *International Journal of Eating Disorders* 26 (1999): 434–47; J. Polivy and C. P. Herman, "The false hope syndrome: Unfulfilled expectations of self-change," *Current Directions in Psychological Science* 9 (2000): 128–31; J. Polivy and C. P. Herman, "If at first you don't succeed: False hopes of self-change," *American Psychologist* 57, no. 9 (2002): 677–89.

53. J. Polivy and C. P. Herman, "If at first you don't succeed: False hopes of self-change" (2002): 679.

54. M. Muraven and R. F. Baumeister, "Self-regulation and depletion of limited resources: Does self-control resemble a muscle?" *Psychological Bulletin* 126 (2000): 247–59.

55. R. M. Wenzlaff and D. M. Wegner, "Thought suppression," *Annual Review of Psychology* 51 (2000): 59–91.

56. T. F. Heatherton and P. A. Nichols, "Personal accounts of successful versus failed attempts at life change," *Personality and Social Psychology Bulletin* 20 (1994): 664–75.

57. Roy F. Baumeister, "How the self became a problem: A psychological review of historical research," *Journal of Personality and Social Psychology* 52 (1987): 163–76; Roy F. Baumeister, "The self," in *The handbook of social psychology*, vol. 1, 4th ed., ed. G. T. Gilbert, S. T. Fiske, and G. Lindzey (New York: Oxford University Press, 1998), 680–740; Roy F. Baumeister, *The cultural animal: Human nature, meaning, and social life* (New York: Oxford University Press, 2005); J. Crocker and L. E. Park, "The costly pursuit of self-esteem," *Psychological Bulletin* 130 (2004): 328–46.

58. Liqing Zhang, "An exchange theory of money and self-esteem in decision making," *Review of General Psychology* 13, no. 1 (2009): 66–76.

59. J. J. Bauer, "How the ego quiets as it grows: Ego development, growth stories, and eudaimonic personality development," in *Transcending self-interest: Psychological explorations of the quiet ego*, ed. H. A. Wayment and J. J. Bauer (Washington, DC: American Psychological Association Books, 2008), 199–210.

60. S. E. Iso-Ahola and C. O. Dotson, "Psychological momentum: Why success breeds success," *Review of General Psychology* 18 (2014): 19–33.

61. S. E. Iso-Ahola and K. Mobily, "Psychological momentum: A phenomenon and empirical (unobtrusive) validation of its influence in a competitive sport tournament," *Psychological Reports* 46 (1980): 391–401.

62. S. E. Iso-Ahola and C. O. Dotson, "Reply: Psychological momentum—not a statistical but psychological phenomenon: Response to commentary by Avugos and Bar-Eli," *Review of General Psychology* 19, no. 1 (March 2015): 112–16.

63. E. Hollander and N. Bakalar, *Coping with social anxiety* (2005).

64. V. S. Maass, *Coping with control and manipulation: making the difference between being a target and becoming a victim* (2010).

65. V. S. Maass and M. A. Neely, *Counseling single parents: A cognitive-behavioral approach* (New York: Springer, 2000).

66. A. Bandura, "Self-efficacy: Toward a unifying theory of behavioral change," *Psychological Review* 4 (1977): 191–215; A. Bandura, *Self-efficacy: The exercise of control* (New York: Freeman, 1997).

Chapter 9

1. Roni Caryn Rabin, "More overdose deaths from anxiety drugs," *New York Times* (Mind), February 25, 2016, http://well.blogs.nytimes.com/2016/02/25/.

2. California State Department of Education, *Toward a state of esteem: The final report of the California Task Force to Promote Self-Esteem and Personal and Social Responsibility* (Sacramento, CA: Author; ERIC Document Reproduction, 1990).

3. PESI, *Anxiety disorder in children and adolescents: Recognizing & treating the emerging epidemic*, workshop announcement, PESI, 2016, https://www.pesi.com.

4. Allen Ivey, "Getting to know (and love) Albert Ellis and his theory," *Counseling Today* (January 2016): 46–54.

5. Victor Raimy, *Misunderstandings of the self* (San Francisco: Jossey-Bass, 1975), 7.

6. V. Raimy, *Misunderstandings of the self* (1975).

7. V. S. Maass, *Finding love that lasts: Breaking the pattern of dead end relationships* (New York: Rowman & Littlefield, 2012).

8. J. P. Tangney et al., "Are shame, guilt, and embarrassment distinct emotions?" *Journal of Personality and Social Psychology* 70 (1996): 1256–69.

9. V. S. Maass, "Single-sided relationship therapy: An alternative," AFTA-IFTA 2005, The International Conference on Family Therapy, Washington, DC, June 22–25, 2005; V. S. Maass, *Facing the complexities of women's sexual desire* (New York: Springer Science + Business Media, 2007).

10. V. S. Maass, *Lifestyle changes: A clinician's guide to common events, challenges, and options* (New York: Routledge / Taylor & Francis, 2008).

11. V. Raimy, *Misunderstandings of the self* (1975).

12. R. Dreikurs, "The Adlerian approach to psychodynamics" and "The Adlerian approach to psychotherapy," in *Contemporary psychotherapies*, ed. M. I. Stein (New York: Free Press, 1961).

13. Robert G. Allen, "Faith and Fear," in *Phobia: A comprehensive summary of modern treatments*, ed. Robert L. DuPont (New York: Brunner/Mazel, 1982), 3–7.

14. Ludwig Binswanger, *Grundformen und Erkenntnis menschlichen Daseins* [Foundations and understanding of the human existence] (Munich, Germany: Ernst Reinhardt Verlag, 1962).

Resources

American Academy of Child and Adolescent Psychiatry, 3615 Wisconsin Ave. NW, Washington, D.C. 20016; (202) 966-7300; www.aacap.org; www.parentsmedguide.org

American Psychiatric Association, 1000 Wilson Blvd., Suite 1825, Arlington, VA 22209; (888) 357-7924; www.psych.org; www.healthyminds.org; www.parentsmedguide.org

American Psychological Association, 750 First St. NE, Washington, D.C. 20002-4242; (800) 374-2721 or (202) 336-5500; www.apa.org

Anxiety and Depression Association of America (ADAA), 8701 Georgia Ave., Suite 412, Silver Spring, MD 20910; (240) 485-1001; www.adaa.org (includes help in finding a therapist)

Association for Behavioral and Cognitive Therapies, 305 Seventh Ave., 16th Floor, New York, NY 10001; (212) 647-1890; www.abct.org

Bazelon Center for Mental Health Law, 1101 15th St. NW, Suite 1212, Washington, D.C. 20005; (202) 467-5730; www.bazelon.org

Brain & Behavior Research Foundation, 60 Cutter Mill Rd., Suite 404, Great Neck, NY 11021; (800) 829-8289; https://bbrfoundation.org

Center for Mental Health Services (CMHS)–SAMHSA, Information Center for Mental Health Services, 5600 Fishers Ln., Rockville, MD 20857; (240) 276-1310; www.samhsa.gov/about-us/who-we-are/offices-centers/cmhs

Freedom from Anxiety by Jerilyn Ross (Chicago: Nightingale-Conant, 2001). Available through www.RossCenter.com

Freedom From Fear Anxiety and Depression Resource Organization, 308 Seaview Ave., Staten Island, NY 10305; (718) 351-1717; www.freedomfromfear.org

International Paruresis Association, P.O. Box 65111, Baltimore, MD 21209; (800) 247-3864; www.paruresis.org

National Alliance on Mental Illness, Colonial Place Three, 2107 Wilson Blvd., Suite 300, Arlington, VA 22201; (800) 950-6264; www.nami.org

National Association of Social Workers, 750 First St. NE, Suite 700, Washington, D.C. 20002; (202) 408-8600; www.socialworkers.org; www.helpstartshere.org

National Association of State Mental Health Program Directors (NASMHPD), 66 Canal Center Plaza, Suite 302, Alexandria, VA 22314; (703) 739-9333; Fax: (703) 548-9517; www.nasmhpd.org

National Institute of Mental Health, 6001 Executive Blvd., Room 8184, MSC 9663, Bethesda, MD 20892; (866) 615-6464; www.nimh.nih.gov

National Mental Health Association, 2001 N. Beauregard St., 12th Floor, Alexandria, VA 22311; (800) 969-6642; www.nmha.org

National Mental Health Information Center, P.O. Box 42557, Washington, D.C. 20015; (800) 789-2647; www.samhsa.gov

Parent Advocacy Coalition for Educational Rights, 8161 Normandale Blvd., Minneapolis, MN 55437; (952) 838-9000; www.pacer.org

Phobics Anonymous, P.O. Box 1180, Palm Springs, CA 92263; (619) 322-COPE (2673)

Shyness Homepage, sponsored by the Shyness Institute, Palo Alto, CA 94306; www.shyness.com; E-mail: clinic@shyness.com

Social Anxiety Association, 2058 E. Topeka Dr., Phoenix, AZ 85024; www.socialphobia.org

Toastmasters International, P.O. Box 9052, Mission Viejo, CA 92690; (949) 858-8255; www.toastmasters.org

Websites

Academy of Cognitive Therapy, www.academyofct.org

American Academy of Child and Adolescent Psychiatry, www.aacap.org

American Psychiatric Association, www.psych.org, www.healthyminds.org

American Psychological Association, www.apa.org, www.apahelpcenter.org, http://locator.apa.org

American Psychological Association shyness page, www.apa.org/topics/topicshyness.html

Association for Behavioral and Cognitive Therapies, 305 7th Avenue, 16th Floor, New York, NY 10001; (212) 647-1890; Fax: (212) 647-1865; www.abct.org

Anxiety and Depression Association of America (ADAA), www.adaa.org

Anxiety Resource Center ARC, 312 Grandville Ave. SW, Grand Rapids, MI 49503; (616) 356-1614; www.anxietyresourcecenter.org

Fearfighter, www.fearfighter.com (helps sufferers to identify specific problems and develop work on treatment of those problems)

Medical Research Network, www.medicalresearchnetwork.com

Mindful Living Programs, www.mindfullivingprograms.com

The Shyness Institute, www.shyness.com

Social Anxiety Institute (SAI), www.socialanxietyinstitute.org

Social Anxiety Research Clinic, Columbia University / New York Psychiatric Institute, 1051 Riverside Dr., Unit 69, New York, NY 10032; (646) 774-5000; www.columbiapsychiatry.org/researchclinics/anxiety-disorders-clinic

TeensHealth, Nemours Foundation, www.teenshealth.org

Bibliography

Abela, J. R. Z., R. P. Auerbach, and M. E. P. Seligman. "Dispositional pessimism across the lifespan." In *Risk factors in depression*, edited by K. S. Dobson and D. J. A. Dozois, 195–220. Oxford, UK: Elsevier, 2008.

Abramson, L. Y., L. B. G. Alloy, G. J. Hankin, D. G. Haeffel, D. G. MacCoon, and B. E. Gibb. "Cognitive vulnerability-stress models of depression in a self-regulatory and psychological context." In *Handbook of depression*, edited by I. H. Gotlib and C. L. Hammen, 268–94. New York: Guilford Press, 2002.

Abramson, L. Y., G. I. Metalsky, and L. B. Alloy. "Hopelessness depression: A theory-based subtype of depression." *Psychological Review* 96 (1989): 358–72.

Ainsworth, M., M. Blehar, E. Waters, and S. Wall. *Patterns of attachment*. Hillsdale, NJ: Erlbaum, 1978.

Ainsworth, M., M. Blehar, E. Waters, and S. Wall. *Patterns of attachment: A psychological study of the Strange Situation*. New York: Basic Books, 1978.

Ajzen, I., and M. Fishbein. "A Bayesian analysis of attribution processes." *Psychological Bulletin* 82 (1975): 261–77.

Allen, J. G., L. Coyne, and J. Huntoon. "Complex posttraumatic stress disorder in women from a psychometric perspective." *Journal of Personality Assessment* 70 (1998): 277–98.

Allen, Robert G. "Faith and Fear." In *Phobia: A comprehensive summary of modern treatments*, edited by Robert L. DuPont, 3–7. New York: Brunner/Mazel, 1982.

Alloy, L. B., L. Y. Abramson, W. G. Whitehouse, M. E. Hogan, C. Panzarella, and D. T. Rose. "Prospective incidence of first onsets and recurrences of depression in individuals at high and low cognitive risk for depression." *Journal of Abnormal Psychology* 115 (2006): 145–56.

Appelbaum, P. S., P. C. Robbins, and R. Vesselinov. "Persistence and stability of delusions over time." *Comprehensive Psychiatry* 45 (2004): 317–24.

Babcock, M. K. "Embarrassment: A window on the self." *Journal for the Theory of Social Behavior* 18 (1988): 459–83.

Baldwin, S. A., and J. P. Hoffmann. "The dynamics of self-esteem: A growth-curve analysis." *Journal of Youth and Adolescence* 31 (2002): 101–13.

Bandura, A. *Self-efficacy: The exercise of control.* New York: Freeman, 1997.

Bandura, A. "Self-efficacy: Toward a unifying theory of behavioral change." *Psychological Review* 4 (1977): 191–215.

Barnard, Laura K., and John F. Curry. "Self-compassion: Conceptualization, correlates, & interventions." *Review of General Psychology* 15, no. 4 (2011): 289–303.

Barrios, B. A., and S. I. O'Dell. "Fears and anxieties." In *Treatment of childhood disorders*, edited by E. J. Mash and R. A. Barkley. New York: Guilford, 1989.

Bauer, J. J. "How the ego quiets as it grows: Ego development, growth stories, and eudaimonic personality development." In *Transcending self-interest: Psychological explorations of the quiet ego*, edited by H. A. Wayment and J. J. Bauer, 199–210. Washington, DC: American Psychological Association Books, 2008.

Baumeister, Roy F. *The cultural animal: Human nature, meaning, and social life.* New York: Oxford University Press, 2005.

Baumeister, Roy F. "How the self became a problem: A psychological review of historical research." *Journal of Personality and Social Psychology* 52 (1987): 163–76.

Baumeister, Roy F. "The self." In *The handbook of social psychology*, vol. 1, 4th ed., edited by G. T. Gilbert, S. T. Fiske, and G. Lindzey, 680–740. New York: Oxford University Press, 1998.

Baumeister, Roy F., Ellen Bratlavsky, and Catrin Finkenauer. "Bad is stronger than good." *Review of General Psychology* 5, no. 4 (2001): 323–70.

Baumeister, Roy F., J. D. Campbell, J. I. Krueger, and K. D. Vohs. "Does high self-esteem cause better performance, interpersonal success, happiness, or healthier lifestyles?" *Psychological Science in the Public Interest* 4 (2003): 1–44.

Baumeister, R. F., and M. R. Leary. "The need to belong: Desire for interpersonal attachment as a fundamental human motivation." *Psychological Bulletin* 117 (1995): 497–529.

Baumeister, R. F., L. Smart, and J. M. Boden. "Relation of threatened egotism to violence and aggression: The dark side of high self-esteem." *Psychological Review* 103 (1996): 5–33.

Beauregard, K. S., and D. Dunning. "Turning up the contrast: Self-enhancement motives prompt egocentric contrast effects in social judgments." *Journal of Personality and Social Psychology* 74 (1998): 606–21.

Beck, A. T. "Cognitive models of depression." *Journal of Cognitive Psychotherapy: An International Quarterly* 1 (1987): 5–37.

Beck, A. T. "Cognitive therapy: A 30-year retrospective." *American Psychologist* 46 (1991): 368–75.

Beck, A. T. *Depression: Clinical, experimental, and theoretical aspects.* New York: Harper & Row, 1967.

Beck, Aaron T., Gary Emery, and Ruth L. Greenberg. *Anxiety disorders and phobias: A cognitive perspective.* New York: Basic Books, 1985.

Bell-Dolan, D., N. M. Reaven, and L. Peterson. "Depression and social functioning: A multidimensional study of the linkages." *Journal of Clinical Child Psychology* 22 (1993): 306–15.

Berckhan, Barbara. *Einfach selbstsicher!* [Simply self-confident!] Munich, Ger.: Gräfe und Unzer Verlag, 2007.

Bering, Jesse M. "Why hell is other people: Distinctively human psychological suffering." *Review of General Psychology* 12, no. 1 (2008): 1–8.

Berry, Rebecca Rialon. "Advances in Cognitive-Behavioral Therapy for youth with anxiety disorders." *Current Psychiatry Reviews* 12, no. 1 (2016): 29–36.

Binswanger, Ludwig. *Grundformen und Erkenntnis menschlichen Daseins* [Foundations and understanding of the human existence]. Munich, Ger.: Ernst Reinhardt Verlag, 1962.

Black, Percy. "Thrust to wholeness: The nature of self-protection." *Review of General Psychology* 10, no. 3 (2006): 191–209.

Blackwell, L., K. Trzesniewski, and C. S. Dweck. "Implicit theories of intelligence predict achievement across an adolescent transition: A longitudinal study and an intervention." *Child Development* 78 (2007): 246–63.

Blaine, R., and J. Crocker. "Self-esteem and self-serving biases in reactions to positive and negative events: An integrative review." In *Self-esteem: The puzzle of low self-regard*, edited by R. F. Baumeister, 55–85. New York: Plenum Press, 1993.

Blankstein, K. R., C. H. Lumley, and A. Crawford. "Perfectionism, hopelessness, and suicide ideation: Revisions to diathesis-stress and specific vulnerability models." *Journal of Rational-Emotive & Cognitive Behavior Therapy* 25 (2007): 279–319.

Blatt, S. J., and D. C. Zuroff. "Perfectionism in the therapeutic process." In *Perfectionism: Theory, research, and treatment*, edited by G. L. Flett and P. L. Hewitt, 393–406. Washington, DC: American Psychological Association, 2002.

Blease, C. R. "Too many 'friends,' too few 'likes'? Evolutionary psychology and 'Facebook depression.'" *Review of General Psychology* 19, no. 1 (2015): 1–13.

Blidner, Rachelle. "Scientists are studying if MDMA, ingredient in Ecstasy, can treat social anxiety in adults with autism." *New York Daily News*, March 26, 2015. http://www.nydailynews.com.

Boden, Matthew Tyler, and Howard Berenbaum. "The bidirectional relations between affect and belief." *Review of General Psychology* 14, no. 3 (2010): 227–39.

Boden, M. T., and J. Gross. "An emotion regulation perspective on belief change." In *Oxford handbook of cognitive psychology*, edited by D. Reisberg. Oxford, UK: Oxford University Press, 2013.

Bohnet, I., and R. Zeckhauser. "Trust, risk, and betrayal." *Journal of Economic Behavior & Organization* 55 (2004): 467–84.

Boivin, M., S. Hymel, and W. M. Bukowski. "The roles of social withdrawal, peer rejection, and victimization by peers in predicting loneliness and depressed mood in childhood." *Development and Psychopathology* 7 (1995): 765–85.

Bolton, G. E., E. Katok, and A. Ockenfels. "How effective are electronic reputation mechanisms? An experimental investigation." *Management Science* 50 (2004): 1587–1602.

Bosson, J. K., C. E. Lakey, W. K. Campbell, V. Zeigler-Hill, C. H. Jordan, and M. H. Kernis. "Untangling the links between narcissism and self-esteem: A theoretical and empirical review." *Social and Personality Psychology Compass* 2 (2008): 1415–39.

Bowlby, J. *Attachment and loss: Vol. I, Attachment.* 2nd ed. New York: Basic Books, 1982.

Bowlby, J. *Attachment and loss: Vol. II, Separation.* New York: Basic Books. 1973.

Bowlby, J. "Developmental psychiatry comes of age." *American Journal of Psychiatry* 145 (1988): 1–10.

Brennan, K. A., and P. R. Shaver. "Attachment styles and personality disorders: Their connections to each other and to parental divorce, parental death, and perceptions of parental caregiving." *Journal of Personality* 66 (1998): 835–78.

Brown, Bene. *I thought it was just me (but it isn't).* 2007.

Burns, D. D. "The perfectionist's script for self-defeat." *Psychology Today* 3 (November 1980): 4–52.

Butler, Gillian. *Overcoming social anxiety and shyness: A self-help guide using Cognitive Behavioral techniques.* New York: Basic Books, 2008.

Buunk, B. P., and F. X. Gibbons. "Toward an enlightenment in social comparison theory: Moving beyond classic and Renaissance approaches." In *Handbook of social comparison: Theory and research*, edited by J. Suls and L. Wheeler, 487–99. New York: Kluwer Academic, 2000.

California State Department of Education. *Toward a state of esteem: The final report of the California Task Force to Promote Self-Esteem and Personal and Social Responsibility.* Sacramento, CA: Author, 1990. ERIC Document Reproduction Service no. ED321170.

Campbell, J. D., and L. F. Lavallee. "Who am I? The role of self-concept confusion in understanding the behavior of people with low self-esteem." In *Self-esteem: The puzzle of low self-regard*, edited by R. F. Baumeister, 3–20. New York: Plenum Press, 1993.

Carducci, Bernardo J. *Shyness—a bold new approach.* New York: Quill, 1999.

Carlson, E. A. "A prospective longitudinal study of attachment disorganization/disorientation." *Child Development* 69 (1998): 1107–28.

Carroll, Patrick, Kate Sweeny, and James A. Shepperd. "Forsaking optimism." *Review of General Psychology* 10, no. 1 (2006): 56–73.

Caspi, A., G. H. Elder, and D. J. Bem. "Moving away from the world: Life-course patterns of shy children." *Developmental Psychology* 24 (1988): 824–31.

Cassidy, J., and P. R. Shaver, eds. *Handbook of attachment: Theory, research, and clinical applications.* New York: Guilford Press, 1999.

Chan, MeowLan Evelyn. "'Why did you hurt me?' Victim's interpersonal betrayal attribution and trust implications." *Review of General Psychology* 13, no. 3 (2009): 262–74.

Charney, David L. "Depression and agoraphobia—chicken or the egg?" In *Phobia: A comprehensive summary of modern treatments*, edited by Robert L. DuPont, 126–39. New York: Brunner/Mazel, 1982.

Ciarrochi, Joseph, Philip Parker, Baljinder Sahdra, Sarah Marshall, Chris Jackson, Andrew T. Gloster, and Patrick Heaven. "The development of compulsive internet use and mental health: A four-year study of adolescence." *Developmental Psychology* 52, no. 2 (2016): 272–83.

Cicchetti, D., and D. J. Cohen. "Perspectives on developmental psychopathology." In *Developmental psychopathology: Vol. I, Theory and methods*, edited by D. Cicchetti and D. J. Cohen, 3–20. New York: Wiley, 1995.

Clore, G. L., and K. Gasper. "Feeling is believing: Some affective influences on belief." In *Emotions and belief: How feelings influence thoughts*, edited by N. H. Frijda, A. S. R. Manstead, and S. Bem, 10–44. Cambridge, UK: Cambridge University Press, 2000.

Cohen, J. B., M. T. Pham, and E. B. Andrade. "The nature and role of affect in consumer judgment and decision making." In *Handbook of consumer psychology*, edited by C. P. Haugtvedt, P. M Herr, and F. R. Kardes, 297–348. Mahwah, NJ: Erlbaum, 2007.

College Board. "College-bound seniors 2008." October 17, 2008. http://professionals .collegeboard.com/data-reports-research/sat/eb-seniors-2008.

Colligan, R. C., K. P. Offord, M. Malinchoc, P. Schulman, and M. E. P. Seligman. "CAVEing the MMPI for an optimism-pessimism scale: Seligman's contributional model and the assessment of explanatory style." *Journal of Clinical Psychology* 50 (1994): 71–95.

Connor, D. B., D. K. Knight, and D. R. Cross. "Mothers' and fathers' scaffolding of their 2-year-olds during problem-solving and literacy interactions." *British Journal of Developmental Psychology* 15 (1997): 323–38.

Conroy, D. D., M. P. Kaye, and J. D. Coatsworth. "Coaching climates and the destructive effects of mastery-avoidance achievement goals on situational motivation." *Journal of Sport and Exercise Psychology* 28 (2006): 69–92.

Crocker, J., and L. E. Park. "The costly pursuit of self-esteem." *Psychological Bulletin* 130 (2004): 328–46.

Crocker, J., and C. T. Wolfe. "Contingencies of self-worth." *Psychological Review* 108 (2001): 593–623.

Crozier, W. R. "Blushing and the exposed self: Darwin revisited." *Journal for the Theory of Social Behavior* 31 (2001), 61–72.

Cummins, R. A. "The domains of life satisfaction: An attempt to order chaos." In *Citation classics from social indicators research*, edited by A. C. Michalos, 559–84. Dordrecht, Neth.: Springer, 2005.

Damon, W., and M. Killen. "Peer interaction and the process of change in children's moral reasoning." *Merrill-Palmer Quarterly* 28 (1982): 347–78.

Darnon, C., J. M. Harackiewicz, F. Butera, G. Mugny, and A. Quiamzade. "Performance-approach and performance-avoidance goals: When uncertainty makes a difference." *Personality and Social Psychology Bulletin* 33 (2007): 813–27.

Das, T. K., and B.-S. Teng. "The risk-based view of trust: A conceptual framework." *Journal of Business and Psychology* 19 (2004): 85–116.

Dayhoff, Signe A. *Diagonally-parked in a parallel universe: Working through social anxiety.* Placitas, NM: Effectiveness-Plus Publications, 2000.

Deci, E., and R. Ryan. "Human autonomy: The basis for true self-esteem." In *Efficacy, agency, and self-esteem*, edited by M. H. Kernis, 31–49. New York: Plenum Press, 1995.

Deutsch, M., and H. B. Gerard. "A study of normative and informational social influences upon individual judgment." *Journal of Abnormal and Social Psychology* 51 (1955): 629–36.

Diagnostic and statistical manual of mental disorders, fifth edition (DSM-5). Washington, DC: American Psychiatric Association, 2013.

DiBartolo, P. M., C. Y. Li, and R. O. Frost. "How do the dimensions of perfectionism relate to mental health?" *Cognitive Therapy and Research* 32 (2008): 401–17.

Diener, E., and M. Diener. "Cross-cultural correlates of life satisfaction and self-esteem." *Journal of Personality and Social Psychology* 68 (1995): 653–63.

Dreikurs, R. "The Adlerian approach to psychodynamics" and "The Adlerian approach to psychotherapy." In *Contemporary psychotherapies*, edited by M. I. Stein. New York: Free Press, 1961.

Dunkley, D. M., K. R. Blankstein, J. Halsall, M. Williams, and G. Winkworth. "The relation between perfectionism and distress: Hassles, coping, and perceived social support as mediators and moderators." *Journal of Counseling Psychology* 47 (2000): 437–453.

Dunkley, D. M., D. Zuroff, and K. Blankstein. "Self-critical perfectionism and daily affect: Dispositional and situational influences on stress and coping." *Journal of Personality and Social Psychology* 84 (2003): 234–52.

Dweck, C. S. "Motivational processes affecting learning." *American Psychologist* 41 (1986): 1040–48.

Dweck, C. S. *Self-theories: Their role in motivation, personality, and development.* Philadelphia: Psychology Press, 1999.

Dweck, C. S., and E. L. Leggett. "A social-cognitive approach to motivation and personality." *Psychological Review* 95 (1988): 256–73.

Dykman, B. M. "Integrating cognitive and motivational factors in depression: Initial tests of a goal-orientation approach." *Journal of Personality and Social Psychology* 74 (1998): 139–58.

Eagly, A. H., and S. Chaiken. *The psychology of attitudes.* Orlando: Harcourt Brace Jovanovich, 1993.

Eidelson, R. J., and J. I. Eidelson. "Dangerous ideas: Five beliefs that propel groups toward conflict." *American Psychologist* 58 (2003): 182–92.

Eisenberger, N. I., M. D. Lieberman, and K. D. Williams. "Does rejection hurt? An fMRI study of social exclusion." *Science* 302 (2003): 290–92.

Elangovan, A. R., W. Auer-Rizzi, and E. Szabo. "Why don't I trust you now? An attributional approach to erosion of trust." *Journal of Managerial Psychology* 22 (2007): 4–24.

Elliot, A. J. "A conceptual history of the achievement goal construct." In *Handbook of competence and motivation*, edited by A. J. Elliot and C. S. Dweck, 52–72. New York: Guilford Press, 2005.

Elliot, A. J. "The hierarchical model of approach-avoidance motivation." *Motivation and Emotion* 30 (2006): 111–16.

Elliot, A. J., and H. T. Reis. "Attachment and exploration in adulthood." *Journal of Personality and Social Psychology* 54 (2003): 5–12.

Elliot, A. J., and K. M. Sheldon. "Avoidance personal goals and the personality-illness relationship." *Journal of Personality and Social Psychology* 75 (1998): 1282–99.

Ellis, Albert. "Rational-emotive psychotherapy." In *Counseling and psychotherapy*, by D. Arbuckle, 84. New York: McGraw-Hill, 1967.

Erdley, C., K. Cain, C. Loomis, F. Dumas-Hine, and C. S. Dweck. "The relations among children's social goals, implicit personality theories and response to social failure." *Developmental Psychology* 33 (1997): 263–72.

Essau, C. A., J. Conradt, S. Sasagawa, and T. H. Ollendick. "Prevention of anxiety symptoms in children: Results from a universal school-based trial." *Behavior Therapy* 43 (2012): 450–64.

Evans, A. M., and J. I. Krueger. "Elements of trust: Risk and perspective-taking." *Journal of Experimental Social Psychology* 47 (2011): 171–77.

Evans, A. M., and J. I. Krueger. "The psychology (and economics) of trust." *Social and Personality Psychology Compass* 3 (2009): 1003–17.

Festinger, L. "A theory of social comparison processes." *Human Relations* 7 (1954): 117–40.

Fisher, C. S. "The 2004 GSS finding of shrunken social networks: An artifact?" *American Sociological Review* 74 (2009): 657–69.

Flavell, J. H. "Cognitive development: Children's knowledge about the mind." *Annual Review of Psychology* 50 (1999): 21–45.

Flett, G. L., and P. L. Hewitt. "Disguised distress in children and adolescents 'flying under the radar': Why psychological problems are underestimated and how schools must respond." *Canadian Journal of School Psychology* 28 (2013): 12–27.

Flett, G. L., P. L. Hewitt, K. R. Blankstein, and L. Gray. "Psychological distress and the frequency of perfectionistic thinking." *Journal of Personality and Social Psychology* 75 (1998): 1363–81.

Flett, G. L., P. L. Hewitt, and M. J. Heisel. "The destructiveness of perfectionism revisited: Implications for the assessment of suicide risk and the prevention of suicide." *Review of General Psychology* 18, no. 3 (2014): 156–72.

Flowers, Steve. *The mindful path through shyness: How mindfulness and compassion can help free you from social anxiety, fear & avoidance.* Oakland, CA: New Harbinger Publications, 2009.

Folger, R. "Reformulating the preconditions of resentment: A referent cognitions model." In *Social comparison, social justice, and relative deprivation: Theoretical, empirical, and policy perspectives,* edited by J. C. Masters and W. P. Smith, 183–215. Hillsdale, NJ: Erlbaum, 2000.

Ford, Emily, with Michael R. Liebowitz and Linda Wasmer Andrews. *What you must think of me: A firsthand account of one teenager's experience with social anxiety disorder.* New York: Oxford University Press, 2007.

Foster, M. D., and K. Matheson. "Perceiving and feeling personal discrimination: Motivation or inhibition for collective action?" *Group Processes and Intergroup Relations* 1 (1998): 165–74.

Fowler, J. H., and N. A. Christakis. "Dynamic spread of happiness in a large social network: Longitudinal analysis over 20 years in the Framingham Heart Study." *British Medical Journal* (2008), advance online publication.

Fox, N. A., S. D. Calkins, and M. A. Bell. "Neural plasticity and development in the first year of life: Evidence from cognitive and socio-emotional domains of research." *Development and Psychopathology* 6 (1994): 677–98.

Fredrickson, B. L. "Cultivating positive emotions to optimize health and well-being." *Prevention & Treatment* 3 (2000), article 0001a.

Freudenberger, Herbert, and Gail North. *Situational anxiety.* New York: Carroll & Graf, 1982.

Froeschle Hicks, Janet. "Empowering youth victimized by cyberbullying." *Counseling Today* 57, no. 9 (March 2015): 48–53.

Gelman, R., F. Durgin, and L. Kaufman. "Distinguishing animates from inanimates." In *Causality and culture,* edited by D. Sperber, D. Premack, and A. Premack, 150–84. Oxford, UK: Plenum, 1995.

Gentile, Brittany, Jean M. Twenge, and W. Keith Campbell. "Birth cohort differences in self-esteem, 1988–2008: A cross-temporal meta-analysis." *Review of General Psychology* 14, no. 3 (2010): 261–68.

Gergeley, G., Z. Nadasdy, C. Gergeley, and B. Szilvia. "Taking the intentional stance at 12 months of age." *Cognition* 56 (1995): 165–93.

Germer, C. *The mindful path to self-compassion: Freeing yourself from destructive thoughts and emotions.* New York: Guilford Press, 2009.

Gernigon, Christophe, Robin R. Vallacher, Andrzej Nowak, and David E. Conroy. "Rethinking approach and avoidance in achievement contexts: The perspective of Dynamical systems." *Review of General Psychology* 19, no. 4 (2015): 443–57.

Gilbert, D. T. "How mental systems believe." *American Psychologist* 46 (1991): 107–19.

Gilbert, P., and C. Irons. "Focused therapies and compassionate mind training for shame and self-attacking." In *Compassion: Conceptualizations, research and use in psychotherapy,* edited by P. Gilbert, 263–325. New York: Routledge, 2005.

Gilbert, P., and C. Irons. "A pilot exploration of the use of compassionate images in a group of self-critical people." *Memory* 12 (2004): 507–16.

Gilbert, P., J. Pehl, and S. Allan. "The phenomenology of shame and guilt: An empirical investigation." *British Journal of Medical Psychology* 67 (1994): 23–36.

Gilbert, P., and S. Procter. "Compassionate Mind Training for people with high shame and self-criticism: Overview and pilot study of a group therapy approach." *Clinical Psychology & Psychotherapy* 13 (2006): 353–79.

Gilbertson, Tina. *Constructive wallowing: How to beat bad feelings by letting yourself have them.* 2014.

Glanville, J. L., and P. Paxton. "How do we learn to trust? A confirmatory tetrad analysis of the sources of generalized trust." *Social Psychology Quarterly* 70 (2007): 230–42.

Glöckner, L., and B. E. Hilbig. "Risk is relative: Risk aversion yields cooperation rather than defection in cooperation-friendly environments." *Psychonomic Bulletin & Review* 19 (2012): 546–53.

Goffman, Erving. *The presentation of self in every day life.* London: Penguin, 1990. First published in 1958.

Goffman, Erving. *Stigma.* Englewood Cliffs, NJ: Prentice Hall, 1963.

Gorn, G. J., M. T. Pham, and L. Y. Sin. "When arousal influences ad evaluation and valence does not (and vice versa)." *Journal of Consumer Psychology* 11 (2001): 43–55.

Grant, H., and C. S. Dweck. "Clarifying achievement goals and their impact." *Journal of Personality and Social Psychology* 85 (2003): 541–53.

Guerin, Bernard. "Individuals as social relationships: 18 ways that acting alone can be thought of as social behavior." *Review of General Psychology* 5, no. 4 (2008): 406–28.

Guerin, Bernard. "Strategies and motives in everyday social life: Integrating the social sciences." Unpublished manuscript, University of Waikato, Hamilton, New Zealand, 2000.

Haeffel, G. J., L. Y. Abramson, P. C. Brazy, and J. Y. Shaw. "Hopelessness theory and the approach system: Cognitive vulnerability predicts decreases in goal-directed behavior." *Cognitive Therapy and Research* 32 (2008): 281–90.

Hafer, C. L. "Do innocent victims threaten the belief in a just world? Evidence from a modified Stroop task." *Journal of Personality and Social Psychology* 79 (2000): 165–73.

Hamamura, T., and S. J. Heine. "Approach and avoidance motivation across cultures." In *Handbook of approach and avoidance motivation*, edited by A. J. Elliot, 557–70. New York: Psychology Press, 2008.

Hampton, N., L. Goulet, C. Marlow, and L. Rainie. "Why most Facebook users get more than they give." Pew Internet and American Life Project, February 3, 2012. http://www.pewinternet.org/~/media//Files/Reports/2012/PIP _Facebook%20users_2.3.12.pdf.

Heatherton, T. F., and P. A. Nichols. "Personal accounts of successful versus failed attempts at life change." *Personality and Social Psychology Bulletin* 20 (1994): 664–75.

Heatherton, T. F., and K. D. Vohs. "Interpersonal evaluations following threats to self: Role of self-esteem." *Journal of Personality and Social Psychology* 78 (2000): 725–36.

Henderson, Lynne. *The compassionate mind guide to building social confidence: Using compassion-focused therapy to overcome shyness & social anxiety.* Oakland, CA: New Harbinger Publications, 2010.

Hewitt, J. P. *The myth of self-esteem: Finding happiness and solving problems in America.* New York: St. Martin's Press, 1998.

Hewitt, P. L., and G. L. Flett. "Perfectionism in the self and social contexts: Conceptualization, assessment, and association with psychopathology." *Journal of Personality and Social Psychology* 60 (1991): 456–470.

Hewitt, P. L., G. L. Flett, S. B. Sherry, M. Habke, M. Parkin, R. W. Lam, B. McMurtry, E. Ediger, P. Fairlie, and M. B. Stein. "The interpersonal expression of perfectionism: Perfectionistic self-presentation and psychological distress." *Journal of Personality and Social Psychology* 84 (2003): 1303–25.

Higgins, R. L., C. R. Snyder, and S. Berglas. *Self-handicapping: The paradox that isn't.* New York: Plenum Press, 1990.

Hollander, Eric, and Nicholas Bakalar. *Coping with social anxiety.* New York: Henry Holt, 2005.

Hoog, Natascha de, Wolfgang Stroebe, and John B. F. de Wit. "The impact of vulnerability to and severity of a health risk on processing and acceptance of fear-arousing communications: A meta-analysis." *Review of General Psychology* 11, no. 3 (2007): 258–85.

Horney, Karen. *New ways in psychoanalysis.* New York: Norton, 1939.

Hovland, C. I., I. L. Janis, and H. H. Kelley. *Communication and persuasion: Psychological studies of opinion change.* New Haven, CT: Yale University Press, 1953.

Hsee, C. K., and Y. Rottenstreich. "Music, pandas, and muggers: On the affective psychology of value." *Journal of Experimental Psychology-General* 133 (2004): 23–30.

Huang, Chiungjung. "Mean-level change in self-esteem from childhood through adulthood: Meta-analysis of longitudinal studies." *Review of General Psychology* 14, no. 3 (2010): 251–60.

Hymel, S., A. Bowker, and E. Woody. "Aggressive versus withdrawn unpopular children: Variations in peer and self-perceptions in multiple domains." *Child Development* 64 (1993): 879–96.

Inzlicht, M., I. McGregor, J. B. Hirsh, and K. Nash. "Neural markers of religious conviction." *Psychological Science* 20 (2009): 385–92.

Iso-Ahola, S. E., and C. O. Dotson. "Psychological momentum: Why success breeds success." *Review of General Psychology* 18 (2014): 19–33.

Iso-Ahola, S. E., and C. O. Dotson. "Reply: Psychological momentum—not a statistical but psychological phenomenon: Response to commentary by Avugos and Bar-Eli." *Review of General Psychology* 19, no. 1 (March 2015): 112–16.

Iso-Ahola, S. E., and K. Mobily. "Psychological momentum: A phenomenon and empirical (unobtrusive) validation of its influence in a competitive sport tournament." *Psychological Reports* 46 (1980): 391–401.

Ivey, Allen. "Getting to know (and love) Albert Ellis and his theory." *Counseling Today* (January 2016): 46–54.

Izard, Carroll E. *Human emotions.* New York: Plenum Press, 1977.

Jackson, Benita, Laura D. Kuhzansky, and Rosalind J. Wright. "Linking perceived unfairness to physical health: The perceived unfairness model." *Review of General Psychology* 10, no. 1 (2006): 21–40.

Janet, Pierre. *The major symptoms of hysteria.* 2nd ed. New York: Macmillan, 1920.

Jetten, J., C. Haslam, S. A. Haslam, and N. R. Branscombe. "The social cure." *Scientific American Mind* 20 (2009): 26–33.

Johnson, E. J., and A. Tversky. "Affect, generalization, and the perception of risk." *Journal of Personality and Social Psychology* 45 (1983): 20–31.

Jones, Laura K. "The evolving adolescent brain." *Counseling Today* 57, no. 7, Neurocounseling: Bridging brain and behavior (2015): 14–17.

Josephs, I. E., and J. Valsiner. "How does autodialogue work? Miracles of meaning maintenance and circumvention strategies." *Social Psychology Quarterly* 61 (1998): 68–83.

Kabat-Zinn, J. "Mindfulness-based interventions in context: Past, present, and future." *Clinical Psychology Science and Practice* 10 (2003): 144–56.

Kagan, Jerome. "Historical selection." *Review of General Psychology* 13, no. 1 (2009): 77–88.

Kagan, J. "Temperament and the reaction to unfamiliarity." *Child Development* 68 (1997): 139–43.

Kahneman, D., and A. Tversky. "The psychology of preferences." *Scientific American* 246 (1982): 160–73.

Kammrath, L., and C. S. Dweck. "Voicing conflict: Preferred conflict strategies among incremental and entity theorists." *Personality and Social Psychology Bulletin* 32 (2006): 1497–1508.

Kaplan, A., and M. L. Maehr. "The contributions and prospects of goal orientation theory." *Educational Psychology Review* 19 (2007): 91–110.

Katon, W., P. P. Bitaliano, J. Russo, L. Cormier, K. Anderson, and M. Jones. "Panic disorder: Epidemiology and primary care." *Journal of Family Practice* 23 (1986): 233–39.

Kawamura, K. Y., and R. O. Frost. "Self-concealment as a mediator in the relationship between perfectionism and psychological distress." *Cognitive Therapy and Research* 28 (2004): 183–91.

Kernis, M. H. "Toward a conceptualization of optimal self-esteem." *Psychological Inquiry* 14 (2003): 1–26.

Kiecolt-Glaser, J. K., L. McGuire, T. F. Robles, and R. Glaser. "Emotions, morbidity, and mortality: New perspectives from psychoneuroimmunology." *Annual Review of Psychology* 53 (2002): 83–107.

Koehler, J. J., and A. D. Gershoff. "Betrayal aversion: When agents of protection become agents of harm." *Organizational Behavior and Human Decision Processes* 90 (2003): 244–61.

Kross, E., P. Verduyn, E. Demiralp, J. Park, D. S. Lee, N. Lin, H. Shablack, J. Jonides, and O. Ybarra. "Facebook use predicts declines in subjective well-being in young adults." *PLoS ONE* 8 (2013): e69841.

Landrum, A. R., B. S. J. Eaves Jr., and P. Shafto. "Learning to trust and trusting to learn: A theoretical framework." *Trends in Cognitive Sciences* 19 (2015): 109–11.

Landry, S. H., P. W. Garner, P. R. Swank, and C. D. Baldwin. "Effects of maternal scaffolding during joint toy play with preterm and full-term infants." *Merrill-Palmer Quarterly* 42 (1996): 177–99.

Lange, Arthur, and Patricia Jakubowski. *Responsible assertive behavior.* Champaign, IL: Research Press, 1976.

Leary, M. R. "Sociometer theory and the pursuit of relational value: Getting to the root of self-esteem." *European Review of Social Psychology* 16 (2005): 75–111.

Leary, M. R., E. B. Tate, C. E. Adams, A. Batts Allen, and J. Hancock. "Self-compassion and reactions to unpleasant self-relevant events: The implications of treating oneself kindly." *Journal of Personality and Social Psychology* 92 (2007): 887–904.

Lee, D. "The perfect nurturer: A model to develop a compassionate mind within the context of cognitive therapy." In *Compassion: Conceptualizations, research and use in psychotherapy*, edited by P. Gilbert, 326–51. New York: Routledge, 2005.

Lerner, J. S., and D. Keltner. "Fear, anger, and risk." *Journal of Personality and Social Psychology* 81 (2001): 146–59.

Leventhal, H. "Findings and theory in the study of fear communications." In *Advances in experimental social psychology*, vol. 5, edited by L. Berkowitz, 119–86. San Diego: Academic Press, 1970.

Lewis, M. *Shame: The exposed self.* New York: Free Press, 1992.

Lockwood, P. "Could it happen to you? Predicting the impact of downward comparison on the self." *Journal of Personality and Social Psychology* 82 (2002): 343–58.

Lockwood, P., P. Sadler, K. Fyman, and S. Tuck. "To do or not to do: Using positive and negative role models to harness motivation." *Social Cognition* 22 (2004): 422–50.

Loewenstein, G., E. U. Weber, C. K. Hsee, and N. Welch. "Risk as feelings." *Psychological Bulletin* 127 (2001): 267–86.

Lyubomirsky, S., C. Tkach, and M. R. DiMatteo. "What are the differences between happiness and self-esteem?" *Social Indicators Research* 78 (2006): 363–404.

Maass, Vera Sonja. *The Cinderella test: Would you really want the shoe to fit?* Santa Barbara, CA: ABC-CLIO/Praeger, 2009.

Maass, Vera Sonja. *Coping with control and manipulation: making the difference between being a target and becoming a victim.* Santa Barbara, CA: ABC-CLIO/Praeger, 2010.

Maass, Vera Sonja. *Facing the complexities of women's sexual desire.* New York: Springer Science + Business Media, 2007.

Maass, Vera Sonja. *Finding love that lasts: Breaking the pattern of dead end relationships.* New York: Rowman & Littlefield, 2012.

Maass, Vera Sonja. "Images of masculinity as predictors of men's romantic and sexual relationships." In *Men in relationships*, edited by Victoria Hilkevitch Bedford and Barbara Formaniak Turner, 51–78. New York: Springer, 2006.

Maass, Vera Sonja. *Lifestyle changes: A clinician's guide to common events, challenges, and options.* New York: Routledge / Taylor & Francis, 2008.

Maass, Vera Sonja. "Single-sided relationship therapy: An alternative." AFTA-IFTA 2005, The International Conference on Family Therapy, Washington, DC, June 22–25, 2005.

Maass, Vera Sonja. *Women's group therapy: Creative challenges and options.* New York: Springer, 2006. First published in 2002.

Maass, Vera Sonja, and Margery A. Neely. *Counseling single parents: A cognitive-behavioral approach.* New York: Springer, 2000.

MacDonald, G., and M. R. Leary. "Why does social exclusion hurt? The relationship between social and physical pain." *Psychological Bulletin* 131 (2005): 202–23.

MacDonald, K., and R. D. Parke. "Bridging the gap: Parent-child play interaction and peer interactive competence." *Child Development* 55 (1984): 1265–1277.

Main, M. "Introduction to the special section on attachment and psychopathology: 2. Overview of the field of attachment." *Journal of Consulting and Clinical Psychology* 64 (1996): 237–43.

Main, M., N. Kaplan, and J. Cassidy. "Security in infancy, childhood, and adulthood: A move to the level of representation." *Monographs of the Society for Research in Child Development* 50 (1985): 66–104.

Main, M., and J. Solomon. "Procedures for identifying infants as disorganized/disoriented during the Ainsworth Strange Situation." In *Attachment in the preschool years*, edited by M. T. Greenberg, D. Cicchetti, and E. M. Cummings, 121–60. Chicago: University of Chicago Press, 1990.

Major, B., M. Testa, and W. H. Blysma. "Responses to upward and downward social comparisons: The impact of esteem-relevance perceived control." In *Social comparison: Contemporary theory and research*, edited by J. M. Smith and T. A. Wills, 237–60. Hillsdale, NJ: Erlbaum, 1991.

Maner, J. K., C. N. DeWall, R. F. Baumeister, and M. Schaller. "Does social exclusion motivate interpersonal reconnection? Resolving the 'porcupine problem.'" *Journal of Personality and Social Psychology* 92 (2007): 42–55.

Manstead, A. S. R., and G. R. Semin. "Social transgression, social perspectives, and social emotionality." *Motivation and Emotion* 5 (1981): 249–61.

Marken, Richard S. "Looking at behavior through control theory glasses." *Review of General Psychology* 6, no. 3 (2002): 260–70.

Marken, Richard S. "The nature of behavior: Control as fact and theory." *Behavioral Science* 33 (1988): 196–206.

Markway, Barbara, and Gregory Markway. *Painfully shy: How to overcome social anxiety and reclaim your life.* New York: Thomas Dunne Books / St. Martin's Press, 2001.

Marsh, H. W. "Age and sex effects in multiple dimensions of self-concept: Preadolescence to early adulthood." *Journal of Educational Psychology* 81 (1989): 417–30.

Marshall, John R. *Social phobia from shyness to stage fright.* New York: Basic Books, 1994.

Mayer, R. C., J. H. Davis, and F. D. Schoorman. "An integrative model of organizational trust." *Academy of Management Review* 20 (1995): 709–34.

McFarlin, D. B., R. F. Baumeister, and J. Blascovich. "On knowing when to quit: Task failure, self-esteem, advice, and nonproductive persistence." *Journal of Personality* 52 (1984): 138–55.

McGregor, H. A., and A. J. Elliot. "Achievement goals as predictors of achievement-relevant processes prior to task engagement." *Journal of Educational Psychology* 94 (2002): 381–95.

McKay, Matthew, and Patrick Fanning. *Self-esteem.* New York: St. Martin's Press, 1987.

McKay, Matthew, and Patrick Fanning. *Self-esteem.* 3rd ed. Oakland, CA: New Harbinger Publications, 2000.

McPherson, M., L. Smith-Lovin, and M. E. Brashears. "Social isolation in America: Changes in core discussion networks over two decades." *American Sociological Review* 71 (2006): 353–75.

Merleau-Ponty, M. "The child's relations with others." In *The primacy of perception*, edited by J. M. Edie. Evanston, IL: Northwestern University Press, 1964. First published in 1951.

Messer, S. C., and D. C. Beidel. "Psychosocial correlates of childhood anxiety disorders." *Journal of the American Academy of Child and Adolescent Psychiatry* 33 (1994): 975–83.

Meyer, J. K., M. M. Weissman, G. L. Tischler, C. E. Holzer, P. J. Leaf, H. Orvaschel, J. C. Anthony et al. "Six-month prevalence of psychiatric disorders in three communities: 1980 to 1982." *Archives of General Psychiatry* 41 (1984): 959–66.

Meyers, Laurie. "Coming to terms with technology." *Counseling Today* 58, no. 1 (July 2015): 22–27.

Meyers, Laurie. "Confronting loneliness in an age of constant connection." *Counseling Today* 57, no. 7 (January 2015): 24–31.

Meyers, Laurie. "Fertile grounds for bullying." *Counseling Today* 58, no. 11 (May 2016): 26–35.

Mickenberg, Kim. "Headhunters for the heart: What do personal matchmakers have over your PC?" *Psychology Today*, May/June 2008, p. 32.

Mikulincer, M., T. Dolev, and P. R. Shaver. "Attachment-related strategies during thought-suppression: Ironic rebounds and vulnerable self-representations." *Journal of Personality and Social Psychology* 87 (2004): 940–56.

Mikulincer, M., and P. R. Shaver. *Attachment in adulthood: Structure, dynamics, and change.* New York: Guilford Press, 2007.

Mills, A., P. Gilbert, R. Bellew, K. McEvan, and C. Gale. "Paranoid beliefs and self-criticism in students." *Clinical Psychology & Psychotherapy* 14 (2007): 358–64.

Modigliani, A. "Embarrassment, facework, and eye contact: Testing a theory of embarrassment." *Journal of Personality and Social Psychology* 17 (1971): 15–24.

Moore, D. W. "Three of four Americans believe in paranormal." June 16, 2005. http://home.sandiego.edu/~baber/logic/gallup.html.

Morgenroth, Thekla, Michelle K. Ryan, and Kim Peters. "The motivational theory of role modeling: How role models influence role aspirants' goals." *Review of General Psychology* 19, no. 4 (2015): 465–83.

Muraven, M., and R. F. Baumeister. "Self-regulation and depletion of limited resources: Does self-control resemble a muscle?" *Psychological Bulletin* 126 (2000): 247–59.

Murayama, K., and A. J. Elliot. "The joint influence of personal achievement goals and classroom goal structures on achievement-relevant outcomes." *Journal of Educational Psychology* 101 (2009): 432–47.

Muris, P., P. Steerneman, H. Merckelbach, and C. Meesters. "The role of parental fearfulness and modeling in children's fear." *Behavior Research and Therapy* 34 (1996): 265–68.

Mustanski, Brian, Rebecca Andrews, and Jae A. Puckett. "The effects of cumulative victimization on mental health among lesbian, gay, bisexual, and transgender adolescents and young adults." *American Journal of Public Health* 106, no. 3 (March 2016): 527–33.

National Psychologist. "College students text a lot." May/June 2015, p. 23.

Neff, K. "The development and validation of a scale to measure self-compassion." *Self and Identity* 2 (2003): 223–50.

Neff, K. "Self-compassion: An alternative conceptualization of a healthy attitude toward oneself." *Self and Identity* 2 (2003): 86–101.

Neff, K., Y. Hsieh, and K. Dejitterat. "Self-compassion, achievement goals, and coping with academic failure." *Self and Identity* 4 (2005): 263–87.

Neff, K., S. Rude, and K. Kirkpatrick. "An examination of self-compassion in relation to positive psychological functioning and personality traits." *Journal of Research in Personality* 41 (2007): 908–16.

Nicholls, J. G. "Achievement motivation: Conceptions of ability, subjective experience, task choice, and performance." *Psychological Review* 91 (1984): 328–46.

Niiya, Y., J. Crocker, and E. M. Bartmess. "From vulnerability to resilience: Learning orientations buffer contingent self-esteem from failure." *Psychological Science* 15 (2004): 801–5.

Nobel, R., K. Manassis, and P. Wilansky-Traynor. "The role of perfectionism in relation to an intervention to reduce anxious and depressive symptoms in children." *Journal of Rational-Emotive & Cognitive-Behavior Therapy* 30 (2012): 77–90.

Nolen-Hoeksema, S., B. E. Wisco, and S. Lyubomirsky. "Rethinking rumination." *Perspectives on Psychological Science* 3 (2008): 400–424.

Pacht, Asher. "Reflections on perfection." *American Psychologist* 39 (1984): 386–90.

Park, Justin H., and Florian van Leeuwen. "The asymmetric behavioral homeostasis hypothesis: Unidirectional flexibility of fundamental motivational processes." *Review of General Psychology* 18, no. 2 (2014): 89–100.

Park, L. E., J. Crocker, and K. D. Mickelson. "Attachment styles and contingencies of self-worth." *Personality and Social Psychology Bulletin* 30 (2004): 1243–54.

Park, L. E., J. Crocker, and K. D. Vohs. "Contingencies of self-worth and self-validation goals: Implications for close relationships." In *Self and relationships: Connecting intrapersonal and interpersonal processes*, edited by K. D. Vohs and E. J. Finkel, 84–103. New York: Guilford Press, 2006.

Pennebaker, J. W. *Opening up: The healing power of expressing emotions*. New York: Guilford Press, 1990.

PESI. *Anxiety disorder in children and adolescents: Recognizing & treating the emerging epidemic*. Workshop announcement, 2016. https://www.pesi.com.

Peterson, C., and N. Park. "Explanatory style and emotion regulation." In *Handbook of emotion regulation*, edited by J. J. Gross, 159–79. New York: Guilford Press, 2007.

Pham, Michael Tuan. "Emotion and rationality: A critical review and interpretation of empirical evidence." *Preview of General Psychology* 11, no. 2 (2007): 155–78.

Piaget, Jean. *The language and thought of the child*. London: Routledge & Kegan Paul, 1926.

Polanchek, Sara, and Sidney Shaw. "Ten intimate relationship research findings every counselor should know." *Counseling Today* 58, no. 6 (December 2015): 34–39.

Polivy, J., and C. P. Herman. "The effects of resolving to diet on restrained and unrestrained eaters: The 'false hope syndrome.'" *International Journal of Eating Disorders* 26 (1999): 434–47.

Polivy, J., and C. P. Herman. "The false hope syndrome: Unfulfilled expectations of self-change." *Current Directions in Psychological Science* 9 (2000): 128–31.

Polivy, J., and C. P. Herman. "If at first you don't succeed: False hopes of self-change." *American Psychologist* 57, no. 9 (2002): 677–89.

Premack, D. "The infant's theory of self-propelled objects." *Cognition* 36 (1990): 1–16.

Putnam, R. D. "Bowling alone: America's declining social capital." *Journal of Democracy* 6 (1995): 65–78.

Putnam, R. D. *Bowling alone: The collapse and revival of American community.* New York: Simon & Schuster, 2000.

Rabin, Roni Caryn. "More overdose deaths from anxiety drugs." *New York Times* (Mind), February 25, 2016. http://well.blogs.nytimes.com/2016/02/25/.

Raimy, Victor. *Misunderstandings of the self.* San Francisco: Jossey-Bass, 1975.

Rhodewalt, F., and K. D. Vohs. "Defensive strategies, motivation, and the self: A self-regulatory process view." In *Handbook of competence and motivation,* edited by A. Elliot and C. Dweck, 548–65. New York: Guilford Press, 2005.

Robbins, B. D., and J. Goicoecchea. "The psychogenesis of the self and the emergence of ethical relatedness: Klein in light of Merleau-Ponty." *Journal of Theoretical and Philosophical Psychology* 25, no. 2 (2005): 191–223.

Robbins, Brent Dean, and Holly Parlavecchio. "The unwanted exposure of the self: A phenomenological study of embarrassment." *Humanistic Psychologist* 34, no. 4 (2006): 321–45.

Robins, R. W., H. M. Hendin, and K. H. Trzesniewski. "Measuring global self-esteem: Construct validation of a single-item measure and the Rosenberg Self-Esteem Scale." *Personality and Social Psychology Bulletin* 27 (2001): 151–61.

Robins, R. W., K. H. Trzesniewski, J. L. Tracy, S. D. Gosling, and J. Potter. "Global self-esteem across the life span." *Psychology and Aging* 17 (2002): 423–34.

Rogers, R. W. "Cognitive and physiological processes in fear appeals and attitude change: A revised theory of protection motivation." In *Social psychophysiology: A sourcebook,* edited by J. T. Cacioppo and R. E. Petty, 153–76. New York: Guilford Press, 1983.

Rosen, Larry. "The power of 'Like' on Facebook." *National Psychologist* 24, no. 2 (2015): 20.

Rosenberg, M. *Society and the adolescent self-image.* Princeton, NJ: Princeton University Press, 1965.

Rothbaum, Fred, Beth Morling, and Natalie Rusk. "How goals and beliefs lead people into and out of depression." *Preview of General Psychology* 13, no. 4 (2009): 302–14.

Rottenstreich, Y., and C. K. Hsee. "Money, kisses, and electric shocks: On the affective psychology of risk." *Psychological Science* 12 (2001): 185–90.

Roxborough, H. M., P. L. Hewitt, J. Kaldas, G. L. Flett, C. Caelian, S. Sherry, and D. L. Sherry. "Perfectionistic self-presentation, socially prescribed perfectionism, and suicide in youth: A test of the perfectionism social disconnection model." *Suicide and Life-Threatening Behavior* 42 (2012): 217–33.

Rubin, K. H. "The Waterloo Longitudinal Project: Correlates and consequences of social withdrawal from childhood to adolescence." In *Social withdrawal, inhibition and shyness in childhood,* edited by K. H. Rubin and J. Asendorpf, 291–314. Hillsdale, NJ: Lawrence Erlbaum, 1993.

Rubin, K. H., and J. Asendorpf, eds. *Social withdrawal, inhibition, and shyness in childhood.* Hillsdale, NJ: Lawrence Erlbaum, 1993.

Rubin, K. H., and Kim B. Burgess. "Social withdrawal and anxiety." In *The developmental psychopathology of anxiety*, edited by M. W. Vasey and M. R. Dadds, 407–34. New York: Oxford University Press, 2001.

Rubin, K. H., X. Chen, P. McDougall, A. Bowker, and J. McKinnon. "The Waterloo Longitudinal Project: Predicting adolescent internalizing and externalizing problems from early and mid-childhood." *Development and Psychopathology* 7 (1995): 751–64.

Rubin, K. H., S. Hymel, and R. S. L. Mills. "Sociability and social withdrawal in childhood: Stability and outcomes." *Journal of Personality* 57 (1989): 237–55.

Rubin, K. H., and R. S. L. Mills. "Maternal beliefs about adaptive and maladaptive social behaviors in normal, aggressive, and withdrawn preschoolers." *Journal of Abnormal Child Psychology* 18 (1990): 419–35.

Rubin, K. H., J. J. Nelson, P. D. Hastings, and J. Asendorpf. "The transaction between parents' perceptions of their children's shyness and their parenting styles." *International Journal of Behavioral Development* 23 (1999): 937–58.

Rusk, Natalie, and Fred Rothbaum. "From stress to learning: Attachment theory meets goal orientation theory." *Review of General Psychology* 14, no. 1 (2010): 31–43.

Rychlak, Joseph F. *Introduction to personality and psychotherapy: A theory-construction approach*. Boston: Houghton Mifflin, 1973.

Sabini, J., M. Siepmann, J. Stein, and M. Meyerowitz. "Who is embarrassed by what?" *Cognition and Emotion* 14 (2000): 213–40.

Salovey, P. "Social comparison processes in envy and jealousy." In *Social comparison: Contemporary theory and research*, edited by J. M. Suls and T. A. Wills, 261–85. Hillsdale, NJ: Erlbaum, 1991.

Salovey, P., and J. Rodin. "Some antecedents and consequences of social comparison jealousy." *Journal of Personality and Social Psychology* 47 (1984): 780–92.

Sampson, E. E. *Celebrating the other: A dialogic account of human nature*. Boulder, CO: Westview Press, 1993.

Sanna, L. J. "Mental simulations, affect, and subjective confidence: Time is everything." *Psychological Science* 10 (1999): 339–45.

Sanna, L. J., and S. Meier. "Looking for clouds in a silver lining: Self-esteem, mental simulation, and temporal confidence changes." *Journal of Research in Personality* 34 (2000): 236–51.

Scaer, R. C. *The body bears the burden: Trauma, dissociation, and disease*. New York: Haworth Press, 2001.

Schurman, R. A., P. S. Kramer, and J. B. Mitchell, "The hidden mental health network: treatment of mental illness by non-psychiatric physicians." *Archives of General Psychiatry* 42 (1985): 89–94.

Schwarz, N. "Feelings as information: Informational and motivational functions of affective states." In *The handbook of motivation and cognition: Foundations of social behavior*, vol. 2, edited by E. T. Higgins and R. M Sorrentino, 527–61. New York: Guilford Press, 1990.

Selfhout, M. H., S. J. Branje, M. Delsing, T. F. ter Bogt, and W. H. Meeus. "Different types of Internet use, depression, and social anxiety: The role of perceived friendship quality." *Journal of Adolescence* 32 (2009): 819–33.

Sen, A. K. "Rational behavior." In *The new Palgrave: Utility and probability*, edited by J. Eatwell, 198–216. New York: Norton, 1990.

Senko, C. M., A. M. Durik, and J. M. Harackiewicz. "Historical perspectives and new directions in achievement goal theory: Understanding the effects of mastery and performance-approach goals." In *Handbook of motivation science*, edited by J. Y. Shah and W. Gardner, 100–113. New York: Guilford Press, 2008.

Shadel, Doug, and David Dudley. "Are you real?" *AARP The Magazine* 58, no. 4C (2015), pp. 40–46, 65–66, 70.

Shapiro, S. L., J. A. Astin, S. R. Bishop, and M. Cordova. "Mindfulness-based stress reduction for health care professionals: Results from a randomized trial." *International Journal of Stress Management* 12 (2005): 164–76.

Shapiro, S. L., K. W. Brown, and G. M. Biegel. "Teaching self-care to caregivers: Effects of mindfulness-based stress reduction on the mental health of therapists in training." *Training and Education in Professional Psychology* 1 (2007): 105–15.

Sharp, H. M., C. F. Fear, M. G. Williams, D. Healy, C. F. Lowe, H. Yeadon, and R. Holden. "Delusional phenomenology—Dimensions of change." *Behavior Research and Therapy* 34 (1996): 123–42.

Sheldon, K. M., M. R. Ryan, and H. T. Reis. "What makes for a good day? Competence and autonomy in the day and in the person." *Personality and Social Psychology Bulletin* 22 (1996): 1270–79.

Shepperd, J. A., J. A. Ouellette, and J. K. Fernandez. "Abandoning unrealistic optimism: Performance estimates and the temporal proximity of self-related feedback." *Journal of Personality and Social Psychology* 70 (1996): 844–55.

Shields, S. A. "The politics of emotion in every day life: 'Appropriate' emotion and claims of identity." *Review of General Psychology* 9 (2005): 3–15.

Shorey, Hal S., and C. R. Snyder. "The role of adult attachment styles in psychopathology and psychotherapy outcomes." *Review of General Psychology* 10, no. 1 (2006): 1–20.

Silver, M., J. Sabini, and W. G. Parrott. "Embarrassment: A dramaturgic account." *Journal for the Theory of Social Behavior* 17 (1987): 47–61.

Smith, R. H. "Assimilative and contrastive emotional reactions to upward and downward social comparisons." In *Handbook of social comparison: Theory and research*, edited by J. M. Suls and L. Wheeler, 48–67. New York: Kluwer Academic, 2000.

Sorotzkin, B. "The quest for perfection: Avoiding guilt or avoiding shame?" *Psychotherapy* 22 (1985): 564–71.

Stein, Murray B., and John R. Walker. *Triumph over shyness: Conquering shyness and social anxiety.* New York: McGraw-Hill, 2002.

Strauss, J. S. "Hallucinations and delusions as points on continua function: Rating scale evidence." *Archives of General Psychiatry* 21 (1969): 581–86.

Sugawara, K. A study on embarrassment in new role situation: Using the data from university students at their probation in nursery school for the first time [in Japanese]. *Communication & Society (Bulletin of Edogawa University)* 2 (1992): 31–39.

Sutter, M., and M. G. Kocher. "Trust and trustworthiness across different age groups." *Games and Economic Behavior* 59 (2007): 364–82.

Swiggett, Chelsea Rae. *Rae: My true story of fear, anxiety, and social phobia.* Deerfield Beach, FL: Health Communications, 2010.

Sykes, C. J. *Dumbing down our kids: Why American children feel good about themselves but can't read, write, or add.* New York: St. Martin's Press Griffin, 1995.

Tangney, J. P. "Self-conscious emotions: The self as a moral guide." In *Self and motivation: Emerging psychological perspectives*, edited by A. Tesser, D. A. Stapel, and J. V. Wood, 97–117. Washington, DC: American Psychological Association, 2001.

Tangney, J. P., R. S. Miller, L. Flicker, and D. H. Barlow. "Are shame, guilt, and embarrassment distinct emotions?" *Journal of Personality and Social Psychology* 70 (1996): 1256–69.

Taylor, S. E., and M. Lobel. "Social comparison activity under threat: Downward evaluation and upward contacts." *Psychological Review* 96 (1989): 569–75.

Tennen, H., T. E. McKee, and G. Affleck. "Social comparison processes in health and illness." In *Handbook of social comparison: Theory and research*, edited by J. M. Suls and L. Wheeler, 443–83. New York: Kluwer Academic, 2000.

Thielman, Isabel, and Benjamin E. Hilbig. "Trust: An integrative review from a person-situation perspective." *Review of General Psychology* 19, no. 3 (2015): 249–77.

Thoits, P. A. "Stressors and problem-solving: The individual as psychological activist." *Journal of Health and Social Behavior* 35 (June 1994): 143–59.

Thompson, Ross A. "Childhood anxiety disorders from the perspective of emotion regulation and attachment." In *The developmental psychopathology of anxiety*, edited by Michael W. Vasey and Mark R. Dadds, 160–82. New York: Oxford University Press, 2001.

Tomaka, J., and J. Blascovich. "Effect of justice beliefs on cognitive appraisal of and subjective physiological, and behavioral responses to potential stress." *Journal of Personality and Social Psychology* 67 (1994): 732–40.

Tompkins, Michael A., Katherine Martinez, and Michael Sloan. *My anxious mind: A teen's guide to managing anxiety and panic.* Washington, DC: Magination Press / American Psychological Association, 2010.

Tullberg, J. "Trust—the importance of trustfulness versus trustworthiness." *Journal of Socio-Economics* 37 (2008): 2059–71.

Turner, S. M., D. C. Beidel, and K. T. Larkin. "Situational determinants of social anxiety in clinic and nonclinic samples: Physiological and cognitive correlates." *Journal of Consulting and Clinical Psychology* 54 (1986): 523–27.

Twenge, J. M. *Generation me: Why today's young Americans are more confident, assertive, entitled—and more miserable than ever before.* New York: Free Press, 2006.

Twenge, J. M., R. F. Baumeister, C. N. DeWall, N. J. Ciarocco, and J. M. Bartels. "Social exclusion decreases prosocial behavior." *Journal of Personality and Social Psychology* 92 (2007): 56–66.

Twenge, J. M., and W. K. Campbell. "Birth cohort differences in the Monitoring the Future dataset and elsewhere: Further evidence for Generation Me." *Perspectives in Psychological Science* 5 (2010): 81–88.

Twenge, J. M., and J. D. Foster. "Birth cohort increases in narcissistic personality traits among American college students, 1982–2000." *Social Psychological and Personality Science* 1 (2010): 99–106.

Twenge, J. M., S. Konrath, J. D. Foster, W. K. Campbell, and B. Bushman. "Egos inflating over time: A cross-temporal meta-analysis of the narcissistic personality inventory." *Journal of Personality* 76 (2008): 875–902.

Uhlmann, Eric Luis. "American psychological isolationism." *Review of General Psychology* 16, no. 4 (2012): 381–90.

Ullmann-Margalit, E. "Trust, distrust, and in between." In *Distrust*, edited by R. Hardin, 60–82. New York: Russell Sage Foundation, 2004.

Van Lange, P. A. M., A. A. E. Vinkhuyzen, and D. Posthuma. "Genetic influences are virtually absent for trust." *PLoS ONE* 9 (2014): e93880.

Vasey, Michael W., and Mark R. Dadds. "An introduction to the developmental psychopathology of anxiety." In *The developmental psychopathology of anxiety*, edited by M. W. Vasey and M. R. Dadds, 3–26. New York: Oxford University Press, 2001.

Vaughn, B. E., G. Coppola, M. Verissimo, L. Monteiro, A. J. Santos, G. Posada, O. A. Carbonell et al. "The quality of maternal secure-base scripts predicts children's secure-base behaviors at home in three sociocultural groups." *International Journal of Behavioral Development* 31 (2007): 65–76.

Verini, James. "Will success spoil MySpace?" *Vanity Fair*, March 2006, pp. 238–49.

Walsh, Roger. "Lifestyle and Mental Health." *American Psychologist* 66, no. 7 (2011): 579–92.

Wells, Polly. *Freaking out.* New York: Annick Press, 2013.

Wenzlaff, R. M., and D. M. Wegner. "Thought suppression." *Annual Review of Psychology* 51 (2000): 59–91.

Whybrow, Peter C. "Adaptive styles in the etiology of Depression." In *Affective disorders*, edited by Frederic Flach, 1–18. Markham, Canada: Penguin Books Canada, 1988.

Wilber, K. *Integral psychology.* Boston: Shambhala, 2000.

Williams, J. G., S. K. Stark, and E. E. Foster. "Start today or the very last day? The relationships among self-compassion, motivation, and procrastination." *American Journal of Psychological Research* 4 (2008): 37–44.

Williams, K. D. "Ostracism." *Annual Review of Psychology*, 58 (2007) 425–52.

Williams, M., G. J. Teasdale, Z. Segal, and J. Kabat-Zinn. *The mindful way through depression: Freeing yourself from chronic unhappiness.* New York: Guilford Press, 2007.

Willie J. *Dancing on the dumpster.* Jesus Hands, 2014.

Wills, T. A. "Similarity and self-esteem in downward comparison." In *Social comparison: Contemporary theory and research*, edited by J. M. Suls and T. A. Wills, 51–78. Hillsdale, NJ: Erlbaum, 1991.

Witte, K. "Putting the fear back into fear appeals: The extended parallel process model." *Communication Monographs* 59 (1992): 329–49.

Wood, J. V. "Theory and research concerning social comparisons of personal attributes." *Psychological Bulletin* 106 (1989): 231–48.

Wright, W. F., and G. H. Bower. "Mood effects on subjective-probability assessment." *Organizational Behavior and Human Decision Processes* 52 (1992): 276–91.

Wyer, R. S., and D. Albarracin. "The origins and structure of beliefs and goals." In *Handbook of attitudes*, edited by D. Albarracin, B. T. Johnson, and M. P. Zanna, 273–322. Hillsdale, NJ: Erlbaum, 2005.

Yngvesson, B., and M. A. Mahoney. "'As one should, ought and wants to be': Belonging and authenticity in identity narratives." *Theory, Culture & Society* 17 (2000): 77–110.

Yu, M., M. Saleem, and C. Gonzalez. "Developing trust: First impressions and experience." *Journal of Economic Psychology* 43 (2014): 16–29.

Zech, E., B. Rime, and F. Nils. "Social sharing of emotions, emotional recovery, and interpersonal aspects." In *The regulation of emotion*, edited by P. Phillippot and R. S. Feldman, 157–185. Mahwah, NJ: Lawrence Erlbaum, 2004.

Zhang, Liqing. "An exchange theory of money and self-esteem in decision making." *Review of General Psychology* 13, no. 1 (2009): 66–76.

Zimbardo, P. G., and S. Radl. *The shy child: Overcoming and preventing shyness from infancy to adulthood.* New York: Malor Books, 1999.

Zitrin, Charlotte Marker. "Combined psychological and pharmaceutical approach to the treatment of phobias." In *Phobia: A comprehensive summary of modern treatments*, edited by Robert L. DuPont, 57–76. New York: Brunner/Mazel, 1982.

Zook, Helen. "Perfectionism is a total confidence killer." *Cosmopolitan*, June 2016, p. 154.

Index

About the Author

Vera Sonja Maass, PhD, is a licensed clinical psychologist, mental health counselor, and marriage and family therapist in private practice in Indianapolis. She holds past certifications as a chemical dependence counselor, sex therapist, and Family Life Educator. Maass has enjoyed adjunct faculty status at local colleges and universities and has conducted personal growth groups addressing popular psychological topics of interest to the community. Practicing within a cognitive behavioral (REBT/RBT) theoretical framework, she has a strong interest in neuropsychology and, after studying with Ralph Reitan, PhD, has conducted evaluations for several years using the Halstead-Reitan Neuropsychological Test Battery.

Dr. Maass is the author of several books, including *Counseling Single Parents*; *Women's Group Therapy*; *Lifestyle Changes: A Clinician's Guide to Common Events, Challenges, and Options*; *Facing the Complexities of Women's Sexual Desire*; *The Cinderella Test: Would You Really Want to Fit the Shoe?*; *Coping with Control and Manipulation: Making the Difference between Being a Target and Becoming a Victim*; and *Finding Love That Lasts: Breaking the Pattern of Dead End Relationships*.